The
Chimp
Paradox

Dr Steve Peters

Vermilion
LONDON

Published in 2011 by Vermilion, an imprint of Ebury Publishing
Ebury Publishing is a Random House Group company

The Random House Group Limited Reg. No. 954009
Addresses for companies within the Random House Group can be found at
www.randomhouse.co.uk

A CIP catalogue record for this book is available from the British Library

The Random House Group Limited supports The Forest Stewardship Council (FSC®), the
leading international forest certification organisation. Our books carrying the FSC label
are printed on FSC® certified paper. FSC is the only forest certification scheme endorsed
by the leading environmental organisations, including Greenpeace. Our paper
procurement policy can be found at www.randomhouse.co.uk/environment

Printed and bound by CPI Group (UK) Ltd, Croydon, CR0 4YY

ISBN 9780091935580

Copies are available at special rates for bulk orders.
Contact the sales development team on 020 7840 8487 for more information.

To buy books by your favourite authors and register for offers, visit
www.randomhouse.co.uk

About the author

Dr Steve Peters is a consultant psychiatrist and has worked in the clinical field of psychiatry for over 20 years. He holds degrees in mathematics and medicine, a Masters in medical education and postgraduate qualifications in sports medicine, education and psychiatry.

Dr Peters has been a Senior Lecturer at Sheffield University since 1994 and is also Undergraduate Dean at the Medical School and a Royal College Examination panel member.

In addition, Dr Peters works in elite sport and has been the resident psychiatrist with the British Cycling team since 2001 and now the Sky ProCycling Team. His mind management techniques have been credited with helping to transform the performance of Britain's elite cyclists, and contributing to bringing home 14 medals from the Beijing Olympics, eight of which were golds.

Sir Chris Hoy, Bradley Wiggins and Victoria Pendleton have all spoken publically about how Dr Peters' unique Chimp Model has helped them improve their performance. He has also been involved in 12 other Olympic Sports, including Taekwondo and Canoeing, as well as England Rugby and Premier League Football.

Outside of elite sport, Dr Peters also works with CEOs, senior executives, hospital staff, patients and university students helping them to understand why they think and act as they do and how to manage their minds to optimise their performance, at work and in their personal lives.

Dr Peters' Chimp Model can work for anyone from any walk of life. *The Chimp Paradox* brings his work to a wider audience for the first time and it is the author's hope that everyone who reads this book will benefit from it.

Contents

Part 3: Your Health, Success and Happiness

Introduction
The Journey
Choosing the Sun

Reading this book will take you on a journey of self-discovery and development. By understanding and applying the concepts within it, you will not only improve the quality of your life, but also significantly increase your chances of being happy and successful in whatever you do. The book is written around a model that I have developed called Chimp Management, which has helped many people understand themselves and learn how to work with their emotions. Some parts of the book will resonate with you more strongly than others. Select those parts that are relevant to you and work with them.

In my work as a psychiatrist and lecturer, people typically present me with comments or questions that are usually centred on problems that they don't understand or can't solve. For example:

- How do I become the person that I would like to be?
- I want to be confident in myself.
- How do I become more organised and successful in what I do?
- Why do I worry so much?
- How do I become a more effective leader?
- I want to be happy.

- How do I stop worrying about what others think?
- Why can't I make decisions?
- How do I motivate myself?
- Why do I have such a low opinion of myself?
- How do I stop emotions that prevent me from reaching my professional potential?
- I drink too much.
- Why do I often act against common-sense?
- My moods just go up and down.
- How do I stop overeating?
- Why do I sometimes become so irrational in my thinking?
- I can't control my anger.
- Why can't I remain faithful?
- I can't get on with my boss.
- Why do I feel judged all the time?
- How do I make my relationship work?

And the list goes on!

How we will go through the journey

Chimp Management is based on scientific facts and principles, which have been simplified into a workable model for easy use. It will help you to answer the above questions, develop yourself and give you the skills, for example, to remove anxiety, have confidence and choose your emotions.

The book will do this by giving you an understanding of the way in which your mind works and how you can manage it. It will help you to identify what is holding you back or preventing you from having a happier and more successful life. Each chapter explains different aspects of how you function and highlights key facts for you to understand. There are exercises for you to work through. By undertaking these exercises you will see immediate improvements in your daily living and over time you will develop emotional skills and practical habits that will help you to become the person that you want to be, and live the life that you want to live.

We will consider seven different areas to work on:

- Your inner mind
- Understanding and relating to others
- Communication
- The world in which you live
- Your health
- Your success
- Your happiness

To help you to understand and visualise these areas better, each will be represented by a planet, some of which have their own moons to stabilise them. The seven planets and their moons come together to form the Psychological Universe within your head! I will introduce each planet as we go through the journey across this Universe, which of course, strictly speaking is a solar system. (See page 339 for a diagram of the Universe).

Just as the sun is the centre of the physical solar system, your Sun is the centre of your Psychological Universe and represents self-fulfilment and what you believe to be the meaning and purpose of your life. The Sun has the best chance of shining when all of the seven planets in your Universe are spinning correctly and in harmony. Therefore, in order to make your Sun shine you have to work on each area in your life and get it into a good place. So let's choose the Sun and begin our journey of self-discovery and life-changing attitudes.

Part 1
Your Inner Mind Explored

Chapter 1
The Psychological Mind

As we begin our journey across the Universe we need to have a basic understanding of what is inside our head and how it works. The human brain is complicated so we will look at a simplified version. It is easiest to consider the human brain as a system of seven brains working together.

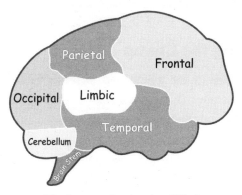

The human brain simplified

Within the Chimp Management model, three of these brains – frontal, limbic and parietal – combine to form the 'Psychological Mind' and we will only look at these brains. Remember that scientifically this is far from accurate but it will give us a working model. Strictly speaking, the other brains significantly contribute to emotions, thinking and memory but for our purposes we will dramatically simplify things.

The three psychological brains in our model, the frontal, limbic and parietal, are called the Human, the Chimp and the Computer. For convenience, we will let the parietal lobe represent many parts of the brain, which makes our diagram more straightforward. Although these three brains try to work together, they very frequently get into conflict and struggle against each other to gain control, with the Chimp (limbic brain) often winning!

The Psychological Mind

Introducing the Chimp

When you were in the womb two different brains, the frontal (Human) and limbic (Chimp: an emotional machine), developed independently and then introduced themselves to each other by forming connections. The problem is that they found they were not in agreement about most things. Either of these two brains, or beings, could run your life for you but they try to work together, and therein is the problem. The Human and Chimp have independent personalities with different agendas, ways of thinking, and modes of operating. Effectively there are two beings in your head! It is important to grasp that only one of these beings is you, the Human.

The Chimp is the emotional machine that we all possess. It thinks independently from us and can make decisions. It offers emotional thoughts and feelings that can be very constructive or very destructive; it is not good or bad, it is a Chimp. The Chimp Paradox is that it can be your best friend and your worst enemy, even at the same time. The main purpose of this book is to help you to manage your Chimp and to harness its strength and power when it is working for you and to neutralise it when it is not.

Key Point
The Chimp is an emotional machine that thinks independently from us. It is not good or bad, it is just a Chimp.

When people have accidents that damage their frontal lobe or where they have a disorder or illness affecting the frontal lobe, their personality alters. Effectively the Human part of the brain stops working and the new personality that presents is the Chimp. Very often, people affected in this way will become disinhibited and lose

The case of Phineas Gage
An early example that demonstrated there could be two different personalities in one head – represented by the Human and Chimp – was that of Phineas Gage. In the late nineteenth century, Gage was employed by a railway company to clear the way for the tracklayers by blowing away any boulders that were too big to move manually. To do this he packed explosives beneath the boulder and then tamped it down with a thick iron rod before lighting the fuse. Gage had been chosen to do this dangerous work because he was judged to be careful, sober and responsible. However, one time, Gage allowed himself to be distracted at a crucial moment and caused the rod to strike the boulder, which created a spark. The resulting explosion jettisoned the iron bar into Gage's eye socket, through the front of his head and out the top of his skull. As it exited, it took with it a clean core of brain tissue from his frontal (Human) lobe.

Apart from being blind in one eye, Gage made a full recovery. However, his personality was completely altered. He became foul-mouthed, aggressive and impulsive. Effectively, his Human had gone and he was now left with just the Chimp!

their judgement or they can become apathetic or have outbursts of aggressive behaviour.

You can recognise the difference between your Chimp thinking and Human thinking without knowing any of the science. How many times have you talked to yourself, reassured yourself or had battles within your own head? Often you have thoughts and feelings that you do not want and even carry out behaviours that you know at the time are not really what you want to do. So why are you doing this? How can it be that you do not have control over what thoughts or emotions you have and what behaviours you carry out? How can you be two very different people at different times?

Technology can go some way to answering this question. Functional brain scanners show the blood supply in your brain going to the area that is being used. If you think calmly and rationally then we can see the blood going to the frontal area, the Human in your head, and you become the person that you want to be and that you really are. If you become emotional and somewhat irrational, especially when you are angry or distressed, then we see the blood supply go to your Chimp, and you would usually say this is not how you want to be and that you don't want this. The truth is that it is your Chimp, an emotional machine, that is overpowering your Human mind.

This starts to explain many things, such as why you worry or why you say things in the heat of the moment and then regret them, or why you can't stop eating or why you don't exercise when you really want to but just can't get your act together. The list is endless. Wonder no more: it is not you doing these things, it is your Chimp that is hijacking you. Having a Chimp is like owning a dog. You are not responsible for the nature of the dog but you are responsible for managing it and keeping it well behaved. This is a very important point and you should stop and think about this because it is crucial to your happiness and success in life.

> ## *Key Point*
> *You are not responsible for the nature of your Chimp but you are responsible for managing it.*

The Chimp within

To reiterate, the Chimp within your head is a separate entity to you. It was born when you were born but actually has nothing to do with you as a Human. It is simply part of your machinery. For example, when you were born you were given a certain colour of eyes. You didn't choose this colour, it was given to you. It was in your genes. There isn't much you can do about it, so you accept your eye colour and get on with your life. Similarly you didn't choose your Chimp, it was given to you and you need to accept it. It has a mind of its own and thinks with original thoughts that are not yours. It is a living machine that is built to serve a purpose, which is to ensure the next generation. It has a personality of its own and it can run your life for you, usually not very well, but it can do it! It is an extremely powerful emotional machine.

You might wish to give your Chimp a name and introduce yourself because it plays one of the biggest parts in your life. Throughout your life, you (the Human) and your Chimp (your emotional thinking machine) will often do battle.

Key Point

One of the secrets of success and happiness is to learn to live with your Chimp and not get bitten or attacked by it. To do this, you need to understand how your Chimp behaves, and why it thinks and acts in the way that it does. You also need to understand your Human and not muddle up your Human with your Chimp.

The Psychological Mind therefore has two independent thinking machines that also independently interpret our experiences.

Human   Chimp

The two beings that think and then interpret

- The Human is you, and you live in your frontal lobe.
- The Chimp is your emotional machine, given to you at birth, and it lives in your limbic system.

The third part of the Psychological Mind

The 'Psychological Mind' also has a storage area for thoughts and behaviours called the Computer, which is spread throughout the whole brain.

Computer

The storage of information for reference

The Computer stores information that the Chimp or Human has put into it. It then uses this information to act for them in an automatic way or it can serve as a reference point.

So now that you have a basic understanding of what is inside your head, let us start the journey across the Psychological Universe. We can see how you are operating with your Human, Chimp and Computer in different circumstances and how you can use them to your advantage and understand yourself better.

Summary key points

- The Psychological Mind is made up of three separate brains: Human, Chimp and Computer.
- You are the Human.
- Your Chimp is an emotional thinking machine.
- Your Computer is a storage area and automatic functioning machine.
- Any one of them can take complete control but usually they work together.

Suggested exercise:
Development time

What is 'development time' and why have it?
Simply put, 'development time' is time specifically set aside that is dedicated to reflecting on how you are managing yourself. You will benefit most from the model of the Chimp, the Human and the Computer if you spend time thinking through the concepts involved and then implementing them. The best way to make sure that you establish 'development time' is to make it into a habit. Habits are formed when they are easy to do.

Therefore, setting aside a specific time in the day that is sacro-sanct for development thinking will increase your chances of it happening regularly. This session must be easy to do otherwise your Chimp won't agree and you won't do it! So making the session just ten minutes long is more likely to establish the habit than making the session an hour long. Try to establish ten minutes a day. By reflecting during development time, the Human is reviewing what is in the Computer and modifying it. As we will see in future chapters, this is critical to managing your Chimp.

What to do
During this time, you need to look back over the last 24 hours and reflect on how you managed it. Keep a logbook and write only one or two lines for each day, which will help focus your mind on how you can improve the way that you do things or how you are thinking. It will also help you to work through the points raised in this book.

An example
Here is a suggestion for the first few sessions. Try to improve your ability to recognise when your Chimp is hijacking you with thoughts, feelings and behaviours that you don't want to have. By doing this, you are learning to recognise the difference between yourself and your Chimp and who is in control at any point in time. This will help to make clear that there are two brains operating within your head and only one of them is you.

Chapter 2
The Divided Planet
(PART 1)
How to understand yourself and your Chimp

The first of the seven planet systems consists of the Divided Planet and the Guiding Moon. It represents your inner mind and the battle that goes on inside your head. This is the most important planet system in your Universe because if it is not in control then it is unlikely that any of the other planets can function properly.

The Divided Planet is where the Human and Chimp live. You and your Chimp typically have an uneasy relationship that frequently involves compromise and conflict. It is often a battle for power between the two of you. As the Chimp is far stronger than you are, it is wise to understand it and then nurture and manage it.

To understand how you and your Chimp work differently, we will approach this in a systematic way by looking at four aspects:

- Ways of thinking
- Agendas
- Modes of operating
- Personalities

Two different ways of thinking

You and your Chimp think in very different ways. As we go about our day we are continually receiving information from around us. The Human and Chimp both receive this information and then interpret it.

The Chimp interprets this information with **feelings** and **impressions**. When it has got a feel for what is going on, it then uses **emotional thinking** to put things together and to work out what is happening and form a plan of action. All of this process is based on emotion. Emotional thinking means that the Chimp makes guesses and fills in detail by assumptions that are typically based on a hunch, paranoid feelings or defensive thoughts. The chances therefore that the Chimp will get the right interpretation as to what is happening may not be so good; however, sometimes the gut feeling it has is right. It can only think and act with emotion.

The Human, on the other hand, will interpret information by **searching for the facts and establishing the truth**. When it has done this, it will then put things together in a logical manner using **logical thinking** and form a plan of action based on this. So logic is the Human's basis for thinking and acting.

Both processes can be healthy, but lead to different interpretations of what is happening and how to deal with it.

Ways of working

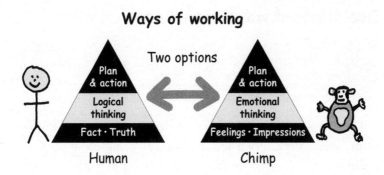

Two options

Human · Chimp

So whatever you are doing, there are two of you interpreting what is going on and forming an opinion as to what you should do. Sometimes the two of you agree on what to do and there is no problem, but often the two of you disagree. When you disagree, the Chimp is the most powerful and therefore gets control of your thoughts and actions. However, if you recognise what is happening, and have strategies for managing this, you will gain control of your thinking and then you can act in a logical manner.

John and the parked car

Let's start with a simple example to demonstrate the differences in thinking between the Chimp and the Human within the head of someone called John.

John is telling his wife, Pauline, that the man next door had blocked his car in by parking across the driveway and he had to go and tell the man to move the car. John (the Human) is telling the story in a matter-of-fact way and his inner Chimp is calmly listening.

Pauline then responds by saying, 'I don't know why you are making such a deal of it; it got sorted didn't it?'

John and his Chimp have both heard this response but have very different interpretations and reactions to Pauline's comment. The Human in John, being reasonable, may think, 'I wasn't really making a deal of it but clearly Pauline doesn't want to hear, so I will just let it go,' or 'It did get sorted so she has probably got a point and I need to move on and not react.' The Human has remained calm and has already moved on without a problem.

The Chimp in John, however, may react in a very different way. The Chimp has taken the remark personally and has become agitated. It may interpret the comment as a direct criticism, and therefore the Chimp will go into defence or attack mode. It is likely to raise its voice and say something like, 'Why do you never support me?' or 'I am not making a deal of it, what is your problem?' or 'I only made a comment that I thought you, as my wife, might be interested in.'

You can imagine how the conversation goes downhill from this point on. If we had stopped the scenario after Pauline gave her remark and we asked John how he would like to respond, then it is likely that he would choose to be Human and let it go. However, as the Chimp within us is far more powerful than the Human, it is more likely that the Chimp will speak before the Human gets a chance to take control, and this will end up leaving John wondering why he didn't just let go of the remark in the first place.

Sarah's comment

Let's have another example of the different thinking patterns between the Human and the Chimp. Rachael is at work when Sarah makes a comment to her, saying that Rachael looks like she is tired.

The message always goes to the Chimp first (this is one of the rules of how the brain works). The Chimp reacts in an emotional way and typically thinks it is being criticised so it becomes agitated, possibly annoyed, possibly upset (it all depends on the nature of that particular Chimp and what mood it is in). The Chimp now uses emotional construction to understand the remark. So it may say something like, 'She really means you are looking old,' or 'She is insinuating that you are not working hard enough,' or it may have any other unhelpful or destructive interpretation. Alternatively, the Chimp might think positively, such as, 'She is concerned for me,' or 'She is probably right and I need to slow down a bit,' or some other constructive thought.

The Human, on the other hand, if it were unsure of what was meant, would have calmly checked what Sarah implied. It would have done this by establishing what the facts of the comment were. Then, having clarified what Sarah meant, it would have responded to it in a rational way. Now we can answer one of the questions posed at the start of the book.

Why do I sometimes become so irrational in my thinking?

One of the opening questions was: 'Why do I sometimes become so irrational in my thinking?' The answer may now be clear. It is not you thinking at all, but your Chimp taking over and thinking for you. The solution therefore is to understand how your Chimp thinks, recognise when it is taking over, and intervene.

What you are experiencing when you have strong emotional reactions is very natural and the sign of a healthy mind. However, emotions can shift ground quickly and therefore the Chimp's thinking is relatively unstable and inconsistent. Therefore, the Chimp is less predictable than the Human when it comes to decision-making and the process is often irrational. Because of this unpredictability, it is usually unhelpful to let the Chimp think for us, so we need to address it. First we will understand how a healthy inner Chimp thinks.

Understanding the Chimp – emotional thinking

The basis of emotional thinking is impression and feeling

The Chimp does not necessarily work with facts but it works with what it believes is the truth or with a perception of the truth or, even worse, with a projection of what might be the truth. It is quick to form an impression on little, if any, evidence and usually won't give way. Of course, some impressions that the Chimp gives us are accurate and helpful, but they can just as easily be wrong. Searching for some accuracy and truth would help us to reach a sensible conclusion.

Your Chimp typically forms first impressions when you meet new people by reading body language. If you know that your Chimp is often wrong then it can be helpful to see if a friend's Chimp is more skilled in doing this and rely on them! We know that some people's Chimps are naturally good at judging the character of people, whereas other Chimps are not so good.

Chimps like to work on feelings and often start their conversations with 'But I feel…' or 'I don't feel like…' Their feelings are very important to them and they usually fail to recognise that all feelings come and go. Of course, it is good to have feelings from the Chimp and they can be a very useful indication for us to know what to do. However, they are not always reliable and can change quickly. So working with feelings can be helpful or unhelpful. Sometimes the Human needs to say to the Chimp, 'I don't care how you feel we have to do it,' or 'I don't care whether you are in the mood or not, it is not about mood.'

Here are some of the traits of emotional thinking

- Jumps to an opinion
- Thinks in black and white
- Paranoid
- Catastrophic
- Irrational
- Emotive judgement

Jumps to an opinion
The Chimp is fast to reach a conclusion and doesn't wait for all of the information to come through before reaching its conclusion. The Chimp forms an opinion based on its feelings and impressions and then fixes its opinion. It then searches out evidence to back up its opinion and prove its point. In doing this, it typically twists the facts to fit its opinion and is very unreasonable and irrational if challenged.

Thinks in black and white

Inner Chimps are very much like children, they think in terms of black and white. They can be very unforgiving and will not discuss shades of grey. Adult Humans are more able to appreciate that very little in life is black or white. As Chimps think in black and white, they become very judgemental and are quick to respond. When you are thinking with your Chimp you tend to see only one possibility. Chimps don't usually consider alternative interpretations of what might be happening.

Paranoid

The Chimp needs to know that it is safe, so it is vigilant and continually looks for danger and therefore is prone to paranoia. It thinks that it is far safer to be a bit paranoid and wary towards others or a situation than to relax and lose your life. Therefore it is not unusual for our Chimps to be suspicious of others and have some mistrust. The more vulnerable that a Chimp feels, the more paranoid it will become in its outlook.

Chimps that are insecure may read lots of things into harmless situations. They can also read intrigue and malice in comments or statements that others make and then allow their imaginations to run wild. When the Chimp has an opinion it will become even more paranoid about defending it. The Chimp will often take things out of context and also become very defensive. Dealing with paranoia in your Chimp is a skilful business and will be addressed in the Chimp Management section.

Catastrophic

As Chimps are constantly vigilant to danger, they tend to think catastrophically. They overreact to situations and fuel them with high and intense emotion. Whenever they perceive something is wrong, they have a tendency to start worrying about what might happen and then get things completely out of perspective. This frequently leads to terrible feelings of gloom and doom and stomach-churning moments. These moments are often linked to black-and-white thinking, which means you are left with a feeling that there is no way out or there can be no recovering from what you are going through.

The emotion the Chimp then offers to the Human is horrendous and extreme, causing much pain. Think how many times you have been through emotional turmoil at the hands of your Chimp, only to look back wondering why you allowed yourself to be put through it.

Irrational

The Chimp does not work rationally. It doesn't try to decide if something is likely or feasible but typically jumps to conclusions and fills in missing details with anything it chooses. It can therefore become very unreasonable and end up looking foolish. If the Chimp manages to get control of your mind and then interprets what is happening to you, the reasoning it offers is likely to be silly and unfounded. There will be little, if any, logic shown. Sadly this irrational approach will lead us into uncomfortable situations and when the truth appears we may want the ground to swallow us up. Let's look at an example of how the Chimp works:

Rob is waiting for his girlfriend, Sally, at a cinema and they have agreed to meet at 8.30. The time is now 9.00 and there is no sign of her. His Chimp has got control and is on the warpath. His Chimp thinks emotionally. 'It is late; she has not told me what is happening; I am wasting my time; I may as well go into the cinema; she isn't worth it; she has let me down; she shouldn't do this to me; she has humiliated me; I am angry; I am upset,' and so it goes on. Suddenly Sally arrives and, before she has the chance to say anything, his Chimp attacks – 'Why have you turned up late? You have made me look like a fool; what's the point of going in now it's too late?' and many more attacks. Then he stops and Sally speaks.

'Someone has been knocked over just round the corner. I went to help and they were using my mobile to get an ambulance and the police. I held the woman's hand as she lay on the floor. The ambulance came and then I rushed to get here. I am sorry I couldn't let you know but they were using my phone to get help.' Now Rob feels pretty bad and his Chimp changes its emotion to being remorseful. But the damage is done.

This simple story represents how the Chimp thinks very emotionally, it did not wait for the facts but just made assumptions and got offended. In this case the Chimp got angry but there are many other ways it could have responded and still left Rob acting inappropriately. This happens a lot to all of us if we don't manage our Chimps. By managing our Chimps we would live in a very different world.

Emotive judgement

Chimps judge others quickly and without mercy. Judgement is based on all of the criteria that it uses to think with. Therefore it can be based on pure feelings or impressions or on its own paranoia. These judgements are not open to reasoning, so the Chimp is unlikely to be persuaded that it may be wrong. Chimps may also judge others to fulfil their own agenda, such as getting revenge or to wield power over someone.

The Chimp's basis for making decisions is by using 'emotional thinking'

When we are thinking with the Chimp, we use 'emotional thinking' to piece together our ideas on what is happening. Very little logic, if any, is used, just emotional energy. So the Chimp pieces together its irrational, black-and-white and catastrophic impressions, feelings and paranoia, in an often nonsensical way to draw up conclusions and then a plan of action. The Chimp does not use sound reasoning. It doesn't take a genius to see that this is not a good basis to work from. Thankfully there is an alternative way of thinking and we can learn to shift the blood supply in our brains in order to use this alternative. The alternative way is that of the Human.

Understanding the Human – logical thinking

The basis of logical thinking is facts and truth

Humans begin to work out what is happening by first establishing the facts. They gather all the information available before beginning to make plans. Having gathered the facts, Humans try to establish the truth and then base their beliefs on the truth.

In society, we spend a lot of energy and discussion finding out the truth, whether it is about something serious or trivial. There is an innate Human desire to try to reach the truth in all situations and when the truth does not come out it can cause distress to both Chimp and Human. Being misrepresented is a particularly unpleasant experience that Humans try to rectify and if this doesn't happen then the Chimp often joins forces with the Human to demonstrate its annoyance!

Here are some of the traits of logical thinking

- Evidence-based
- Rational
- In context and with perspective
- Shades of grey and balanced judgement

Evidence-based

Humans work with evidence and they search for proof. They remain open-minded and have the ability to change their mind and to see someone else's point of view. They don't personalise their viewpoint or belief, and therefore do not become defensive if challenged.

Rational

Rational thinking is when we use common-sense and decide if something is feasible and realistic. Ironically, rational thinking is often prompted by the Chimp, which activates the Human. The Chimp does this by an intuitive prompt; a bell ringing in your head saying that something just doesn't sound true. However, the Human must remain in charge and search for evidence to back up the Chimp's prompt. If we don't do this and allow our Chimp to take over, common-sense disappears and at some point in the future the Chimp's prompt may work against us. We will then look back and say, 'What was I thinking?'

In context and with perspective

Keeping situations in context and perspective demonstrates Human thinking. Wanting to understand how things came about and what was happening at the time is a Human trait. This helps us to give actions and remarks a context. Humans also appreciate that all events come and go and therefore gain a perspective on what is happening and how important it is in the scheme of things.

Shades of grey and balanced judgement

Typically, when we are very young we work via the Chimp and see most things in black and white. Children demonstrate this by being quite harsh in their judgements of situations.

Adult Humans think in shades of grey. As adults, we learn to appreciate that there may be many factors involved when we are trying to understand something and we accept that we may not have all of them in our possession. Therefore, we are less likely to judge harshly and we are more likely to see things in shades of grey or not judge at all. We also modify our thinking with the experience that life gives us.

Humans accept that they may be wrong, and reflect on this, becoming more open to suggestions. They also accept that some-times they may not reach the truth, there may not be an answer or it may be just a matter of opinion.

The Human's basis for making decisions is by using 'logical thinking'

Logical thinking means that we follow patterns of thinking that are linked and make sense and then reason out conclusions on which to act. If someone is upset, for example, then we can say that there must be a reason for this. The counter-argument would also be true, that if someone experiences something unpleasant then they are likely to become upset. There are several forms of logic that we use. Examples include:

- Deducing things by going through steps
- Working with evidence and facts, to reach a conclusion
- Following arguments by piecing together information
- Employing reasoning to work things out

A summary of the two different ways of thinking

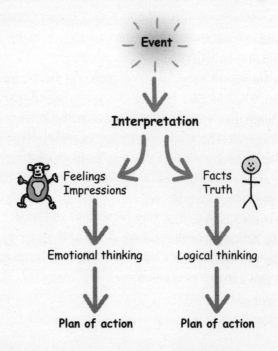

Two different agendas

The purpose and agenda of the Chimp is survival.

The Human's agenda is to achieve self-fulfilment. This is usually about becoming the person you want to be and achieving the things you want to achieve. The Human will often search for the meaning of life.

Many people might consider the Human as having the soul or spirit of the person. As we consider the differences between the agenda of the Chimp and the Human we will see why there is frequently a severe clash between the two beings.

Understanding the Chimp's agenda

- Perpetuation of the species and self-survival
- Other objectives

Perpetuation of the species and self-survival

The Chimp may have many objectives and these may vary at different times but the main agenda of the Chimp is to produce the next generation. It's nature's way of perpetuating the species.

The Chimp uses its sex drive along with other drives to try and fulfil this agenda. Therefore your Chimp has this drive high on its priority list! A strong sex drive indicates a healthy Chimp.

A very close second agenda of the Chimp is self-survival, which includes protecting itself from harm.

These two agendas of the Chimp play a very big part in the way that it acts. All Chimps are different and may have different agendas but we will consider the typical Chimp.

These two extremely strong drives are common to all higher species, not just ourselves and are necessary for survival of the species. Therefore, they must want to produce the next generation, or at least have some drives (such as the sex drive or a parental drive) that will result in the next generation being produced. We must also want to survive ourselves in order to do this.

If the typical Chimp is really pushed, it is quite likely to protect the species rather than protect itself. The black widow spider demonstrates this principle. Here there is a clash between the drive to produce the next generation and the drive to survive. The drive for the male to have sex and therefore perpetuate the species overrides his own safety and he will mate with the female knowing that he is highly likely to be eaten, if he can't escape quickly enough.

We can also see this clash of drives in people, though hopefully not quite so dramatically! For example, those who have unprotected sex despite being in a situation where there is a high risk of contracting the HIV virus. Thankfully, with medication, this virus is not the killer that it once was. However, when it first arrived people took incredible risks, knowing that this may have deadly consequences.

For many people the drive for sex cannot be underestimated, it is nature's way of ensuring the species continues. This is why some people who are in a loving relationship and wish to remain monogamous find it almost impossible to remain faithful. The Human is saying and wanting one thing, and the Chimp is saying and wanting another.

Other objectives

Clearly the Chimp will have other objectives that support species or individual survival, and these objectives may vary from time to time. Examples include: attracting a mate, establishing a territory, searching for food and finding shelter. We will cover the drives behind these agendas later in this chapter in the 'Jungle Centre' section.

Understanding the Human's agenda

- Self-agenda
- Society agenda
- Other objectives

Self-agenda

Human beings are very diverse about what they feel is their purpose in life. Some live a life that is based on establishing the basics of living and stop there. Other Humans go on to try to gain self-fulfilment and satisfaction in life, which may be by helping others.

Self-fulfilment can be achieved in many different ways and it is really up to you to work out what it is that you want to do with your life. Everyone is unique and there are no rights and wrongs here. Many people look at self-development, and it seems that those who work on this and on self-fulfilment are more likely to be content in life. One thing is clear: that having a purpose in life is something that Humans thrive on.

Society agenda

Humans are by nature typically social animals, although there are clear exceptions. One of the main agendas of the Human is to build a society where Humans can live in harmony and in peace. This agenda is seen across all Human societies. Therefore, Humans by their nature will constantly try to establish society rules and society living. These rules are based on equality and opportunity and are really there to contain the Chimp within people. The Human looks for justice and structure, and works with ethical and moral principles to establish Human rights and Human values to live by. They are based on value judgements of right and wrong, with consequences attached to them.

Other objectives

Other Human objectives vary greatly from individual to individual but most are based around happiness and success, however these are defined. The problem with these agendas is that if we are not careful the Chimp takes them up and employs 'jungle laws' to achieve them. For example, Humans would like businesses to be based on ethical principles and have an agenda to succeed. However, often bullying and intimidation take place as the Chimp takes over this Human agenda to succeed, and mixes in its own agendas, such as fulfilling its own ego or establishing its own territory.

Two different modes of operating

The Chimp and Human have different agendas and to fulfil these they operate by using two very different principles. The Chimp operates by the laws of the jungle and it does this by having powerful drives and instincts. The Human operates by the laws of society and it does this by using powerful ethical and moral drives, typically with a conscience.

By far, the biggest challenge for the individual Human is to live with an animal within that is determined to live by the laws of the jungle and to use extremely powerful drives and instincts to fulfil its own agenda.

Understanding the Chimp – the Jungle Centre

The Chimp operates with a 'Jungle Centre' that is based on instincts and drives. The Jungle Centre is an area within the Chimp brain that gives the Chimp the characteristics and attitudes needed to survive in a jungle. This Centre contains beliefs and behaviours that work well in the jungle but not so well in a society! Major problems arise when the Chimp applies its jungle drives in a Human society.

Here are some of the operational features of the Jungle Centre

- Instincts
- Drives
- Vulnerable stance
- Male and female Chimps
- Body language

Instincts

An instinct is a built-in response or reaction, usually present from birth, to a particular stimulus or trigger. Instincts are in place to ensure that we survive. They are pre-programmed automatic behaviours and do not require us to have a say in what happens, they just need a stimulus.

For example, when a baby is born it has an automatic (instinctual) response to being touched by a finger on the cheek. It will turn towards the finger and begin to suck. This suckling response ensures that when it is near a nipple it will search out the nipple and suckle on it. All young animals have an array of instincts to help them survive. Your Chimp uses very strong instincts to keep both it and you safe.

The Fight, Flight or Freeze (FFF) response is arguably the most frequently used and most important instinct that our Chimps possess. The entire animal kingdom shares this one particular instinct and it is used every day by all species, including humans. This FFF instinct is nature's automatic response when danger or perceived danger threatens. The response takes place instantly in order to protect you. It is a very powerful reaction and it provokes intense emotion to make you act quickly. It is meant to evoke intense emotion because it is there to ensure survival in situations that can be life-threatening. In our Psychological Mind it is the Chimp that works with the FFF response and offers this to the Human.

The FFF response
Fight – attack
Flight – run away
Freeze – don't move

Quickly choosing the right response is critical to survival. If you choose to fight when you should have run then you wouldn't survive. **Fight** is taking on the threat; **Flight** is running away from the threat; **Freeze** is keeping still and hoping the threat will go away and you won't be noticed. Freeze can also be interpreted as avoiding, siding with or giving in to the threat in the hope that it won't be too damaging.

Which one of the responses the Chimp chooses depends on how vulnerable the Chimp feels. So most Chimps will choose Flight and run away whenever they can or they choose Freeze to avoid any conflict.

In the jungle, a chimpanzee's FFF instinct is a successful survival response. The problem for us, as humans, is that your inner Chimp still believes it is in the jungle and it tries to use this in everyday life. The use of the FFF mechanism is not always appropriate in modern-day society.

For example, when we have to walk into a room full of strangers, many of our Chimps start to go into Flight mode and want to get out. Some go into Freeze mode and try to remain unnoticed, whilst others may take on the Fight mode and try to establish their presence. These responses occur because our Chimp has sent a message saying, 'I feel under threat and need to do something.' Occasionally these responses become intense and cause us gross anxiety. In order to calm the Chimp, the Human needs to speak to it and use logic to reassure the Chimp. Some people's Chimps don't perceive any threat and therefore they have little, if any, reaction.

If your Chimp is trying to tell you to react to a situation, and you don't respond in some way by choosing one of the FFF options reassuring the Chimp, then your body will naturally release adrenalin.

When this adrenalin is coupled with negative thoughts your Chimp will go into an anxiety state. Anxiety in this example is nature's way of prompting us to make a decision when under threat. Anxiety typically occurs when you don't make a decision. It is a perfectly natural response from your Chimp showing that it is healthy. The answer therefore is to make a decision or reassure the Chimp!

Nature throws in anxiety as a means of forcing
the Chimp to make a decision

As FFF is about survival the intensity of emotion is massive and typically out of proportion to the event. For example, if you have to give a public speech, you may experience gut-wrenching feelings and gross anxiety as the moment approaches. This is because the Chimp has gone into FFF because it senses danger and is saying to you that this is a matter of life and death and you need to run away. Therefore, by thinking emotionally, it has a catastrophic reaction in order to make you safe; the reality is that it is not life and death but the Chimp does not know this. So when you are about to get up and speak, the Chimp, for many of us, is typically going hysterical and saying, 'What are you doing? This is a terrible danger and you are walking straight into it. You may lose your life.' If you, the Human, try to reassure the Chimp then it still comes back at you with, 'What if I look stupid?', 'What if I make a mistake?', 'What if it goes wrong?' And so it continues. The Human, by contrast, is saying, 'This is just a speech,' 'I can deal with criticism,' 'I can only do my best,' 'Stop overreacting and stop getting things out of perspective,' and so on. With these examples, we can begin to appreciate the struggle for thinking between the Chimp and the Human.

Drives

Apart from instincts, the Chimp has strong drives. A drive is something that compels us to get up and do something. If we didn't have drives we would just sit around and do nothing. Drives fulfil needs that we have, both physical and emotional.

The Chimp has powerful drives such as sex, dominance, food, security, parental, territorial and the search for a troop. The purpose of these drives is to perpetuate the species. Like instincts, drives are in-built, they are there from birth, but they don't require a trigger or stimulus. As drives are necessary for survival, their compelling nature makes them difficult to resist. For example, the drive to eat is extremely powerful and your Chimp will probably gorge itself if food is available because there may be no guarantee when the next meal will be. Again, the Human within you will be saying that one doughnut is fine whereas the Chimp will crave as many as it can eat before it feels full, leaving the Human to pick up the guilt!

Arguably, female chimpanzees are more prone to having stronger feeding drives than males, possibly because they are normally pregnant or nursing a youngster. They therefore need to eat heavily in order to do this. A developing youngster within the womb can drain the mother's physical resources and she needs to replace these quickly. In nature, the normal state for a female is to be pregnant or to be nursing and therefore it would be no surprise if the eating drive were to be powerful. The inner Chimp's drive for food is very healthy and normal. However, we are not in the jungle but in a society and the strength of the eating drive becomes inappropriate. It therefore needs to be contained and managed carefully. Many people, men and women alike, suffer horrendously trying to manage their Chimp's eating habits and it can cause terrible distress with weight control problems. If the Human understands the consequences of overeating and being overweight but is happy with this, then there is no problem between Human and Chimp. When the two disagree there are significant inner battles taking place.

Drives have to be strong in order to keep the species going and the individual alive, so they have strong reward pathways in the brain to enforce them. These pathways release chemicals that usually have a good or compelling feeling attached to them and this makes the individual want to repeat the behaviour. Hence eating food is a pleasurable experience that is not only part of a primitive drive to survive but is also an addictive habit.

Some typical drives

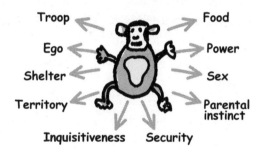

When we begin to look at how drives impact on our day-to-day lives we can see why there is a clash for power between the Human and the Chimp.

Vulnerable stance

In the jungle, the chimpanzee is not at the top of the food chain so it needs to keep constant vigilance: there are always leopards about. It is aware that it is potentially in danger at any moment, therefore it relaxes only when it is fairly sure that it is safe; almost always when it is among the troop. As it is constantly looking for any danger it is frequently on edge, gets easily upset or aggressive and is typically emotionally unstable.

This helps to explain why most inner Chimps become anxious when they are unsure or in unfamiliar territory. It is a very natural reaction from their Chimp, warning them of potential danger. It is, however, inappropriate and unhelpful most of the time. It also helps to explain why many people search out hidden meanings from things that are said to them because their Chimps are searching for potential threat. The Chimp is insecure by nature.

Male and female Chimps

We could say there are two different types of Chimp, male and female. Both of these emotional machines within us have drives and instincts. However, they serve different roles in the male and female and therefore the emphasis on the drives is different and they do not function in exactly the same way, physically or psychologically within the brain. Every Chimp is unique but to help understand the Chimp we will make generalisations about the typical male and female Chimps.

It is important to note that although male and female Chimps differ considerably, male and female Humans do NOT differ very much at all. There is also a great overlap between the characteristics of the male and female Chimps.

This section is not written to offend but is based on physical and physiological differences found in the brains of men and women. For example, in men the right amygdala (an emotional centre in the brain) has more right-sided brain connections. Whereas in women the left amygdala has more left-sided brain connections. This helps us to understand where a lot of our emotions come from. It is also to help a significant number of people to appreciate that many of the emotional features within themselves that they may not like are not coming from them but being imposed on them by their Chimp.

If we think of the purpose of the female and male in the jungle it then becomes apparent why specific drives and instincts need different emphases.

In nature the male chimpanzee must be muscled up and strong and he must impress the female and the troop to give them security. He will walk the boundaries of the territory that he must protect every day, with only the males from his troop.

The female chimpanzee is only half his size and is no match for his strength; however, she can be strong and aggressive if the need arises. This means that she must be wary of the male and be very good at weighing up his mood and anticipating his actions. In other words, she can read body language extremely well. She needs to do this to protect herself.

The male chimpanzee must be driven sexually, otherwise, if he is indifferent, the species will fail. He can be good or bad as a father. He will, however, see the female as his property and ward off other males.

The female must have a strong maternal drive and stay close to the male if she is to get his genes and fulfil her maternal drive. By staying close to the male she will remain safer from predators, as he is physically stronger. He will remain with her to obtain sexual gratification.

The female chimpanzee has an amazingly powerful maternal drive; otherwise the young would not survive. She will protect her young to the death if need be. She also has a strong nesting instinct to provide shelter for the young. If you think about it, a female chimpanzee that is highly insecure is the one that is most likely to survive and be vigilant enough for their offspring to survive. A confident female chimpanzee is probably not going to make it!

It seems reasonable then that female inner Chimps are frequently lacking in confidence and wary. They can be quick to become anxious and therefore avoid decision-making for fear of getting it wrong.

Some women complain bitterly that they find decision-making difficult, even just choosing what to wear. They then beat themselves up because they don't like this aspect about themselves. In reality it is not an aspect of them at all, it is merely an out-of-control Chimp that they can learn to manage. The woman is easily capable of making decisions; her emotional Chimp is just hijacking her.

The reason that I mention this is that, over the years, I have met many distressed women who seek help to understand why they lack the confidence to make decisions or constantly put themselves down. I am hoping that by understanding the inner Chimp they will come to realise that these features are not coming from them but from their Chimp. It is natural for the inner Chimp to be uncertain but it's very destructive for the woman, and clearly there are men also who suffer similarly. The Chimp needs managing so that the individual can be free from these influences.

Key Point
The Human male and Human female are extremely similar but are being influenced by the inner Chimp, which is more typically male or female in character.

Hormones enforce these differing roles by boosting the genes and systems within the brain. Men and women both have levels of oestrogen and testosterone. The main female hormone, oestrogen, functions to promote maternal drives, nesting instinct and passivity. The main male hormone, testosterone, gives a high sex drive, aggression and builds muscle. Many years ago, before the practice became illegal, male prisoners were given oestrogen, which calmed them down and made them more passive. The oestrogen given may have calmed them down but had some odd side effects. Understandably, breast development is not usually welcome in males!

Different emphasis rather than male and female?
So the differences between male and female inner Chimps are based on the roles that they play in perpetuating the species and in looking after themselves, along with the hormones that fuel these drives. The drives and instincts are different in that they are given

different emphases but there is a great deal of overlap. It would be wrong to say that certain characteristics are male and certain female but rather that some characteristics are found more frequently in females than in males and vice versa. There are therefore no specific characteristics that are purely male or purely female. Also, therefore, it would imply that there is not a feminine side to men or a masculine side to women, there are just characteristics.

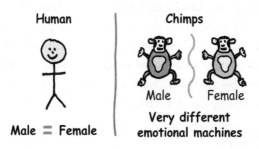

Understanding the Human – the Humanity Centre

The Humanity Centre is based on ethics and morals and is the part of the brain in the Human that lights up on a brain scanner when we show the characteristics of what it takes to live in a society. So, for example, when people show empathy or guilt this Centre will light up because it receives an increased blood supply and uses more oxygen to function. This demonstrates that it is activated. This Centre contains the unwritten rules of Humanity.

Here are some of the operational features of the Humanity Centre

- Honesty
- Compassion
- Conscience
- Law-abiding
- Self-control
- Sense of purpose
- Achievement and satisfaction

It has to be said that not all Humans possess these qualities, as some Humans are inherently unpleasant and dishonest. However, generally the Humanity Centre gives the potential for these qualities to emerge.

Honesty
Being honest and showing integrity is necessary for a society to work. Humans show sincerity and truthfulness in varying degrees, along with loyalty and reliability.

Compassion
The basis of society is compassion. An empathy and understanding of what others are going through and altruistic, selfless support for them are the hallmarks of a developed society. How human society treats its most vulnerable members sets us apart from most animal societies.

Conscience
Having a conscience is a cornerstone for a Human. Without a conscience, we lack remorse and fail to develop ourselves. The presence of a conscience gives rise to feelings of guilt and shame, which can lead to regret and the desire to change or to make recompense. Interestingly, much research has been done on the personality generally known as the psychopath. There is a substantial body of scientific evidence to show that the psychopathic individual does not demonstrate the activation, or possibly lacks the presence, of the Humanity Centre. The individual therefore effectively has no conscience.

Law-abiding
Societies have laws, whether they are written and stated or whether they are unwritten but acted out. Humans are law-abiding and accept responsibility and accountability for their actions, but in varying degrees. You cannot blame the Chimp for causing all of your problems. Sometimes it is the Human that rationally decides to break the rules and stifle its conscience.

Self-control

Self-control is probably the biggest factor that marks us out from the chimpanzee. The real chimpanzee works on impulse and lacks emotional control. These two factors are arguably the two main factors that keep a real chimpanzee in the jungle. Humans have the potential to control impulse and emotion that the inner Chimp is throwing at them. The inner Chimp has little self-control and demands immediate gratification whereas Humans can delay rewards and can choose not to work with impulse and emotion.

This factor is graphically demonstrated in the 'Stanford Marshmallow' experiment. This experiment on pre-school children has been replicated in various forms and consistent results found. In essence, children were offered a marshmallow to eat but told that **if they waited** they would receive more marshmallows at a later time. The children who delayed eating the marshmallow were found to be more successful in later life and those who could not control their impulse for immediate gratification were less successful.

Key Point

Managing your impulsive, emotional Chimp as an adult will be one of the biggest factors determining how successful you are in life.

Sense of purpose

Humans work best when they have a sense of purpose. It doesn't seem to matter what it is, as long as there is one! Without a sense of purpose the Human lacks direction and meaning to life.

Achievement and satisfaction

These are two qualities that the Human seems to be fulfilled by. Generally, achievement and satisfaction are dependent on the sense of purpose. They can come from a career, work or leisure activities.

Two different personalities

We will look at your personality, and how it can be changed, in greater detail later in the book once we have a full picture of the entire psychological mind. Here I just want to remind you that there are two distinct personalities in your head: you and your Chimp. They operate via two different brains, which are trying to work together. They may have similar personalities or they may be very different. If one of them gets control of the decision-making then this personality will dominate and this is what you will present to the outside world.

Recognising the two different personalities will help you to understand yourself better and also to manage each of them to get the best out of both. Most people can recognise that when they are not emotional but calm, they think and behave quite differently to when they are emotional and under stress.

Summary key points

- You, the Human, have a personality, agenda and Humanity Centre. You think logically and work with facts and truth.
- Your Chimp has a personality, agenda and Jungle Centre. It thinks emotionally and uses impressions and feelings.
- The Chimp is an emotional machine that will hijack you, if you allow it to. It is not good or bad: it is a Chimp. It can be your best friend or your worst enemy. This is The Chimp Paradox.

Suggested exercise:
Learning to understand yourself and your Chimp

Choosing the Chimp or the Human

In order to implement changes in your life it is important to recognise the differences between the Chimp and the Human, in terms of agendas, thinking and operating methods. Look back at situations that have happened during your day and revisit them and work out the different ways that the Chimp and Human could have handled them.

Emotional or logical thinking?

For example, consider a common scenario where someone may have said something that disturbed or troubled you and how you responded to it. If you later thought that your response was unhelpful, think through how the Chimp responded and then think through how the Human could have responded. Remember that the Human will choose to establish the facts and then gain perspective before reacting. Relate the way your Chimp reacted to typical Chimp operating and then consider how a Human response would have been more appropriate. Use this chapter as a reference to compare the modes of thinking.

Time spent thinking

The amount of time you spend reflecting on how your mind is operating, the more likely it is that you will improve your future functioning.

Chapter 3

The Divided Planet
(PART 2)
How to manage your Chimp

Now that you have an understanding of the two different beings in your head and how they operate, you can start working with them. You can begin by using a three-step process:

1. Recognise who is in charge: the Human or the Chimp.
2. Understand the rules of how the brain works and ACCEPT these.
3. Nurture and manage your Chimp to get the best results for you.

Step 1: How to recognise who is in charge

The first step is to be able to recognise who is in control, the Chimp or the Human. You can ask a very simple question that will give you an easy way of recognising who is in charge.

Key Point
The golden rule is that whenever have you feelings, thoughts or behaviours that you do not want or welcome, then you are being hijacked by your Chimp.

The very simple question, therefore, is to begin with 'Do I want...' and then finish the sentence. For example: 'Do I want these feelings?' or 'Do I want these thoughts?' or 'Do I want to be behaving this way?' If the answer is 'no' then you are in Chimp mode and if the answer is 'yes' then you are in Human mode.

Here are some examples:

- You are worrying about something. You ask yourself, 'Do I want to worry?' If the answer is 'no' then it is not you worrying but your Chimp. You now have a choice to manage your Chimp and stop it hijacking you.
- Something has happened to make you angry. You may agree that an injustice has been done and therefore your Human agrees with the Chimp. You want to do something about it but you don't want to be angry, as it is an emotion that is upsetting and unpleasant for you. Therefore you ask, 'Do I want to have this angry emotion?' If the answer is 'no' then it is your Chimp who is feeling this way. You can now thank the Chimp for the emotion but let it know that you do not want to feel this way. However, you will be taking action to address the situation that caused your Chimp to be angry but will act via the Human in a calm manner.
- You want to do something but you have feelings that are stopping you. Here the Chimp could just be refusing to engage. For example, you may want to catch up on emails or get some work done and the Chimp is giving you negative thoughts or emotions that are demotivating you. You ask, 'Do I want these indifferent and negative feelings?' The answer is 'no', therefore you recognise that they do not belong to you, the Human, and can now manage the Chimp to get rid of them.

Everyone is different, so what is right for one person may not be right for the next. There are no right or wrong answers. Only you can learn to recognise the difference between your Chimp and your self but you need to learn to do this, as it is critical if you are going to manage your Chimp.

Some typical Chimp thinking

There are some typical Chimp phrases worth watching out for that will give away when it is thinking for you.

'But what if…?'

'But what if…?' is the Chimp's favourite way to open a question.

'But what if it goes wrong?'

'But what if I can't do it?'

'But what if the sky falls down?'

The Chimp very often unsettles you with 'what if' questions. Occasionally the Human asks 'what if' questions but these are usually constructive in order to plan rather than useless worrying about things that often can't be controlled or may not even happen.

'But I feel…' or 'But I don't feel…'

'But I feel tired so I won't do it.'

'But I feel lacking in motivation therefore I can't start.'

'But I feel concerned that bad things might happen.'

The list is endless. Basically the Chimp is going on its feelings and then suggesting how you should act or what will happen because of those feelings. Again, the Human may agree with the feelings that the Chimp is offering when they are logical and wise. For example, if you have come down with a flu bug then it is probably wise to say, 'But I feel unwell so I had better not start digging the garden.'

Key Point

Remember that Chimps like to go on how they feel to decide on future actions, whereas Humans tend to go on what needs to be done and also how they will feel at the end of the day when they look back on how they used their time. These are two very different approaches.

Step 2: Understanding the fixed process of how the brain receives information

All information goes to the Chimp first

The process is always the same as you go about your daily routines: in every situation and action, all input goes to the Chimp first. The Chimp then decides if there is anything to worry about. If there is no concern then the Chimp goes to sleep and hands over to the Human. If the Chimp is concerned, then it will hold on to the blood supply in the brain and will make its own decisions on what is going on.

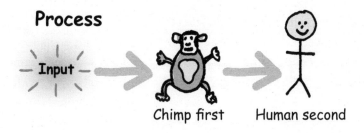

Process

Input → Chimp first → Human second

The Human and the Chimp both think in the here and now and both interpret situations as they happen. The Human interprets things in a calm and logical manner. The Chimp interprets things in an emotional manner.

The Chimp and the Human can work effectively together. The Chimp with its instincts and drives can keep us safe and healthy. It can tell us when to eat and sleep, and warn us of danger and how to deal with it, or when there is something it would like to engage with to fulfil its own desires. It is the norm for most of us to run on emotion throughout our day and there is nothing wrong with this. Problems arise when the Chimp gives us a suggestion that is not appropriate and we then allow it to control us and don't know how to stop the Chimp from dominating us.

Why can't we take the power off the Chimp and make decisions?

The simple answer is that the Chimp is more powerful and acts more quickly than the Human. A real chimpanzee has five times the strength of a human. In the same way, you can think of your emotional inner Chimp as having five times your strength. Therefore, you must learn to manage the Chimp if you are to be the person that you want to be.

It is no use trying to control a Chimp with willpower. I call this 'arm-wrestling the Chimp'. We all learn at about the age of three that willpower is not a very good way to do most things. It only works when the Chimp is asleep, indifferent or agrees. When the Chimp has a different agenda then willpower goes out of the window. So we must learn different ways to deal with the Chimp.

Arm-wrestling the Chimp

> ## *Key Point*
> *Willpower is not a good way to try and manage your Chimp – don't arm-wrestle the Chimp!*

So when you go about your daily routine the Chimp continually scans for danger and if it perceives any threat, or gets worried or concerned, then it refuses to release control of your thinking. It now works with emotion to deal with the situation. You, the Human, can recognise this but are often powerless to do anything because your Chimp hijacks you and you are left with unpleasant emotions. We can see this happen on a brain scanner with the blood supply being used by the Chimp and the Human trying to get control. The inner battle between Chimp and Human is on! The Chimp is five times as strong as the Human so the Human has no chance if it is just a battle of strength.

Don't try to control your Chimp... MANAGE it

Key Point

A chimpanzee is five times as strong as a human being. Similarly, your emotional Chimp is five times stronger than you are. Don't try to control it, manage it. You need a management plan!

Amy's road rage

Let's look at a common example of how the Chimp overrides the Human, even when the Human is present and trying to function. This example involves road rage.

Amy is driving to work in a car and another driver cuts in front of her. Her two thinking brains (Human and Chimp) now go into action.

The Human is saying, 'How ridiculous, I feel sorry for people who behave like that, it doesn't reflect on me and the best thing to do is just forget it, it's not important to me.'

However, the Chimp within her is saying, 'I am outraged, that man has just belittled me and I am angry. He needs teaching a lesson, this is all about him trying to be bigger than me, I am going to win this battle, he is not going to get away with it. I am going to let him know that I am angry, I am going to get back at him.'

If the Human doesn't know how to manage the Chimp, the Chimp now takes over. The Chimp pushes the accelerator pedal and drives as close as possible to the back of the enemy Chimp and hassles him. The enemy Chimp recognises what is happening and gestures back. The Chimp battle is in full swing. This goes on for several miles until the enemy Chimp turns off and 'waves' good-bye. Amy's Chimp is now even more agitated and irritated when she turns up for work. It takes her several hours to get over it. The Chimp keeps wittering on about the incident and how it makes her upset and angry. On the drive home her Chimp is waiting for some-one else to do it again and woe to him or her if they do!

That night Amy meets up with a friend and tells her what happened. The friend says, 'Why don't you just let it go?'

As Amy's Chimp has tired itself out the Human in Amy can finally get some control of the situation. As her Chimp is now sleeping, Amy responds in a more logical manner, and her Human says: 'I know it's really stupid; I don't know why I get so uptight. At times I hate myself for being so out of control.'

If Amy doesn't understand how her mind works she ends up beating herself up and feeling bad about it. If she understands how her mind works then we have a very different scenario and interpretation. What really happened, and how it could have been interpreted more accurately, is as follows.

Amy's road rage revisited

Amy and her Chimp are driving along. The enemy Chimp cuts in front of her. Amy is calm and accepts it is no big deal, irritating as it is. Amy says to herself: 'I will ignore this, as there is no point in getting upset over a Chimp in front of me.' However, as we have seen, the Chimp within Amy immediately wakes up and goes into screech mode.

What Amy could have done at this point is to talk to her Chimp, calm the Chimp down and then go on her way. However, she didn't know how to do this. (We will be looking at managing the Chimp later on in detail.) Amy could have dealt with the Chimp at work and again with her friend if she knew how to do it. When the Chimp did finally settle by becoming exhausted, the blood supply in the brain moved from the Chimp to the Human.

Amy then could have interpreted the situation differently and explained how frustrating it is trying to manage an ill-mannered Chimp who keeps hijacking her and taking her places that she doesn't want to go. She could also say how especially irritating it is to experience the emotions her Chimp kept offering all the way through the morning, following the incident. Amy could then say: 'I need to practise my Chimp training.' She could smile and not beat herself up, even though the Chimp is whispering in her ear: 'You are just an out-of-control person and everyone can see that.' Instead Amy could say, 'I am sorry that my Chimp got the better of me but I will continue to learn how to manage it and things will improve but I am certainly not going to beat myself up.'

The inner battle: the clash and struggle for power between the Human and the Chimp

Either you or your Chimp will make the decisions in your life. If you both agree then there will be peace. When you don't agree with the Chimp, then it typically attacks you and the attack can be emotionally very painful. Managing this struggle is critical to happiness and success.

The basic way that your emotions work is that the Chimp interprets what is happening and then offers the Human an emotion and a suggestion of how to deal with the situation. The Human then makes the decision on whether to accept the Chimp's offer or reject it.

If the Human agrees with the Chimp's offer and accepts, then there is no problem and we act on our emotions. However, if the Human decides to reject the Chimp's offer then we have a problem because the Chimp is very likely to kick off and refuse to behave. It will then create havoc emotionally until either it gets its way and hijacks us or until we learn how to manage the emotion without acting on it.

Part of the problem is that most people don't realise that the Chimp is merely making an **offer** and not a **command**. You do not have to follow your emotions; you have a **choice**.

The Chimp makes an offer

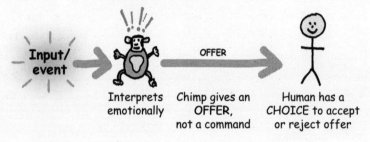

Interprets emotionally — Chimp gives an OFFER, not a command — Human has a CHOICE to accept or reject offer

The Human and Chimp may disagree

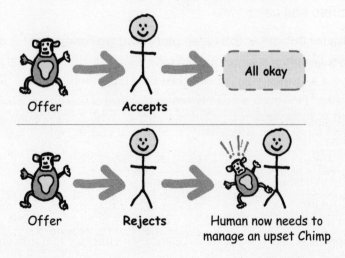

Offer — Accepts — All okay

Offer — Rejects — Human now needs to manage an upset Chimp

The taxi driver and the Chimp

Suppose you have set off too late to get to the train station and you could miss the train. You have taken a taxi to try to get there as quickly as you can. The taxi driver drives sensibly and takes his time at junctions. You are sitting in the back of the taxi watching this. The Human in you will be saying, 'The taxi driver is driving sensibly, if I don't get there on time it is nobody's fault but my own. I am the one who left it too late and I will have to deal with the consequences.' So the Human relaxes and says, 'It's not the end of the world.'

The Chimp, however, is having none of this. It gets very angry when the taxi driver slows down at the junctions and starts to criticise what is happening and may start making comments. It may even go as far as getting annoyed with the taxi driver and blaming him.

In your head the two of you are now battling for control. The Human will decide who wins but only if it knows what to do. If the Human has the skill then it can calm the Chimp down and deal with the situation. If the Human hasn't got the skill then the Chimp will take over and the Human may feel upset by the way the Chimp acted.

Coffee and cake

Imagine that you are going for a coffee with a friend and the friend says, 'Would you like a piece of cake with your coffee?' If you are trying to watch your weight then the Human will answer, 'No, thanks.' However, if you happen to like the cake, then the Chimp will answer, 'Yes, please.' Who will actually answer then, the Human or the Chimp?

Typically the Chimp will answer and the Chimp will then use emotional thinking with rationalisation to justify its decision. 'It is only a piece of cake,' and 'I want to be happy,' and 'It's ridiculous not to eat what you like.' In fact it can have a million excuses. What happens is that you eat the cake and then either try to numb your conscience or about thirty minutes later feel awful and become perplexed as to why you ate the cake in the first place. Your Chimp hijacked you. You didn't say, 'Yes, I want cake,' the Chimp did. The Chimp gets away with it and it is the Human who picks up the guilt and frustration. Of course you might actually agree to eat the cake, so you and the Chimp are happy and then there is no problem. However, if you were hijacked then we have a problem involving Chimp Management.

Sex and the roaming Chimp

Sometimes the Chimp's drives land us in big trouble. Eating a piece of cake is one thing; involving yourself in an affair is a much more serious problem. In this case there is the potential for lots of people to get hurt.

Many people have Humans that are determined to be faithful and monogamous. However, their Chimps have a different agenda with a powerful sex drive and this frequently takes them in search of encounters. Recognising and dealing with seriously powerful drives such as this is a skill and one that takes effort. We will look at this under Chimp Management.

Your Chimp – YOUR Responsibility AND ACCOUNTABILITY!

Remember: you can't use your Chimp as an excuse. If you had a dog and it bit someone, you couldn't just say, 'Sorry but it was the dog, not me.' You are responsible for the dog and its actions.

Likewise, you are totally responsible for your Chimp and its actions. So no excuses! You cannot say, 'Well, sorry, but it was just my Chimp so how can I be to blame?' or 'Oh well, I said and did some terrible things, therefore it was my Chimp so don't blame me.' **You have a responsibility to manage your Chimp.** You can work on managing the Chimp so that you can stop it making you feel bad and also harming others. Chimp Management is a skill and takes time and you may need help from someone who knows how to help you to deal with your emotions and impulses. There is little excuse for not taking responsibility, by helping yourself or getting help.

Key Point

You can't change the nature of your Chimp BUT you are responsible for managing it.

Step 3: How to manage the Chimp and develop the Human

The Chimp's drives won't change but its behaviours can

A crucial step in Mind Management is accepting that your Chimp's fundamental drives do not change. You can't change the nature of the Chimp that you are working with. It is an emotional machine that is never going to be programmed differently. Your Chimp will always act on drives and according to its nature, with emotions and actions such as aggression, neurosis or impulsivity.

With the eating drive, for example, you have to accept the Chimp wants to eat and you are always going to have that drive and associated emotions. It is not about trying to remove the drive or battle with it using willpower. It is about accepting and working with the drive. This can be done by smiling, relaxing and employing Chimp Management. You can then use the drive as you want to and not how the Chimp wants to.

So rather than trying to change the Chimp you need to manage its emotions and impulses by recognising what it needs and how it works. This means you may always experience thoughts and feelings from the Chimp that you don't welcome. Your Chimp will mature and it will learn some basic behaviours but its drives remain the same.

Nurturing before managing

There are two aspects to working with the Chimp: *nurturing* the Chimp and *managing* the Chimp, and they have to be addressed in that order.

The order of dealing with the Chimp

Nurture first → Then manage

Calmer and happier

This is a really important point so please think carefully about it. If you have a Chimp that is well looked after by being nurtured and having all its needs met, then it is very likely that this happy little animal will not cause you any trouble. This makes managing it very easy. If you do not look after your Chimp then it is very likely that it will kick off at any time and cause you a lot of pain. Nurturing and managing the Chimp is an emotional skill, and will take time and commitment to develop and maintain it.

Nurturing the Chimp

If you meet the needs of the Chimp first then the Chimp is in a position where you can talk to it and it will listen. For example, if your Chimp is insecure, you need to make it feel secure so that it is in a position to be managed. If you have an aggressive and dominating Chimp, doing something simple like playing a sport can be a socially acceptable way to fulfil this primitive drive of dominance behaviour.

The main drives and needs of the Chimp are unique to your Chimp but for most Chimps these are a combination of power, territory, ego, dominance, sex, food, troop, security, inquisitiveness and parental drives. These are common examples, so let's look at a couple of them.

Territorial drives

Chimpanzees like to have their own clearly delineated territory as it gives them the security of food, knowledge and familiarity of the area. This knowledge will help reduce the potential for predators to hide and catch the chimpanzee unawares. So chimpanzees that have their own territory will feel more secure and relaxed.

Our inner Chimp no longer has a jungle area to live in but will search out the equivalent in our society. We can have territorial instincts that are applied to our homes or gardens. The fight between neighbours over conifer hedging or even disputes over as little as six inches of driveway can be lethal. There are plenty of documented cases where this dispute results in the death of one of the neighbours. So severe is this drive to establish our territory that our Chimps will engage quickly to protect it and when uncontrolled this drive can result in disasters.

The territorial drive doesn't have to be just at home or physical. It can be at work too, and psychological. Chimps get frustrated if they feel that others are encroaching on their area of responsibility, such as a job role. At the most primitive level, experiments have shown that we can even get upset or feel encroached upon by someone just sitting at a table with us. An experiment had two people sitting at either side of the table and then one would deliberately move their belongings so that they were over the invisible halfway mark in the middle of the table. The second person, who was not aware of the nature of the experiment, would show signs of agitation that this person was invading their area. Clearly there are no lines drawn onto the table but our Chimps instinctively draw them up for us. The Chimp also receives support from the Human by the laws of etiquette, where the unwritten law is that everyone should have equal amounts of the table. Therefore the Chimp, with possible Human support, will become agitated and potentially react.

The territorial drive is strong in both male and female Chimps, though male Chimps tend to fight boundaries, whereas female Chimps tend to defend the 'nest'. These instincts are very strong in order to perpetuate the species so it is no surprise that we deal with them on a daily basis. They may be subtly disguised but with a bit of thinking you can learn to recognise them.

The territorial instinct can still be applicable in today's world and it is not good or bad. What you have to decide is whether you need to apply this instinct or whether it is not applicable to the situation or out of perspective. Once you have recognised the need for the Chimp to have this territory then you can help the Chimp by establishing it in a civilised way. This way, the Chimp will be happy and you can get on without it pestering you. The important point is to recognise the Chimp's needs and to look after it. Therefore, establishing a sensible territory for the Chimp that is compatible with the society in which we live is the way forward. Hence, establishing our homes and jobs is very reassuring to the Chimp.

This is the method for fulfilling many of the Chimp drives. First: **recognise** that the drive is present and then **find a solution** that will make the Chimp feel fulfilled and happy in a way that is acceptable in the world in which you live.

So if you recognise that your Chimp has territorial drives then you need to nurture the Chimp by providing it with some territory and space. This can be a room, a flat, a house, a job with a role that is clearly defined or even just psychological space by escaping from the world into a book. Whatever you choose should satisfy your Chimp and should be carried out. It is the Human who carries the actions out and not the Chimp!

As an example of how to deal with territories, let's look at your role at work. If your Chimp is telling you how insecure it feels because it does not know its role then it is your duty to go and establish this role with your line manager and make sure that you are happy and the Chimp is feeling settled. Otherwise the Chimp will become insecure and start acting out because you haven't looked after it. Once you have established your territory at work then your Chimp will calm down and feel secure in its part of the jungle, as it sees it.

Parental drives

Parental drives are a mixture of drives and instincts. We could look at it as the desire and need to be a parent and the instinct to protect the offspring.

How do people deal with these parental drives if they are not fulfilled? Sublimating the drive can fulfil it. Sublimating means constructively redirecting the energy and drive somewhere else. Some people will sublimate this drive by taking on professions that care for others, especially youngsters. Others may sublimate with pets; the dog is easily recognised as a classic substitute for a child. However, for some, the dog may represent another sublimated drive and is a status symbol; for others it may represent a companion. What is important for you is to recognise your own Chimp drives and to make sure that they are fulfilled in the way that you want them to be and to ensure that the sublimation is appropriate without you crossing boundaries.

Praise and recognition in nurturing the Chimp

An important point in nurturing the Chimp is to recognise the different ways that Chimps think compared to Humans when it comes to recognition and praise. Chimps are like children in that they look for external praise, whereas Humans are like adults and use internal praise and assess themselves. Of course, Humans can enjoy recognition and praise but they don't generally look for it.

Chimps like to have praise and recognition from the alpha Chimp (i.e., people they see as important). The Chimp isn't wrong in wanting this, so although you as a Human do not need praise and recognition from others, your Chimp probably does, so do not let it down. In order to look after your Chimp you really should seek out praise from those whose opinion you respect or think is important. This will settle down your Chimp. The consequences of not politely asking for recognition and praise (where it is worth it, of course!) is that your Chimp will kick off and feel resentful and undervalued. This will typically lead to some negative emotional interactions. Nurture the Chimp and get the recognition that it needs by asking for constructive feedback from someone whose opinion you believe is important.

Managing your Chimp

Three ways to manage your Chimp

Exercise   Box   Banana

Exercising the Chimp

If your Chimp is agitated or upset about something, the first thing it has to do is to release this emotion or opinion. This is called 'Exercising the Chimp'. You must allow it to do this if it is to listen. Allowing the Chimp to express emotion will calm it down and then the Chimp will be able to listen to reason or just go to sleep.

Expressing emotion means saying exactly what you think, no matter how irrational it may be and doing this for as long as it takes. Remember that the Chimp is irrational, so just let it express its feelings and then when it has finished let the Human select the sensible things that have been said and ignore the nonsense. Most Chimps will take less than ten minutes to express fears or emotions and then will go silent and listen. Occasionally they may need a second exercise.

If you were going to exercise a real chimpanzee you would take it to a fenced compound and let it loose. You wouldn't take it to your local supermarket and let it off the chain! Don't exercise your Chimp in the supermarket!

Exercising the Chimp

1 Take the Chimp to a locked compound

2 Let it all out

3 Listen to the Chimp for as long as it takes

4 Don't comment

Letting your emotions be expressed inappropriately, in a public place, at the wrong time or in front of the wrong person is like letting your Chimp loose in a supermarket. Exercising your Chimp in a fenced compound is the equivalent of expressing your emotions in private with the right person. By the right person, I mean someone who recognises that this is just a Chimp letting go and not you. Therefore, you can say what you like and they will not react to whatever you say, get worried or repeat things. They recognise that it is just your Chimp, not you. The wrong person is someone who will interact with what your Chimp is saying, and that could make matters worse.

When the Chimp has finished exercising you will feel better and can then allow your Chimp to go to sleep while you have a conversation that is Human and calm. If someone interrupts the Chimp while it is exercising, it is not likely to listen but will just get more agitated. So if you are listening to someone else's Chimp then wait until it has finished exercising!

Some people find it hard to express emotion and this can be helped by leaving them alone to do it or they might find it useful to write down their feelings. You can exercise your Chimp very successfully by yourself, but most Chimps want someone to hear what they have to say and to understand them and to console them or agree with an opinion. Expressing emotion doesn't have to be shouting and screeching. It can be done effectively in a very calm way. The crucial point is to get things off your chest, and then be able to think them through and act on the legitimate points. Remember that the Chimp may have some very good points that it is unhappy with and these need to be taken forward by the Human.

Boxing the Chimp

Once the Chimp has finished exercising you then have a chance to deal with it in a more measured way. If we assume the Chimp has exercised enough and is now in a place to receive information, we can address its fears and concerns by speaking to it.

Using facts, truth and logic we can continue to calm the Chimp down and reason with it. This reasoning by the Human is called 'Boxing the Chimp'.

The misrepresentation of John

Let's look at a scenario involving an injustice, as this almost invariably would get most of our Chimps out.

John is a foreman at a road repair site and has two men allocated to the job. He meets with the men and explains clearly what they have to do and emphasises that they must let him know if there are any problems, as the work must be finished that day. He then has to leave to oversee another project. When he returns some hours later, the two men have failed to do the work, have been sitting waiting for him to return and have not phoned him. John is agitated by this but says he will speak to his boss to let him know of the problem. When John phones his boss, John is horrified to learn that the boss called by and had already seen the two men and spoken with them. They told him that John had not left instructions or a contact number and they were therefore innocent and John was to blame. John's boss refuses to listen to John and fires him. John learns later that one of the two workmen happens to be the nephew of his boss.

If we now consider the reaction of both John and his Chimp to this situation we can work through how best to deal with this scenario. Clearly, John has fallen victim to an injustice. His Chimp will correctly interpret this situation as such and we might expect it to react with both anger and distress. This would be a reasonable response from the Chimp. John needs to first exercise the Chimp and get this injustice off his chest. He has tried to speak to his boss, who is not prepared to listen. He might decide to take this to arbitration and fight for his job and for compensation. The avenues open to him need exploring but not by his Chimp! He needs to get the emotion out by exercising his Chimp in a safe place. This might be with a friend or relative who can listen, understand and acknowledge the injustice. This will go some way to settling the Chimp. However, the Chimp may want revenge against the two men and also compensation. Compensation is again reasonable but might not happen. The Chimp needs boxing, so now it is the turn of the Human to think and plan.

John boxes the Chimp

The Human in John will need some facts and truths that will satisfy the Chimp in order to box it. The Human in John will acknowledge that, although it is uncomfortable, injustice happens and often doesn't get put right. The fact is, it may be worth fighting your corner but there is a time when you need to recognise it is not going to work the way you want it to and you must cut your losses. It is a fact that life is not fair.

John needs to talk to his Chimp and agree that there will be a limit on how much energy and time he is going to put into trying to get justice. He will confront his Chimp with the uncomfortable truths of life. The rational plans John makes will help the Chimp to accept the situation and to let go at the right time.

If John does not come up with a solid, truthful answer based on fact then it is unlikely that the Chimp will settle. For example, if the Chimp wants revenge on the two men then John cannot say to the Chimp, 'Just get over it, lots of people suffer like this.' This answer is not very helpful as it is based partly on the truth and partly on a command or wish from John to his Chimp: 'just get over it'. A better and logical answer might be, 'There has been an injustice but this particular injustice may never be resolved and we need to set a limit on the efforts to resolve it.' He can add other truths, such as, 'It is not the end of the world if justice does not get served;' ' I am an adult and I can deal with this problem;' 'I do not have to remain upset if I choose not to be;' 'This event will soon be history and I will move on.'

Clearly, John needs to find answers that will satisfy his Chimp and none of these answers might be powerful enough. What is definite is that to move on and box the Chimp he must find answers. Otherwise he will act on his Chimp feelings and find he gets nowhere and cause himself even further distress.

Sometimes you can't win. The importance here is to recognise this fact and to accept it. Then you can remind the Chimp about this. Remember that the Chimp is making an OFFER. You the Human have the CHOICE. You can either go with your emotions or you can refuse them and let the Chimp know that you want it to offer some more helpful emotions. It is not easy but at the end of the day there are many times when things in life will not go your way. Boxing the Chimp is therefore telling it *truths that it will accept* in order to calm it down.

Andy's visit to the dentist

Another example of boxing the Chimp might help to drive home the concept of how to calm the Chimp. Let's assume Andy is going to the dentist for a filling and he is very anxious about this and it is making him ill. He knows it's silly because it's only the dentist but this isn't helping at all.

First, Andy must recognise that it is his Chimp that is worrying and not him. His Chimp is acting naturally by being overanxious. He knows it is the Chimp because he answers the question, 'Do I want these anxious feelings?' with a simple 'no'. Therefore we have a very anxious Chimp. What does Andy want? He says he wants to get this in perspective and to go to the dentist in a calm and positive state. So the Human is saying, 'I want to be calm, it is only a filling.' The Chimp is saying, 'I can't cope, I am terrified and I don't want to go.'

We now have a battle that is taking place between the Chimp and the Human.

Andy exercises his Chimp

In order for the Human to get what they want they must follow the procedure in the correct order. We begin by exercising the Chimp.

Andy's Chimp begins his exercise. He says:

'I am so stupid and this is pathetic. I can't believe I am so afraid of a dentist. I know I am going to make a fool of myself. Why did I have to get a cavity in my tooth? If only I didn't have this. Why do we have to need teeth anyway, why couldn't we have something stronger?'

The rambling gets more and more stupid but less and less powerful. After about ten minutes he stops and then we hear the Human saying, 'I have had enough of this moaning.' The Chimp is getting tired, if not exhausted. Please note that this rambling was very important to get the Chimp tired. If you suppress this rambling then it is less likely that you will be able to talk to the Chimp. So don't hold back!

Andy boxes his Chimp

Now Andy can box the Chimp by talking to it using truth and logic. He might say the following to the Chimp:

'If you really don't want to go then we won't go, we can just stay with a hole in the tooth and deal with the inevitable problems from this. If we do go it may be painful to a certain extent. I agree with you.'

(Sometimes it is right to agree with the Chimp if it is telling you the truth. There is no point in having 'positive thinking' if this is really just ignoring the truth. Let's stick to reality thinking, which is more like it!)

'If we go and get the tooth fixed then it will all be over in about 30 minutes and the benefits will be great. After it is over we will be happy again. The treatment and discomfort won't last forever. Let's get some perspective on this, we are having a tooth filled, it is not the end of the world. I actually want this done.'

As you can see, there are many answers and truths that Andy can tell the Chimp. These truths will only settle the Chimp down if they are significant to it. Everyone needs to find the truths that are meaningful and powerful to **their** Chimp. So some truths will settle one person's Chimp, whereas other Chimps will need different truths. Again, the important point for you is to find the truths that will settle **your** Chimp down and make it go into its box and sleep.

If you do this well you will find that you are training your Chimp to understand there are rules for it to live by and that you, the Human, are making those rules. The Chimp will eventually start responding on a regular basis. At first it may refuse to cooperate and *it may take several repeat episodes of exercising the Chimp for any one problem* before you can box it. You may also need to *keep putting the Chimp back into its box several times for any one problem* but with practice and skill the Chimp will respond and finally the Human can manage the situation.

Andy may find that his Chimp gets out of the box again and so he needs to be patient and go through the same procedure to put his Chimp back into the box.

We never control the Chimp; we manage it. There is a difference. Remember that the Chimp is five times stronger than you; so do not use willpower to try to control it. It will defeat you in the long run. Instead manage the Chimp by exercising and boxing it.

> ## Key Point
> *It may take several repeat episodes of exercising the Chimp for any one problem before you can box it. You may also need to keep putting the Chimp back into its box several times for any one problem.*

Do I always need to exercise my Chimp?

Sometimes the Chimp does not need to be exercised and will go straight into the box with truth and logic. So don't provoke the Chimp unnecessarily by making it exercise. Also, recall that the Chimp is irrational, which means that it may be unpredictable and sometimes get very anxious for no particular reason, while at other times it may be very calm, again for no particular reason. Don't try to understand why this is so as the Chimp is not rational and in many cases is not understandable. Just deal with emotion rather than always trying to understand it.

Dealing with emotional thinking by the Chimp

The Chimp uses emotional thinking, which has traits such as jumping to conclusions, thinking in black and white and coming up with paranoid ideas. It is important to have a way of recognising when you are allowing the Chimp to think for you and then have a means to deal with it.

The easiest way of recognising that the Chimp is thinking for you is when either you are becoming emotional or you are calm but have uneasy feelings. Remember that the Chimp offers you its feelings and then you have to decide what to do with them. If you can recognise that the Chimp is using emotional thinking then you can address it with some specific techniques. For example, if the Chimp is thinking in black-and-white terms, stop and ask yourself what the alternatives are or if there is any middle ground. It might be that you are in a difficult relationship and it is upsetting you greatly not knowing whether to continue in the relationship or not. This is never a good place to be and can devastate you emotionally. The Chimp is trying to solve this situation by thinking that it has to make a choice and the choices are clear: either I leave this person and it is all over, or I stay with them and try to make things work better. This dilemma and inability to decide is being offered to the Human, who needs to recognise that this is black-and-white thinking. The Human can now look for middle ground. Ask yourself if there is any alternative. One possibility is not to see the situation as needing a definite answer right now. This would mean you could, for example, have time out where both of you have time away from each other while you gather your thoughts so that you can see the picture more clearly. Time out is a compromise giving the Human within you a chance to talk to the Chimp and settle it down. It also gives the Chimp time to express itself and exercise so that it feels better.

Paranoid thoughts can be dealt with by first recognising that you may have an overreacting Chimp offering you ideas that are too sensitive or imaginative. This often happens because the Chimp feels insecure and also hasn't got the facts, so it fills in the missing gaps. As a first step you can let the Chimp express its paranoid thoughts and then see if they still feel real. If they do, then the Human can search out facts and evidence not only to support the idea (which the Chimp will agree with) but also to dispute the idea. Running this evidence past a friend can help to clarify things. Often when we talk things out a few times the picture becomes clearer. The most important thing is to establish the facts and this usually means approaching the person or people concerned to clarify what is happening in a constructive way. All too often when we have feelings of paranoia or persecution, they disappear rapidly when we ask the right questions in a neutral way and listen to the answers.

Bananas

A third way to manage the Chimp is to feed it bananas. These are things the Chimp wants that are given either as a distraction or a reward. So there are two types of banana: distractions and rewards. Feeding the Chimp bananas is not a very powerful way to solve problems but in some circumstances they can be a very effective way to manage the Chimp.

The banana of distraction

Here is an example of a distraction banana. Imagine you are finding it hard to get out of bed in the morning. The moment you wake up, your Chimp immediately starts the dialogue: 'I can't get up, it's warm in here, I'm still tired, my body is heavy, just five more minutes…'

The problem in this circumstance is that you are allowing your Chimp to think and this is not helping. In order to distract it you can override it by saying: 'We don't think before we are on our feet.' So when the alarm goes off, immediately say firmly to the Chimp: 'We don't think, we just get up on the count of five… five, four, three, two, one and feet on the floor.' If you prepare yourself the night before and go straight into this programme with a rapid countdown, you will be on your feet before the Chimp has the chance to discuss things with you. For this to work you must prevent the

Chimp from thinking. So the distraction is by counting and moving at the same time. For example, on five you would immediately (without thinking) draw back the sheets, on four you would sit up on the edge of the bed (without allowing any thoughts), on three you would stand up, on two you would walk to the bathroom and on one you would congratulate yourself on doing what you wanted and keeping the Chimp occupied. This banana (which is a rapid pattern of actions that prevents thinking) keeps the Chimp from thinking but it must be activated quickly. Many people have used this banana with good effect to get out of bed in the mornings. Reasoning with the Chimp about getting out of bed generally doesn't work. Blocking the Chimp from thinking can be used in a lot of different scenarios with good effect.

The distraction banana can also be a way of occupying an agitated or impatient Chimp when you have to pass time waiting for something. Simple distractions such as reading a book or listening to music are often the most powerful.

The banana of reward

Giving rewards to your own Chimp can be surprisingly powerful. For example, suppose you have to write ten emails but can't get started and want to have your coffee. If you say to your Chimp: 'When you have written five emails you can have your coffee,' it is not unusual for your Chimp to suddenly give you the incentive to start the emails. This 'banana' of having a cup of coffee at the end of the five emails will make the Chimp energised to get you to write the emails. The Chimp will make you focus powerfully on the task and will help and not hinder you. This may seem bizarrely irrational but then the Chimp is irrational and the technique usually works.

Common bananas for most Chimps come in the form of praise or approval from other people. Most Chimps look for recognition and approval from others; therefore to put this in place, as a reward, can be very powerful. For example, your room at home needs painting and you know that you want to get it painted but are struggling to get started. You can reward the Chimp by phoning a friend and inviting them round to view the new paint work in your room. It is no surprise that the Chimp will jump up and make you paint the room because it wants the praise (and also because it doesn't want to look bad in front of the friend).

Bananas can be a useful way to manage your Chimp in the short term to get things done, or distract you from concerns, or allow you to have time out. They are generally not as powerful as boxing the Chimp because they don't usually tackle the cause of the problem.

Developing the Human

In the battle and struggle for power between the Human and the Chimp on the Divided Planet you mustn't forget yourself. You are a separate entity to your Chimp. You as a Human have needs just as the Chimp within you has needs. The Human needs could be worked out by looking at the characteristic features of the Human within. So we expect Human fulfilment by constructive accomplishments, such as hobbies and interests that are not crucial to survival but bring us satisfaction and a richness to our lives.

Key Point
Chimps like to survive; Humans like to have a purpose.

When we have a sense of purpose in life it brings with it a sense of meaning and this in turn leads to achievement, satisfaction and well-being. We will look at success and happiness in great detail later in the book but here the message is that in order to look after your machine well, you must consider the needs of both the Chimp and the Human. All too often we stop at the Chimp because it takes up our time and shouts the loudest.

Summary key points

- 'Do I want…?' is the question to ask in order to recognise if your Chimp is hijacking you. If the answer is 'no' then you are being hijacked.
- You are always responsible for your Chimp.
- The Chimp is five times stronger than you are.
- Nurture your Chimp before you try to manage it.
- Manage your Chimp, don't try to control it.
- There are three common ways to manage your Chimp: Exercise, Box and Bananas.

Suggested exercise:
The 'NEAT' exercise

- **N**ormal
- **E**xpected
- **A**ccepted
- **T**aken care of

Learn to be NEAT in life

It is **Normal** to have Chimp outbursts and activity that you will not manage well. Therefore, you should **Expect** this to happen from time to time. **Accept** that you are not perfect and this animal is very powerful. **Take care of** the outburst or activity by appropriate means, such as apologies if you have affected others, or by forgiving yourself if you feel you have let yourself down.

Being **NEAT** means being reasonable with yourself. Whenever you experience any form of Chimp activity that you do not manage well, stop and think **NEAT**. Accept that this is the way the machine works and then take care of the situation without getting down. Guilt, shame, frustration and other negative emotions are there to help us make repairs not to destroy us. Nobody gets it right all of the time and many of us get it wrong quite a lot of the time.

Work on implementing **NEAT** thinking as a way of dealing with poor Chimp Management. If you have negative emotions, turn these round and use them to move forward. Think of ways to appropriately deal with negative emotions rather then engaging with them.

Chapter 4
The Guiding Moon
(PART 1)
How to understand the Computer in your mind

The Guiding Moon is your brain's computer. In the Universe, the moons all act as stabilisers to the planets that they are orbiting; the Guiding Moon therefore stabilises the Divided Planet. This means that if we can get the Computer in your mind to work well, it will give your mind stability and make managing your Chimp much easier.

The Computer: some basic facts

What is the function of the Computer?

Your Computer has two functions:

- It can think and act automatically for you using programmed thoughts and behaviours.
- It is a reference source for information, beliefs and values.

How does information get into the Computer?

When you are born, effectively the Computer is an empty hard drive. It is merely a store for behaviours and beliefs that the Human or Chimp will input into it. It doesn't have any original thinking or power of interpretation but will act on stored information. Often the Human or Chimp may not even be aware that they have put these conscious or unconscious thoughts or behaviours into the Computer. How successful it is in functioning depends on how helpful and truthful the inputs were.

Potentially the Computer is more powerful than the Chimp and the Human because it is the reference source that both of them look to for help and guidance.

Therefore, it is advisable to get to know how it works and how to maintain it, so the guidance it gives leads to success and happiness.

Are the Computers in men and women the same?

The short answer is yes. They function in a very similar way but there are some differences. The typical female Computer can work with language at a higher level than the typical male Computer. Female brains have many more areas than male brains, called association centres, for working with language. In contrast, the male brain has an area for dealing with mathematics and map-reading that is around four times the size than in the female brain (whether it works better is another matter!). It does mean that it is likely, since the two brains typically do show physical and physiological differences, that they will work differently and be better suited to specific tasks or learning.

These discussions always seem to evoke high emotions with people feeling judged or categorised, which is a shame, as all that scientists are trying to do is to help us to understand ourselves better. There are of course always exceptions to the rule with both sexes, and research continues to throw more light onto this as we go forward. So, anatomically and physiologically, there are differences between the male and female Computers. There are also different responses to some neurotransmitters (chemicals that send messages) in different parts of the brain.

How fast is the Computer?

We can think of the Computer as running at a speed around four times that of the Chimp and twenty times that of the Human. Therefore, if the Computer is operating well, it can execute commands at an amazing speed with complete accuracy and before the Chimp or Human has a chance to finish thinking.

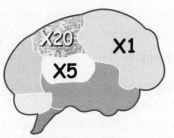

Speed of reaction

These values reflect the speed of what actually happens in the Human brain, where some areas literally operate at a much faster speed than others.

What is in the Computer?

Autopilot Gremlin Goblin Stone of Life

- The Autopilot is a constructive or helpful belief or behaviour.
- The Gremlin is an unhelpful or destructive belief or behaviour that is removable.
- The Goblin is an unhelpful or destructive belief or behaviour that is firmly fixed and extremely difficult to remove.
- The Stone of Life contains the values and beliefs by which you live your life.

The Computer's functions in detail

- Automatic functioning
- Acting as a reference source

Automatic functioning

Automatic functioning, which is exactly what it sounds like, is based on learnt behaviours, learnt beliefs and automatic programmes. It is when we just act with behaviours or thoughts that we have already worked out and can almost carry them out in our sleep. There is little effort on our part as a Human to think. When we combine actions, we can form complicated programmes, such as making a cup of coffee or riding a bike, which we eventually do automatically without thinking.

The Chimp and the Human both input into the Computer and therefore programme it. Once the Computer has programmes to run with, it will take over and allow the Chimp and Human to take a break from thinking and interpreting. The Computer is programmed to think and act for us but only with information that we have told it to use. These stored beliefs and behaviours are therefore learnt by the Human and Chimp and put into the Computer. This is in contrast to the Chimp's instincts that are inherited in the genes giving rise to instant reactions from the Chimp.

The Computer does most of the work in taking us through our day. How well it gets us through the day will depend on what has been put into it. We can of course add and remove things from the Computer, if we stop and take time to maintain it. The problem is that most of us do not do this.

Autopilots

Autopilot

Autopilots are all the positive, constructive beliefs, behaviours and automatic functioning that help us to be successful and happy in life. They can be placed into the computer at any age. So Autopilots could include, for example: riding a bike; staying calm when something goes wrong; focusing on solutions rather than problems; tying a shoelace; being organised and disciplined as a routine; having a positive self-image.

Goblins and Gremlins

Gremlin   Goblin

Goblins and Gremlins are more or less the opposite of Autopilots. They are unhelpful and destructive behaviours, beliefs or automatic programmes that are stored in the Computer.

A Goblin is usually put into the Computer when you are very young. During the very early part of your childhood your Computer tends to hard-wire any information put into it. So Goblins are more or less hard-wired into the Computer and are very difficult to remove, so you need to learn to contain them. As a rule, Goblins occur before the age of about eight and Gremlins usually occur after the age of eight. As Gremlins are soft-wired, when you find them you can remove them. The distinction between Goblins and Gremlins is only made because it is important to know which ones can be removed and which ones probably can't be removed. That way you are not trying to do the impossible. Either way you can deal with these unhelpful creatures once you have detected them.

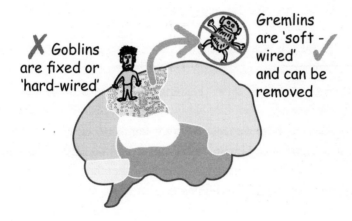

An example of a Goblin

Let me give one example of a Goblin. The Fridge Door Syndrome depicts the most common example of a Goblin and this one affects most people in the Western world.

It is the first day of school and the young child is full of emotion. The teacher says to the child, 'Let's paint a picture for your parents.' After painting the picture the child runs home to show the parent. As the child runs up to the parent, the parent says, 'What is that you've got?' The child hands over the painting. The parent responds, 'This picture is fantastic, you are very clever, I am so proud of you, I want the world to know just how good you are,' and then puts the picture on the fridge door for all the world to see just how clever the child is.

What has happened is that the child now has a great big Goblin to share life with!

Let's look at the same scenario with a different approach. The child returns from school with the painting and runs to the parent. The parent responds with, 'Hang on,' and moves the painting to one side and hugs the child. Then the parent says, 'I am so proud of you and you are clever and I want the world to know just how proud I am of you.' 'Now, what is this that you have got?' The parent and child now have a discussion about the painting and the parent compliments the painting and the child, and asks the child if they would like to put it on the fridge door because it is pretty.

In the first scenario what the parent did was to tell the child that it was clever and that the parent was proud of it *because of what the child had achieved*. In other words, implying that the child's worth is dependent on the painting. Then the parent went on to tell the child that they wanted to let the world know by putting the picture on the fridge door. The message to the child was: '*It is what you can achieve in life that will make you worthy*. It is what you do that will make others see you in a good light.'

The message to the second child was that *you are worthy just as you are. It is who you are that is being loved and respected and you don't have to achieve anything in order to get this*. The parent then went on to say that achieving things is good but these shouldn't be mixed up with your own self-worth. It is of course always good to praise a child if it has done its best, whatever the level it has achieved.

Of course there is a balance to be had and in these two scenarios I have taken an extreme view to drive the point home, but all too many of us are fearful of how we do and what others will think.

Many students when taking exams become very anxious and fear the results. If you ask them how they would feel about taking the exam if the result were secret and known only to them and if it were not good they could retake it, in secret, until they passed, they would then usually say, 'I wouldn't be afraid or worried at all.' Clearly the exam is not the problem for these students, it is the fear of others knowing the result and the implication this has for them.

If we knew nobody thought badly of us then we would have little fear, it would be more of a nuisance to fail and we would then deal with the consequences. We would also not weigh our own self-worth by an exam result. This is the Fridge Door Goblin at its best!

This syndrome is extremely common and the majority of the population seems to be affected by it. However, we can manage it and work around it, not letting it control us. Part of the problem is that the Chimp helps the Goblin. The Chimp has a very powerful troop drive that ensures our survival by being part of the troop. To be part of the troop means that we must be accepted. To be accepted means that we must be strong and useful. Therefore, from the primitive Chimp instinct we want to impress others. Clearly if we link this drive with the Goblin, it becomes very strong indeed. Therefore many people suffer emotionally because they are constantly worried about what others think of them and they would love to just live their lives and not be concerned, but the Chimp and Goblin won't let them.

An example of a Gremlin

One example of two very common Gremlins that most people have in their Computers and experience from time to time: the twins of unrealistic expectation and unhelpful expectation.

The Gremlin twins

Unrealistic expectation | Unhelpful expectation

Checking to see if you are being realistic and reasonable about any expectation you have is always well worth doing. If your expectations are unrealistic or unhelpful then it is almost guaranteed to lead to very strong negative emotions within you. Typically, emotions such as frustration, anger or disappointment rush in.

Consider a simple Gremlin that says, 'I believe that I should always be on time.' If you are late, for whatever reason, then you are likely to become stressed, as you are going on a belief that you should always be on time. You could replace the Gremlin with an Autopilot that says, 'I would like to be on time whenever I can but sometimes this can't happen and it is not the end of the world and I will deal with it.' This is a more realistic belief that is likely to relax you and help you to act more like an adult than a child if things don't go according to plan!

Another example of an unrealistic expectation is that you always have to win to prove yourself. Playing a game of tennis can be good fun if you have a belief that it is just a game and the outcome doesn't really matter. This doesn't mean that you won't try but it means that you have perspective. However, if you have a belief that you have to win because it reflects on your worth as a person then the game will become intense and probably unpleasant. What you hold as a belief will definitely affect the way in which you handle outcomes or respond to them, whatever they are. It is better to have realistic expectations or in some cases hold no expectations at all.

Examples of other Gremlins include:

- Overreacting to situations
- Eating every time you feel like it but don't need to
- Beating yourself up
- Worrying about decisions and not making them
- Getting angry when you don't want to

The Computer acting as a reference source

There are three aspects to the Computer acting as a reference:

- General reference with Autopilots and Gremlins
- The Stone of Life with the 'Truths of Life', 'Values' and the 'Life Force'
- The Mindset

General reference with Autopilots and Gremlins

Both the Human and the Chimp use the Computer as a memory bank for decision-making. When any experience occurs, the Human and the Chimp interpret what's happening and then look into the Computer to see the previous experiences, beliefs or memories that are stored. A decision or course of action can be influenced by this stored information.

Here is an example to demonstrate how this works. Adam works for a very tough boss who calls him in only to criticise and warn him that his job is not secure. The Human in Adam is unsettled by the behaviour of the boss and inputs into the Computer that 'when you see this boss, expect to have criticism and be prepared for this emotionally'. This is a true belief that seems to be backed up by experience. It is a helpful interpretation of what is happening to put into the Computer and therefore would be an Autopilot (a truthful and helpful belief on which to base your future behaviour).

The Chimp in Adam quite reasonably gets very disturbed by meeting the boss and the Chimp might put into the Computer the belief that 'whenever you meet someone who is the boss, expect to be very disturbed and receive bad news'. This is a generalisation because not every boss will be like this and even the same boss may act differently depending on the occasion. So the Chimp inputs into the Computer a not-so-helpful belief that '**ALL** bosses are going to be critical and make you feel bad.'

This interpretation by the Chimp is not that helpful and could be very destructive in the future. It is not the truth and is therefore a Gremlin (an unhelpful belief that is likely to lead to unhelpful behaviours in the future).

What we now have are two very different messages in the Computer. These will be used as a reference for the future.

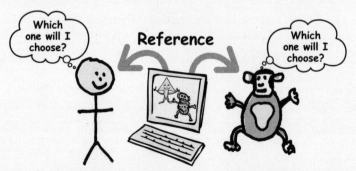

The Human and the Chimp could choose either an Autopilot or a Gremlin. What happens depends on what is chosen

While Adam stays in his current job with the same boss, either message will work when he gets called in to see the boss, as the boss is very likely to be unreasonable again. However, let's assume Adam now moves jobs and has a new boss. The new boss does not work like the old one and is very understanding and likes to compliment and support his staff. Adam receives a call to say that the new boss would like to meet him. The Chimp in Adam immediately senses potential danger and looks into the Computer to see if there is any reference to work from. The Chimp talks to the Gremlin and the Gremlin says 'ALL bosses are going to be critical and make you feel bad.' The Chimp now says, 'This is bad news because every boss will be critical and make you feel bad and you may lose your job.' The Human doesn't get a chance because the Chimp and the Gremlin are more powerful. So Adam enters the room with fear and is unlikely to have a good conversation with the boss because he is too anxious and already believes he knows the outcome. The alternative outcome is that Adam's Human looks to the Autopilot and then reassures the Chimp and says, 'I'll give this new boss a chance as he may not be like the old one.'

This is one way (through experience), by which Gremlins and Autopilots come into being. Either the Chimp or Human has put them into the Computer for future reference and use. It also demonstrates the way in which the Chimp works very closely with the Gremlins. Other ways Gremlins and Autopilots appear can be by education, or by discussion with others about their experiences.

The Chimp and the Human are therefore using stored beliefs in the Computer as a reference point to help to make decisions. If the Computer has lots of Autopilots then it will moderate or stop the Chimp in its tracks and settle it down. This gives the Human a chance to look for and use the Autopilots and stabilise the entire system giving the person a calm feeling. This system can be seen at work on a brain scanner with blood flowing to different parts of the brain, as they are being used. Having lots of Gremlins in the Computer is very destabilising to both the Human and the Chimp.

The Stone of Life with the 'Truths of Life', 'Values' and the 'Life force'

The Stone of Life is your ultimate reference point. It is where your 'Truths of Life', 'Values' and 'Life Force' are all inscribed. The Chimp and Human gauge everything by the Stone so let us look at these three things in detail.

The Truths of Life

The Truths of Life are how you believe the world works and you can 'prove' they are true by examples and experience. You have either worked them out or accepted them from somewhere (parents, education, experience and so on).

Everyone will have different truths but many of us share some of the same truths. The truths may be the same as some Autopilots or even some Gremlins, but they are the ones that you have chosen to live by. They are a set of beliefs that you believe are true.

For example, suppose you have the rule that 'life is not fair'. This seems reasonable as a 'Truth of Life' to most of us because we know it is 'true'. If we then say that this is true and we live by it, then we would not get particularly upset or not even get upset at all if something was unfair, because that is how we believe that life works. It doesn't mean that we don't try to be fair in life but it does mean that when life is unfair we accept it and deal with it.

If someone holds as a truth that 'life is fair' and tries to live by this 'truth', then it is obvious that this person is very likely to get annoyed and upset quite often, when life is not fair. For example, if they buy a set of playing cards from a shop and get home and find that one is missing they will shout, 'This is not fair.' They will return to the shop and explain and expect to get a new pack of cards. This is a reasonable expectation. However, the assistant says she is sorry but there are no refunds because you should have checked before you left the shop. You can imagine the protests now. At the end of the day protesting that it isn't fair won't get them anywhere apart from angry. Sometimes it is best to sigh and say, 'Life is not fair, and on this occasion it wasn't, so I will accept it because there is nothing I can do.' Your choice; you can fight the case and possibly win or you can write it off as experience and save the hassle that might be undignified and fruitless.

My first three Truths of Life are:

1. Life is not fair.
2. The goal posts move.
3. There are no guarantees.

If I manage to live by these 'truths' or rules then very little upsets me. When I don't live by these 'truths', and have days where I say, 'But life is fair,' then I come unstuck and have to remind myself of the reality. Of course these truths don't mean that I just roll over in life, far from it, but it does mean that at the end of the day if I have to accept injustice then I can accept it and move on unscathed.

Where did the idea that life is fair or SHOULD be fair come from? Most likely from early childhood when you were probably brainwashed! As a child you were read or watched fairy stories. The prince always married the princess and the wicked witch died and everyone lived happily ever after (except the witch, of course, but she got what she deserved). In other words, good always wins in the end. But that was a fairy story and you have been brainwashed into believing that it really does happen this way. It doesn't. In fact we might do our children a favour by changing the ending to let the witch kill off the princess and marry the prince. Then after several horrendous years they get a divorce and the prince mourns for the rest of his life while the witch smirks happily. This is a bit more lifelike. But be warned, if you tell it to children who already have a strong belief that good always wins then they might attack you, so keep your distance!

In reality not everything works out. I think it is worth trying to make good win and to be fair, but it is unwise to believe it SHOULD happen and something is wrong if it doesn't. Hence, my own number one truth of life, 'Life is not fair'.

Values

Within the Computer you have unwritten values that you believe to be important to you. Just as with the Truths of Life, it is very helpful for you to work out your values, as these values will be the guide for the Human and Chimp to work to. The values will act as a constant reminder of where your heart and soul lie and will settle down both the Human and Chimp in times of distress. Values are judgement calls that you have made and reflect moral and ethical principles that you intend to uphold. For example, you may hold the value that 'lying is wrong'. This is not a truth of life as you can't prove it, but it is a value judgement. Common values that some people hold could be:

- Being unfaithful is wrong.
- Family is more important than work.
- Being selfless is a virtue.

So the difference between 'Truths' and 'Values' is that 'Truths' are evidence-based, whereas 'Values' are personal judgement calls.

The Life Force

To discover the Life Force on your Stone of Life, imagine that you are 100 years old and on your death bed with one minute left to live. Your great-great-grandchild asks, 'Before you die, tell me what I should do with my life?'

Pause for a moment now and try to honestly answer the question immediately within the next minute. You have just one minute, start now and then when the time is up and you have worked out what you would say to them, continue reading.

Answering this question will identify what is important to you, what is the essence of the Sun within your Universe. It is what life is all about to you. It is your 'Life Force'.

Many of you will answer with statements such as, 'it doesn't matter what you do', 'be happy', 'don't worry', and 'make the most of it'.

Whatever your advice was to your great-great-grandchild is really the advice to yourself. If you are not living by this advice, which is the essence of your existence, you are living a lie. Don't live a lie; it will unsettle you more than anything else.

Summary of the Stone of Life

- The Truths of Life are statements that you believe are true for the way that the world works.

- The Values are the principles and ideals that you believe in.
- The Life Force is what you believe life is all about and how it should be lived.

The Mindset

The final aspect of the Computer acting as a reference is the Mindset. To understand a Mindset it is helpful to ask three specific questions.

- How do you see yourself?
- How do you see others?
- How do you see the world?

The way in which we approach life is greatly influenced by the way in which we see ourselves, others and the world in which we live. These three viewpoints represent the Mindset that we hold. So a Mindset is the basis that we work from when dealing with ourself, others and the world.

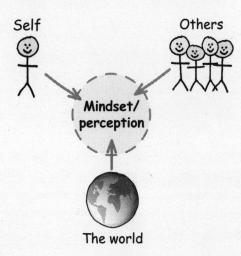

Mindset is based on perception of self, others and the world.

Self Others

Mindset/ perception

The world

These beliefs tend to come in clusters (of Autopilots and Gremlins), which group together to form a characteristic presentation. It is important to note that this is not your personality, although it will influence it. It is a pathway in the Computer based on beliefs that are changeable.

For example, suppose you see yourself as a very intelligent person whom everybody loves and the world as a place of fun and opportunity, then your Mindset means that it is likely that you will get up every morning feeling good and will look forward to new experiences. It also means that if you meet someone who doesn't like you then you will probably think that something is wrong in their world and that when it comes right they will like you again. As you can imagine, this particular Mindset will probably be a great advantage to you most of the time and get you into difficulties only very occasionally. Certainly, it is very likely that you will be a happy person.

Now let's reverse the situation. Suppose you believe that you are not intelligent and that you have to try and hide this so that others won't find out. You also believe that others are better than you and that they are usually trying to uncover your own inadequacies. Finally you believe that the world is a hostile place that you must survive each day. With this Mindset, it doesn't take too much imagination to see how destructive this will be to you. You will not want to try anything new for fear of looking silly and being found out and confirmed as an idiot. You may be very cautious with other people, often resenting and finding fault with them, as you may feel they are patronising you. It is likely that you will have few friends and either withdraw feeling depressed from a world that you feel you don't belong in, or you may become a very aggressive person always feeling like you have to prove yourself or defend yourself against others.

These two Mindsets are very severe but they do represent two ends of a spectrum within which we all tend to fall. It is well worth spending some time thinking about the Mindset that you have because it will affect the Chimp, the Human and what goes into the Computer by distorting your perception of what is happening in everyday events.

Let's look at another extreme example to drive the point home. Imagine that you believe you are Miss World or Mr Universe and are going into a nightclub; it is likely that you would walk in feeling positive and confident, striding in, head held high, wanting to meet other people. Now imagine that you believe you are a Quasimodo look-a-like. You may not feel too confident and would possibly slink in, trying to avoid other people. Your Mindset greatly influences the way in which you act and portray yourself to the world.

Summary key points

- The Computer has two principal functions: running automatic programmes and acting as a reference source for the Human and Chimp.
- The Computer can be thought of as being twenty times faster to act than the Human and four times faster than the Chimp.
- Autopilots are constructive and helpful automatic behaviours and beliefs.
- Gremlins are destructive and unhelpful automatic behaviours and beliefs that are removable.
- Goblins are destructive and unhelpful automatic behaviours and beliefs that are firmly fixed.
- The Stone of Life contains your Truths of Life, Values and Life Force.
- The Mindset you hold is based on your perception of how things are and therefore influences your approach to life.

Suggested exercise:
Reviewing your Computer and Stone of Life

Reviewing your Computer for Gremlins
As the Computer is the steadying influence on both Human and Chimp, it is important to regularly review what is in it. Search for the Gremlin twins of unrealistic expectation and unhelpful expectation in your day-to-day life. You may be surprised to find how often they are behind many emotionally unpleasant feelings. If you have become upset by something, let this be a prompt to check on whether your expectations are realistic and helpful regarding the situation or others involved. Your Chimp is likely to have very high expectations of others. Recognise this and replace them with Human expectations. For example, expecting friends to always agree with you is Chimp, instead of expecting friends to have an opinion and hoping it will agree with yours, which is Human.

Making the Stone of Life visible
Consider your Stone of Life and take time to very clearly work out what is written on it. Make sure that you have specific Truths and Values that you are working with. Write down your Life Force statement. When you have done this, draw up the Stone of Life onto a poster and put it somewhere prominent to remind you of what you believe and want to live your life by.

Chapter 5
The Guiding Moon
(PART 2)
How to manage your Computer

Managing your computer is mainly about establishing constructive thoughts and behaviours. We will look at managing the Computer by working through these four themes:

- Identifying and replacing Gremlins with Autopilots
- Stopping any more Gremlins from going into the Computer
- Perfecting the Stone of Life
- Establishing your Mindset and living by it

Identifying and replacing Gremlins with Autopilots

Automatic functioning relies on stored beliefs and behaviours. In order for you and the Chimp to go to sleep and let the Computer take over, you have to programme it properly. If it doesn't run smoothly or it doesn't know what to do, then you and the Chimp stay awake and interfere.

Useful, constructive behaviours and beliefs are the Autopilots. Useless, destructive behaviours or beliefs are the Gremlins. So you will first need to identify the Gremlins in your Computer and then remove them by replacing them with Autopilots. Remember that the reason this is so important is because whenever the Human or the Chimp receives any information, they first look around the Computer to see if there is anything they should know or remember before acting. If they are given constructive and helpful comments from an Autopilot they will settle down and act appropriately; if they are given information from a destructive Gremlin they are likely to act on this. The Gremlin is likely to rouse the Chimp into an unwelcome emotional state and unsettle the Human, which will lead to a negative outcome and probably regrettable behaviour.

The Chimp and Human always look into
the Computer before acting

Gremlins are often hidden so you need to search for them. For example, if you have a hidden belief that you are not as good as other people, it may not be obvious to you, so you have to find it. Let's say you are waiting in a queue to buy a cup of coffee and someone pushes in front of you. You, the Human, may want to politely say, 'Excuse me there is a queue;' your Chimp might want to say the same thing, but in a much more aggressive manner! However, before either of you get a chance to speak, you and the Chimp look into the Computer. Here you will see the Gremlin who says, 'You are not as good as other people.' This is the reference for the Human and the Chimp to act on. So this Gremlin prevents you from speaking because you feel you do not have the right or you fear the person's response.

This Gremlin is very destructive and it is compromising your ability to act as an adult. What if you had a Gremlin that said, 'You are better than everybody else'? This Gremlin may give you a lot of confidence but you may well come across as arrogant and domineering, which in the long run is just as unhelpful as the first Gremlin.

Gremlins must be replaced with Autopilots

If you can recognise these Gremlins then you can remove them. To replace a Gremlin you must introduce an Autopilot. In other words, if you have a belief that is unhelpful, you must replace it with a helpful belief. In this case, that helpful belief is likely to be that 'all humans are equal and we are all worthy of respect'. If this Autopilot were in your head in the example above when someone barged in front of you, then when the Human and Chimp looked into the Computer to check for guidance they would have seen an Autopilot that says 'we are all worthy of respect' and then either the Chimp or Human could have spoken up. (Hopefully the Human would have silenced the Chimp and said, 'Let me handle this politely!')

Finding your Gremlins

Whenever a Gremlin is at work it will typically leave you with a negative experience, which will be either an unwelcome emotion or a negative outcome. This often means that the Gremlin will stop you doing something you want to do or have you doing something that you don't want to do. Only you can decide if a belief you have is helpful or not, depending on what makes you happy and how you want to live your life.

To find your Gremlins, think of a time when you had an emotion that you didn't want. This is usually a negative emotion – people don't normally complain about being too happy or excited! Such an emotion could be: anger, frustration, upset or disappointment. Next, re-live the situation. What happened? What were you doing? What were others doing? What were you thinking? Focus on what you were thinking and ask yourself if this was a helpful thought or not. Also, was it a truthful thought or not? If it is causing you a negative emotion it is likely to be an unhelpful Gremlin and could be removed. Gremlins and the Chimp can be hard to distinguish between if they are both saying the same thing. This is not too surprising since it was the Chimp that put the Gremlin into the Computer in the first place! The Chimp thinks in the here and now. The Gremlin merely recalls what the Chimp has previously said in the form of a belief. For example, someone asks you to help him or her with a job. Your Chimp might react on the spot with a negative feeling or a Gremlin might recall that every time you get asked to do a job it is hard work and therefore the Gremlin gives you an automatic negative feeling because of this negative belief.

Removing your Gremlins

Let's take a common example of how to remove a Gremlin and turn it into an Autopilot.

You might complain that you just can't say 'no' to people and this eventually makes you feel upset because you take on too much or feel a bit angry that you have more work to do. The Gremlin is the behaviour of inappropriately saying 'yes' whenever you are asked to do something. Other Gremlins, which are destructive beliefs, will be behind this one and we need to find them.

To find the Gremlins that are causing you to say 'yes', every time you are asked to do something, try asking yourself two questions:

- What do you believe saying 'no' to someone will imply about you?
- What are the consequences of you saying 'no' to someone?

If your answers are something like this: 'If I say "no", then this implies that I am selfish and the consequences are that I will be seen as lazy,' then these two Gremlins are making the Human within you make poor decisions.

Try to replace these Gremlins with some truths. For example:

- Saying 'no' is the appropriate response of an adult who is respecting his or her own exhaustibility or boundaries.
- Saying 'no' is a powerful thing to do by a balanced person.
- People who are realistic will accept being turned down and appreciate that you have the right to say 'no'.
- People respect those who can say 'no'.

A helpful way forward for not saying 'yes' to everything is to break the cycle early. So when you are asked to do something, give your Human a chance to think by saying an automatic response such as 'I need a moment to think if I can fit this in,' or 'I need to think if it is appropriate for me to do this.' Once you get used to responding, by stopping and letting people know you need time, they will respect this and you have a chance to make wise decisions.

Gremlins can take several efforts, and some time to remove them, but with persistence they will go. The number of 'truths', or Autopilots, to help with this problem is significant. In order for it to work you have to find these truths and then continually reinforce them until they are firmly fixed in the Computer and become second nature. Going back to the above example, most people will understand and accept if you say that you cannot help them. There are no medals for those who continually say 'yes' and then get upset by it. The fact you recognise you are having problems saying 'no' means there is a need to change.

You have to decide on what is your 'truth'
Let's consider a mother who gets repeatedly angry with her teenage daughter about her room being untidy but doesn't want this emotion. This anger and the untidiness is affecting their relationship. The

mother could ask herself: 'What are the beliefs that I hold causing me to be angry?'

The beliefs that caused the anger might be:

- My daughter is lazy if she doesn't tidy her room.
- There will be germs in the room if it is untidy and germs are bad.
- It is my house and these are the rules.

She could then challenge these beliefs to see if they are actually true or not. Even if she still thinks they are true, she can ask herself:

- What is more important, a battle about the room or a good relationship with my daughter?
- Is there another way of approaching this problem?

The mother can't expect to be angry and not evoke a reaction from her daughter and this may not be the one that she wants. The mother can change the beliefs listed above and replace them with more helpful ones such as:

- Having an untidy room is not the same as being a lazy person; it's just an untidy person who happens to be a teenager.
- My daughter is learning to be an adult and she learns best by discovering things for herself.
- If I explain that an untidy room upsets me then she may tidy it for me.
- It may be my house but it is my daughter's room.

Of course the mother might still choose to get angry and lay down the law and it might all work out. However, she can't complain if she puts the rules before her relationship with her daughter and the relationship disappears.

This example shows that we all have to decide for ourselves what we want and how we want to act and what we want to believe.

This is a choice, and with all choices come consequences. Only you can decide how you want to act in your world. If you want things to change then you have to look at things differently. If you are unwilling to challenge your beliefs then the Gremlin will remain and you must accept the consequences.

Remember that when you have identified the belief that sits behind your negative emotions you have to replace it with something. You are trying to create a new automatic thought, an Autopilot, or pathway, in the brain. You need to replace the Gremlin with a positive Autopilot statement and you need to think about this regularly, rehearsing it until it becomes your automatic response.

Mothers still need a life

A common Gremlin inputted by some female Chimps comes from the maternal drive. This is the belief that the only role she has is to look after her children and family. The Chimp could have programmed the Computer to have a Gremlin that says, 'You have to put your family first on every occasion, otherwise you are a bad mother.' The consequence of this is the mother spends all her time running around after the family and has no time for herself. Anything she does for herself makes her feel guilty. This is not a helpful or healthy belief and it begs the question: what role model is this offering her daughter if she becomes a mother?

Replacing your Gremlins

Let's assume that you are on your way to work and driving into town. You have set off in good time and all is going well. Suddenly you come across a man who has reversed his car into the middle of the road from a driveway. The car has stalled and won't work and is blocking the road. You are now in a queue and the traffic can't move. Time is going by and the man, for whatever reason, isn't moving the car. The oncoming traffic isn't giving way for you, so you are stuck. Ten minutes have passed and you realise that you are now going to be late for work. You also know that your manager is very intolerant of people who turn up late. How would you react?

A typical person might do something like this:

First the Chimp starts to screech a little, 'What is this idiot doing?'; 'Why can't he move his car?'; 'He must realise we are all going to be late'; 'Oh great, just what I need,' and so on.

The Human tries to calm the Chimp with thoughts such as, 'Well, he can't help it'; 'He's not doing this deliberately'; 'It will soon be okay.'

As time passes, the Chimp gets worse and the Human is losing control. They both now look to the Computer to see what the beliefs are. Are they Gremlins or Autopilots?

The Gremlins will be beliefs such as:

- I expect to go to work without being stopped.
- I set off early therefore this is unacceptable.
- Nothing in my world should go wrong.
- If something in my world goes wrong because of somebody else then I should get angry.
- I should have control of my journey to work.
- If something has happened beyond somebody's control then they are still guilty.

These are all quite ridiculous beliefs if you think about them but if you have them hidden inside your head then no wonder the Chimp gets angrier when it speaks to these Gremlins who tell it absurd things.

Let's reverse these beliefs and give some truthful Autopilots and remove these Gremlins. So the counter beliefs are:

- I hope to get to work without being stopped but there is no guarantee.

- I set off early but this doesn't mean I will be there on time.
- I can't always expect everything to go right in my world.
- If someone does something in my world that is unhelpful to me, I don't have to get angry but I can deal with it in a calm way.
- I don't have control of my journey to work.
- If something happens outside my control then I can hardly be guilty.
- If my manager gets angry if I am late then I can deal with this.

If these Autopilots were in the Computer, then when the Chimp began to get angry or upset it would look into the Computer and recognise that this was an inappropriate response and it would calm down. However, this needs to be reinforced by rehearsing these responses so that the pathways in the Computer override and remove the previously unhelpful ones.

A giant Gremlin called 'SHOULD'

A common and destructive Gremlin is often brought into being by the word 'should'. Gremlins are often statements that contain rigid words such as 'must' and 'should'. Think carefully about using these words as they are often inappropriate and can be damaging.

'Everyone *should* be pleasant with me, if I am pleasant with them.'

If this belief is present in the Computer and the Chimp looks into the Computer when someone is not being pleasant to you then it is likely to make you feel angry, frustrated or hurt. In reality, people do not necessarily have the same values as you or live their life according to your beliefs. By accepting this as a fact, you may want to replace the Gremlin with an Autopilot. By replacing the word 'should' with the word 'could' you will have a truth that you will find easier to live by. So the Autopilot becomes, 'Everyone could be pleasant with me if I am pleasant with them.' Now if it doesn't happen you are not disappointed or surprised.

Here are some examples to think about. Consider the difference in feelings that the two statements make just by swapping the word over.

SHOULD	COULD
I should eat sensibly all the time.	I could eat sensibly all the time.
I should be more organised.	I could be more organised.
I should manage my Chimp better.	I could manage my Chimp better.

The differences between the two statements are that using the word 'should' often evokes a sense of judgement, a command, guilt or a feeling of failure, whereas using the word 'could' usually evokes feelings of possibility, hope, an option, a choice, empowerment and potential for change. The equivalent word for 'must' is 'might'. Try some sentences for yourself with this.

It is reasonable to have some expectations of what **might** happen but it may be unreasonable to demand that these **must** happen. Clearly there are some occasions when the words 'must' and 'should' would be appropriate, so I am not suggesting that we remove them from the English language!

Dancing with the Gremlins

When a number of Gremlins get together it can be hard to separate them. Each Gremlin seems to reinforce the next Gremlin. As you jump from one false or unhelpful belief to another you end up dancing with the Gremlins.

For example, let's assume that you are about to meet some of your partner's relatives. Your Computer has a few Gremlins in it that are starting to wake up and speak to you. This will agitate the Chimp. The Gremlins may be the following:

- I have to make a good impression.
- I am about to be judged.
- We are unlikely to have anything in common.
- If I make a fool of myself they will think I am stupid.

These are all possibly true, though unhelpful beliefs that will dance around together.

The way in which to recognise each Gremlin and how they are working together is to write them down as they appear. Putting them down on paper means that you can work to remove each one individually. Trying to do them all together is very unlikely to work, as each one needs its own answer that is based on truth and logic in order to remove it and replace it with an Autopilot (the acceptable truth).

So in this case let's do it!

The answers that you give must be ones that ring true for you, otherwise they won't remove the Gremlins. So you have to think each one out with an answer that is powerful enough, based on the truth that you believe. When you have found your answers you must write them down and remind yourself of them until they become ingrained into your way of thinking. Whatever you do, don't try to brainwash yourself, or fool yourself into something that you don't believe, because it will fail to stop the Gremlins.

It can take several weeks or months to reinforce an Autopilot and remove the Gremlin. Gremlins have a nasty habit of returning so watch out for them. You need to be vigilant and try to address them every time you recognise them.

GREMLIN	REPLACE WITH AUTOPILOT
I have to make a good impression.	I can only be myself and what they make of that is up to them.
I am about to be judged.	They are going to meet me and whether they judge me or not I can't control, but I can enjoy being me.
We are unlikely to have anything in common.	It doesn't matter whether we have anything in common or not, I can always ask about them and listen to them.
If I make a fool of myself they will think I am stupid.	If I make a fool of myself, it wasn't intentional, all I can do is my best and what they make of that is up to them.

Stopping any more Gremlins from going into the Computer

Putting Autopilots or Gremlins into the Computer is done by experience, including discussions and education. So when you experience anything in life you will interpret this. If you interpret it in a negative and unhelpful way then Gremlins will appear in the Computer for future reference. If you interpret the event or experience in a positive or constructive way then Autopilots get put into the Computer. **Therefore it is important when inputting into the Computer that you think carefully through the experience that you have had and interpret it correctly.**

For example, if you go to work and somebody is brisk and quite cold towards you, it is quite easy for the Chimp to interpret this emotionally and jump to conclusions such as: 'this person doesn't like me;' 'There is something wrong with them;' 'There is something wrong with me;' and 'I knew I was unpopular with everyone.' There are infinite possibilities for the interpretation.

The Human, being logical, is likely to think differently and more along the lines of, 'I'm not sure why that person seems cold towards me; I need to find out,' or 'It doesn't really matter to me as long as I remain pleasant;' or 'Maybe something is wrong and they are not well or worried about something,' or 'Maybe I have upset them and I need to apologise.' Again the list is endless.

The point here is that if we listen to the Chimp then inevitably new Gremlins will be put into the Computer and old ones will be reinforced. If we go with the Human and silence the Chimp, then we will first try to search out the truth of the matter and then allow Autopilots to go into the Computer. The key here is not to listen to the Chimp but to listen to the Human and check out the facts first. This will then put Autopilots into the Computer for future reference.

Using the example above, when you speak to the person, you may find that they had a bad headache and they apologise for giving you an impression of coldness. You can now input a healthy Autopilot into the Computer that says: whenever someone seems cold, check out the facts first before jumping to conclusions.

On the other hand, let's be extreme and say that the person turns on you and says they don't like you and they have every intention of being rude to you. At least you can put into the Computer a new

Autopilot that says: not everyone is going to like me and I have to live with that and sometimes no matter what I do I can't win.

Either way, the important point is to recognise the interpretations and way of thinking by the Chimp and by the Human.

Key Point
Humans don't always get it right and Chimps don't always get it wrong.

Helpful and unhelpful information is inputted into the Computer from either the Chimp or the Human. Generally, the Human puts in Autopilots and the Chimp puts in Gremlins but there are exceptions. If the Human is given information that it doesn't or can't understand, then using logic it may analyse this information incorrectly and inadvertently put a Gremlin into the Computer. For example, you may go to see your family doctor who becomes agitated and tells you that you are wasting their time. Later in the year you see another family doctor who also becomes agitated and tells you that you are wasting their time. The Human logic interprets this by saying I am wasting the time of my family doctors because two of them can't both be wrong. However, it could be that in fact you met two very unhelpful doctors and you were not wasting their time at all. However, the Human has used logic to misinterpret what happened and has put a Gremlin in the Computer, that is, when I go to the doctors I am wasting their time.

Similarly the Chimp's emotional thinking may be correct and input an Autopilot. For example, you may meet someone that your Chimp reads emotionally, by body language, and tells you that it doesn't trust them. Your Chimp may well be right and puts into the Computer: 'This person is not trustworthy, be careful.' This is in fact an Autopilot if the Chimp is right in its interpretation and you would be wise to listen to it.

Perfecting the Stone of Life

The whole point of getting your Universe in order is to let the Sun, which is at the centre of your Universe, be the focal point of everything. This Sun is what you believe life is all about and is about self-fulfilment. Of course, many people have a strong faith and this will be the meaning of their life and most, if not all of their values, will be based on this faith. Again, if you have strong religious beliefs it is worth making it clear to yourself what your beliefs are, and then making sure that you are in tune with these and live your life accordingly.

If you do not have strong religious beliefs then you must define what you feel is the ultimate goal that you are trying to achieve, as this will define your Life Force. Many people, regardless of beliefs, would agree that life is about self-fulfilment and about being happy. Only you can decide what is important to you.

Key Point

It is the Stone of Life that holds the key to stabilising your entire Universe.

Establishing your Mindset and living by it

It is worth challenging your Mindset by experimenting. Whilst working with a group of medical students in a hospital setting, we tried an experiment. Several students were asked to believe that he or she were the Clinical Director of the hospital. The students were then observed to see what they did. Most of them walked down the centre of the corridor and greeted staff and patients with a polite 'Good morning' and were seen to initiate the interaction.

Then we asked them to walk down the corridor again but this time as if they were the cleaner of the hospital who was on a temporary contract and likely to lose their job very soon. This time most of the students were observed to walk down the edge of the corridor and not to engage with others they passed. The students did not know that they were being observed for behaviours in the corridor. When shown their change of behaviour based on the perception of themselves they were surprised.

One way to see how you are really coming across is to see the effects you are having on others. Do others find you good company? Do others feel energised when they have met you? Decide which thoughts about yourself are constructive and which ones are destructive. Be sure you have realistic expectations of yourself.

Remember: the values you hold in yourself are likely to be far more important than what you look like or what you can achieve.

Key Point
True friends like us for our values and personalities not for our achievements, position and possessions.

If you believe values and attitudes are the important things in your life then clarify these and work on them when you want to develop a picture of yourself, as they are what is important to you and define you. I am not saying we shouldn't try to achieve things or have possessions and feel good about having these things, but I am saying that these things need to be in tune with your values. If your values are based on having specific characteristics in your personality and holding certain outlooks, then make sure you spend time developing these.

You can always check how you are coming across by asking a number of friends but be prepared for some uncomfortable truths. If you do receive comments that seem quite critical then at least you have a starting point to begin to work from and change these perceptions.

The Mindset is not just about how you perceive yourself but also how you perceive others and the world. I will take two extremes to try and drive this point home.

Let's start with the person who believes that they own the world in which they live. They will be confident and assertive because it is their world. Of course, while no one owns Planet Earth, each of us owns our own world. We decide how it is run and who can enter it to a very large degree.

Now let us look at the person who believes that they are in another person's world and that they don't belong there. This person will lack assertiveness and feel that they have no right to be there. This is likely to result in them being unhappy and protective of themselves and to see the world as a dangerous and threatening place in which to live. They may also go further and feel that they have to fight their corner because others are oppressing them. You can imagine many other beliefs that might appear purely as a result of the person seeing the world as belonging to others. Most of us fall in the middle of these two stances but can drift either way if we are not careful.

Summary key points

- It is vital to get the Computer into correct working order.
- You can search out and replace Gremlins with Autopilots.
- The Stone of Life is the most powerful part of your mind.
- The Stone of Life is something that you can work on.
- Reinforcing the Stone of Life by making it visible every day is a major settling influence on you.
- You can choose the right Mindset to approach life.

Suggested exercise:
Managing your Computer

Replace 'should' Gremlins with 'could' Autopilots

If you are experiencing some form of pressure or stress, try to see if the 'should' Gremlin is behind it and is inappropriate. Replace this with a 'could' Autopilot and think about the differences in emotion that it gives you. This exercise needs to be done repeatedly if you are to embed the Autopilot into the Computer so that it operates without your input.

The ultimate stabiliser

I cannot urge you enough to return to your Stone of Life and if necessary perfect and redraw your poster. When you get this clear in your mind it will be the most settling influence on your Chimp, your Human and your very existence. Remember that the *Stone of Life is by far the most powerful stabiliser for your Psychological Mind and indeed for your entire Universe.*

Chapter 6
Personality and the Mind
How your mind works and influences your personality

You now have an understanding of the three brains in your head: the Human, the Chimp and the Computer. Next we can look at the way in which the Guiding Moon (Computer) stabilises the Divided Planet (the struggle between Human and Chimp). To optimise the system, you can learn to move the blood supply in your head and operate with either the Chimp, Human or Computer, depending on which one will be right for the task. We can also look at your personality and understand how it is formed and then develop it.

How the Computer interfaces with the Chimp and Human

If the Chimp and the Human are relaxed and are not worried, then you will automatically work with the Computer, which means you can perform routine daily tasks without conscious effort as your Computer works according to an automatic programme. However, if any danger or unusual circumstances appear then the Chimp or Human will wake up and take over.

How the Chimp, the Human and the Computer deal with input

The diagram shows that it is the Chimp's perception of whether there is danger or not which starts off the process. Which part of the brain deals with the situation depends on two main factors:

- Whether the Chimp senses danger or threat
- Whether the Human is familiar with the situation or not

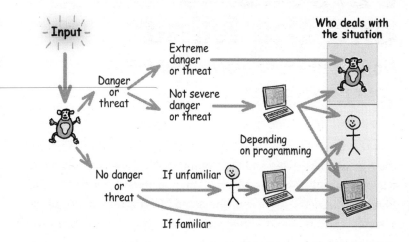

The end result shows that in extreme danger the Chimp will take over. When there is a threat, the Chimp will first look into the Computer to see what is stored there. If the Computer does not reassure the Chimp then the Chimp will take over. If the Chimp is reassured then either the Human or Computer will act. In circumstances where the Chimp does not see any threat then it will hand over to either the Human or the Computer. To give a simple illustration of how the three brains interact we will consider someone playing the piano.

The piano player
Let's assume the pianist is playing their favourite piece, knows it well and has played it easily many times before. This task is firmly programmed into the Computer and the Computer can make their fingers play without any thought involved. It is in automatic mode. Let's also assume that the Human is relaxed and fine, the Chimp is a highly strung animal and that the Computer is just doing its job. We can look at three scenarios.

The first scenario

I walk into the room and pose no threat to the person, who continues to play the piano. I ask them if they would like a cup of coffee and the Human in them answers with a yes or no. The Computer continues faultlessly playing the music. The Chimp is asleep because there is no threat. The Human is relaxed and allowing the Computer to do the work.

The second scenario

I walk into the room and say to the person, 'Can you talk me through the way that your fingers are moving up and down the piano?' This time, as I pose no threat, which means the Chimp is still resting, I have asked the Human to think. So the Human has woken up and the blood supply in the brain is now going to the Human. The Human now thinks very slowly (20 times slower than the Computer). The Human also has to work things out from first principle, so starts to go wrong. The person now stops and says, 'I can't think that quickly but if you just watch I can play easily.' They then pick up where they left off and immediately play well again. (The Human is not a good place to send your blood supply if you have to think quickly or perform a familiar task!)

The third scenario

I walk into the room along with a group of famous pianists and say to the person, 'We are just going to see how well you can play the piano,' and then I lean on the piano and watch the pianist intently! This time the Chimp within the pianist wakes up and panics because it perceives danger. So the blood supply goes to the Chimp. The Chimp is now emotional and unpredictable and the Chimp, who will start the conversation, might typically defend itself and will now overtake the Human within the person. 'I am not at my best today,' would be a typical response from the Chimp, with either a cessation of the music or the Chimp trying to play the piano, which will be poorly done!

The mathematical challenge

Here is another example and this time we will demonstrate the three brains trying to work together. The Computer thinks the fastest because everything is already stored in place. If someone asked you to do a simple multiplication, such as three times three, then you would answer immediately because the answer is stored in the Computer. The Chimp wouldn't have felt threatened because it was an easy sum to do.

However, if you were asked 13 times 17, assuming that you don't know the answer, then you would have to stop and think, using the Human with help from the Computer. If you did that sum every day you would soon know it and it would be automatic. The more you rehearse things, the more they become automatic, robust and quick.

If we now ask you to do the next complicated sum in front of a group of strangers then it is very likely that the blood supply in your brain will go straight to the Chimp because you will feel under threat. Who knows what the Chimp will do with this! It may scream, it may laugh or it may just refuse to engage. What we do know is that if you feel under threat then the blood supply will go to your Chimp first and then onto either the Human or the Computer. So in this example, if you want to work well on mathematical multiplications, you would first manage the Chimp, then get the Human to input the correct answers into the Computer and get the Computer to learn these well.

How you can change this default programme?

Now that we have an understanding of how the machine works we can learn how to intervene and make it work for us.

There are three main ways to adjust the way the machine deals with information. The first is when the Human intervenes by managing the Chimp to stop it acting out on its thoughts, the second is by getting the help of others and the third is by using the Computer to manage the Chimp.

The Human intervenes

Here is the diagram that we saw in the Human and Chimp chapter.
This time we have added an intervention line. **You cannot stop the
Chimp from reacting to anything that happens (shown as the
first step on both pathway options),** however, you can stop the
Chimp from acting on this reaction.

So after the Chimp reacts to some experience and then is about
to employ emotional thinking to make sense of the situation, the
Human needs to intervene. The Human needs to use 'facts' and
'truth' in order to take the person into logical thinking and stop the
Chimp from progressing with emotional thinking.

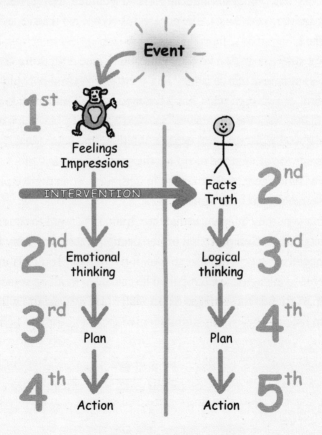

Two pathways to choose from

The broken leg and lost holiday

Here is an example in practice. Tony has booked a holiday abroad with friends and is really looking forward to it. With one week to go he falls and breaks his leg.

This information will first go to his Chimp. He can't stop the Chimp receiving the information first and reacting to it, so needs to accept this and work with it. Inevitably and reasonably his Chimp reacts. His Chimp screeches, 'It's not fair,' 'I can't believe this has happened,' 'This is the last thing that I need,' and so on.

At this point Tony has a choice. He can let the Chimp take over with emotional thinking and it will create an even gloomier picture with lots of complaints and anger and generally have nothing constructive in its plans. Or he can get his Human to intervene, and give the Chimp some facts and truths to stop it from reacting, and to allow his Human to take over with some logical thinking and to form some constructive plans. His facts to the Chimp could be, 'Nothing can change what has happened,' 'I can either make the best of this and choose to enjoy the next few weeks or I can keep complaining and remain miserable,' 'Although it's not ideal, I can still find something good to do for the next few weeks.'

Now Tony needs to follow this up with some constructive plans with something to look forward to.

What generally happens is that the Chimp is allowed to continue and gets things even more out of perspective and leaves Tony in a very negative place with little to look forward to. If Tony's Human isn't able to manage the Chimp then he can always call on someone to help. A friend who is not as emotionally involved as him will be able to listen to his Chimp and then give facts and truth to help to turn the situation into a logical one with a constructive outcome.

The Human continually talking to the Chimp and settling it down is very emotionally exhausting. It is useful and powerful, but tiring. There is a less draining way to deal with the Chimp by using the Computer.

The Computer as a powerful reminder and reference

The problem with using the Human to keep the Chimp from acting on its feelings is that the Human is slow to act. It also takes a lot of energy to intervene with facts and truth and at the time the Chimp reacts we may not be able to think about the facts to settle it down. If we recall that the Chimp thinks quickly and is five times quicker than the Human, then the Human is constantly on catch-up with the Chimp.

But there is an easier way to manage the Chimp's emotional reaction to any situation, which doesn't involve the Human. As we have seen, the Computer thinks at twenty times the speed of the Human and four times the speed of the Chimp. Consequently, if we can get the Computer to act before the Chimp thinks then we will avoid the battle between the Human and the Chimp. In order to do this you need to have thought through what situations might happen and have a response programmed into the Computer ready to act.

Let's use road rage again as the example. Somebody cuts in front of you on the road.

The Chimp says: 'This is a deliberate invasion of my territory and a challenge. I must fight back and win.'

The Human says: 'This is a rude person or someone who has misjudged what they are doing. Either way, I don't want to be bothered by trivia, as it is really unimportant.'

If the Computer receives these inputs it will go with the Chimp, as the Chimp is the strongest. Therefore the person will begin the battle. The battle usually isn't of any use and typically leaves the person frustrated. The Computer registers this.

The next time it happens the Computer reminds the Chimp that the battle isn't very helpful but the Chimp still doesn't listen and repeats the same behaviour of reacting aggressively. If the battle ends in an aggressive confrontation where the Chimp gets hurt, then the Computer registers this. The next time the Chimp may still be angry but when it looks into the Computer, the Computer reminds it that it is not a good idea to fight back, so the Chimp stops. This still leaves the Chimp angry and frustrated.

An alternative can now occur. This time the Human sits down and thinks about what road rage is all about and logically decides it does not want to act like a Chimp and be fooled into Chimp mentality. It would rather act like a civilised person and accept that we have to share our civilised world with some not-so-pleasant people but it isn't worth fighting with them over trivia.

The Human now inputs this Autopilot into the Computer and the Computer is now ready to remind both the Human and the Chimp. The next time that an incident occurs the Chimp immediately reacts but this time when it looks into the Computer it hears the Autopilot saying that it doesn't help to act on primitive drives because you can't win and they are not appropriate. The Chimp now either stops and listens to the Autopilot or it pauses, and this is enough time for the Human to reinforce this message and take over the thinking. The Chimp now relaxes and the Human drives on.

In Tony's situation he broke his leg and began to react. However, let's assume that he has got the Stone of Life in place and has some truths that he has decided to live with. In these truths he has the following absolute beliefs that include:

- I am an adult and I can deal with any situation.
- Life is not fair.
- Everything that happens comes and goes.
- Disappointments are tough but they need to be kept in perspective.
- Happiness can be found in many ways.
- It's the way you deal with things, not what happens, that gives peace of mind.
- Every day is precious.

If he really believes these truths, then when the Chimp gets the bad news it will look straight into the Computer and find them. Remember that this is what the Chimp and Human do every time they receive information. They first check with the Computer before reacting. This will happen so quickly that Tony himself may not even be aware that it has happened. He may just experience calmness in dealing with the situation. On a brain scanner the speed of these reactions is estimated at less than 0.02 of a second! If we rehearse our beliefs and truths regularly then the Computer will stop the Chimp from reacting. This takes little, if any, energy and is the best way to deal with the Chimp. The Stone of Life is the ultimate power source in our Psychological Mind.

The Chimp checks the Computer

Your personality

Defining personality is never easy. We all have a good idea of what it is but it is hard to put it into words. Personality is broadly defined as ingrained behaviours and responses that are predictable in a person. So if someone becomes anxious every time they confront something new, then we say that they have an anxious personality, because that is what they are portraying to the world. If someone seems calm in every situation then we would say that they are a calm person by nature. So what is really happening in these people? There are lots of explanations and debates about this but we will use our model to understand it.

Effectively, the personality that you display to the world is a mixture of the Human, Chimp and Computer. Humans and Chimps have separate personalities and they can be constructive or destructive, pleasant or unpleasant. Humans are not necessarily good and Chimps bad, but generally the Chimp is usually less helpful! You can have compassionate Chimps and very cold Humans. They are both a mixture of lots of characteristics and both the Human and Chimp can be constructive or destructive, and both can vary the presentation of their personalities from day to day.

It is critical to understand that your Chimp's personality has nothing to do with you; it is a machine that was given to you to work with. You may have a very different personality to your Chimp. The Computer merely modifies what the Human and Chimp are presenting, and depending on how you have programmed it, it can be a helpful or unhelpful influence.

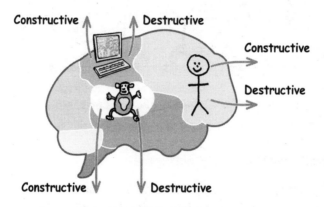

All three are independent influences
and can be constructive or destructive

Personality development through the years

As you grew up and as your hormone levels varied, the brain went through many structural changes and stages of development. Different hormones influence different parts of your machine to start functioning and operating at different points in your life. The Chimp and the Human will begin to change and to perceive things differently. Perhaps the most recognisable example of this is the difference between a child who accepts maternal and paternal ideas, and a teenager whose brain naturally begins to challenge those ideas presented to it.

Clearly social factors play a large part in developing personality. For example, gaining responsibility or independence can change how you present yourself to the world; your personality can apparently suddenly change by being asked to take responsibility for something. Due to the various factors influencing our lives, including our continually ageing brain, our personalities keep modifying, though our blueprint usually runs true! The Chimp and Human both grow up and constantly develop.

Nature and nurture

Chimps, Humans and Computers are a mixture of nature and nurture. We can define nature as the genetic package given to each of us at birth, inherited from our parents, which will run its course unless interrupted. We can define nurture as the experience that life gives us, and our reaction and interpretation of that experience, and how it then influences us in the future.

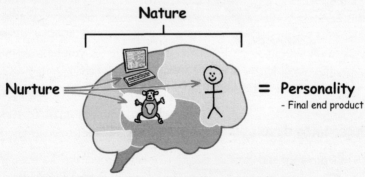

The Chimp, Human and Computer, with nature and nurture, interacting to give final end product

Nature

The Human, Chimp and Computer all have inherited traits handed down to them. For example, the Chimp inherits various emotional traits, the Human inherits the ability to think logically or artistically and the Computer inherits the ability to form programmes for languages or music. These traits are of different strengths in different people, so those who inherit anxiety traits will find it harder to remain calm than those who inherit more relaxed traits.

Nurture

The experiences that we have in life and the way in which we are nurtured or react to these experiences is a learning process. Our parents and society clearly have a very large influence on this. The experiences we have may be very severe and have a great influence on us or they can be very uneventful and therefore have little influence on us. Very often the way that we interpret our experiences is more important than the experiences that we have.

Generally most Chimps are dominated by nature with some input from nurture, whereas most Humans are dominated by nurture with some input from nature. Your Computer is a good mix of the two. All three are different and when they interact they give the final personality presented to the world. So, sometimes you present your Chimp and other times you present your Human. No wonder at times we feel like a split personality! The real personality, that is truly you, is the Human. The Chimp merely hijacks you and presents something that is often not what you want and indeed is not the real you.

Other factors contributing to your personality

Apart from your genes and the experiences you have, there are other main factors found in the Human and Chimp that influence the way in which you act. For example, the **tenacity** that you have to fulfil your drives and ambitions is a major factor for success and is part of your personality. How **flexible** and **adaptable** you are to different situations will also determine how successful you will be in your ventures. Repeated ingrained behaviours, or **habits**, are generally accepted as the way in which your personality is demonstrated, so behaviours are often worth changing if they are unhelpful!

We have discussed the **Mindset** under the Computer chapter. Clearly the Mindset that you hold, constructed in the Computer, will also contribute to the personality that you have and influence the way that the Human and Chimp act and think. People who have a positive image of themselves and of others, and who live in a world that is perceived as pleasant, are far more likely to have the same kind of personality.

Altered Mindset = Altered personality

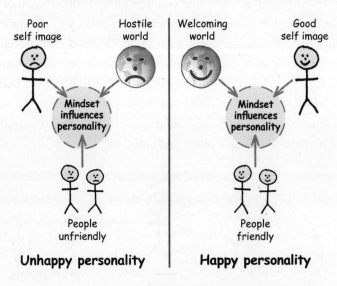

| Poor self image | Hostile world | Welcoming world | Good self image |

Mindset influences personality

Mindset influences personality

People unfriendly

People friendly

Unhappy personality

Happy personality

Your Mindset affects the presentation of your personality

So who are you?

With all of these factors having varying degrees of influence on your final personality, how can you determine who you really are? To work out who you really are as a person is easy to do. If you wrote a list of all the things you would like to be, you may write things like calm, compassionate, reasonable, positive, confident and happy, then *this is who you really are*. Any deviation from this is a hijacking by the Chimp. This is a very important point.

Key Point
Remember: the person that you want to be is the person that you really are.

It is vital that you understand you are simply being hijacked and therefore we need to just stop this. What is happening is that as you are trying to be you, the Chimp keeps interfering or hijacking you with emotion or emotional thoughts and making you present yourself to the world in a way that you don't like. If the Computer has Gremlins in it, then even the Computer can affect you and turn you into someone that you don't want to be. If you do not recognise this hijacking then you may become disillusioned with yourself and feel like you are constantly failing. This in turn may lead to you beating yourself up. This is such a worthless thing to do. Beating yourself up for perceived failure, or self-loathing, is a destructive and useless waste of time and emotion.

You can be hijacked by your Chimp or Gremlins

I would like you to see yourself as the person that you want to be, but the Chimp and some Gremlins are stopping you. With this understanding you can move forward by getting frustrated with the Chimp and Gremlins and not yourself, and then work on managing the Chimp and removing the Gremlins. This is far more constructive.

Let's move on for a moment and forget this hijacking by the Chimp and look at you instead. Let's say that on your list you have put honest, happy, confident, reliable, friendly and so on. The chances of being happy, calm and whatever other characteristics you have written down, even without Chimp activity, are slim unless you work on this. Most of us have got the capacity to be happy and calm but we have not developed this side of our personality. To develop yourself into the real 'you' will take time and effort. The characteristics that you want to flourish within you need action plans to bring them out. They are there but probably only come out by chance on a few occasions. It is time to make them come out most of the time. We can now address how to do this.

Changing and developing your personality

The question most people will want to ask is, 'Can I change my personality or can others change theirs?'

I once had a question from a colleague who said, 'How do you change people?' The answer is that I can't. I am helping people manage their Chimp and adjust and maintain their Computer. I haven't changed the Chimp, I *can't* change the Chimp and I'm not even attempting to. However, when they manage their Chimp and maintain their Computer then the real person emerges.

Let's assume a miracle has happened and that the Chimp is no longer on the move, whatever you do. It has permanently gone to sleep or only offers helpful emotions. Let's also assume that we have removed all Gremlins from the Computer. What you would now be is a more relaxed individual showing Human characteristics. However, to be happy means that you must cultivate this mood and to do this you need to define how you will make yourself happy. Likewise, to be calm we need plans to deal with stress and to carry them out. Developing any aspect of your personality will need time spent on it. It is easiest to work on each aspect one at a time and to monitor your progress.

Developing the Human and bringing out the best in you is about:

- Developing yourself
- Managing your Chimp and removing the Gremlins
- Communicating effectively
- Having the right people around you
- Creating a world for yourself to live in
- Looking after yourself
- Getting quality in your life

If you consider these areas carefully, you will see that these are covered by the planets in the Psychological Universe. Therefore, in order to develop and bring out your true personality, you need to work through each of the planets and get them in good working order. This is why there is the Psychological Universe because it represents the areas in your life that you can address to gain self-fulfilment and to release the Human from within.

Summary key points

- The Chimp always interprets first before the Human.
- The Chimp only hands over to the Human if there is no danger or perceived threat.
- The Human can intervene to stop the Chimp reacting by using facts and truths.
- The Computer can be programmed to settle the Chimp down before it acts.
- Personality is a mixture of Human, Chimp and Computer.
- Nature and nurture both influence your personality.
- Your Mindset affects the way that you come across.
- You can work on the Human, Chimp and Computer to adjust your personality.
- You are the person that you want to be but you are being hijacked by your Chimp into being someone else.

Suggested exercise:
Getting to know the real you

Write down the characteristics of the person that you would ideally like to be. Now write down how you believe you are in reality. Get a close friend, who knows you well, to also write down what they think your personality is like. Now compare all three. See what Gremlins you can start removing and what Chimp behaviours you can start to manage in order to stop the interference from them and allow you to be your ideal person.

Part 2
Day-to-day Functioning

Chapter 7
The Planet of Others

How to understand and relate to other people

Troop
Moon

Planet of Others

Understanding others:

- Understanding the mind and personality of others
- Different physical brains
- Different Mindsets
- Meeting others
- First impressions
- Why do you want to understand others?
- Having realistic expectations

The Planet of Others covers the relationships and interactions that we have with other people in various settings. It explores some fundamental aspects about people to give us a better understanding of them and how we can form meaningful and useful relationships with them.

I was working with a man who understood the Chimp model but was still having trouble with his wife. He said that at times she was difficult with him and said some unpleasant things and then apologised. One day it dawned on him that his wife also had a Chimp that may go out of control without her approval. Her Chimp would suddenly take over and make remarks that she later regretted because she had lost control of the Chimp. He would then react to her Chimp's remarks and go Chimp himself. It was their two Chimps who were talking to each other, not the two Humans. Once they recognised this, they were able to help each other to manage the Chimps and the two Humans then worked together.

Understanding the mind and personality of others in your world

It is up to you whether you want to try and understand others but it would ultimately be to your advantage to do so. Think about it. If you had a cat you wouldn't throw sticks for it to fetch and then get frustrated with the cat for not responding. Who is being foolish here? Again, if you had a dog you wouldn't expect it to sit around all day and not want to go for a walk with you. You need to understand the dog's needs. So understanding the person in front of you, and working with realistic expectations, will help you to help them and also stop you getting frustrated.

I am not proposing that we excuse everyone from all responsibilities but we have to live in the real world. We can't change the way others present themselves to us, they have to want to do this, but we can decide if we want to work out how to get the best out of them and accept their limitations. Of course, the alternative is to move on if we can't tolerate their behaviour or if we have done our best and we still can't get on with them. Those who have unrealistic expectations of others and shout, get frustrated, angry or upset are unlikely to get anywhere and often end up looking pretty foolish. There are times when we have to work with people and can't move on, so here are some ideas on how to deal with this. Very simply speaking, you need to discover who the person is in front of you. You can choose to help them to manage their Chimp and recognise Gremlins, or alternatively you can judge them for how they present themselves to us. It is your choice.

Different physical brains

We often make the assumption that the person in front of us has a brain that is wired the same as ours. Most of us have the same type of physical brain but there are some people who are different. As examples, I would like to look at two of these differently functioning brains. The first type is the brain of someone who has a diagnosis of autistic spectrum disorder. In autism, some areas of the brain do not function well and some areas are very highly sensitive. For example, a child or adult with autistic spectrum disorder has great difficulty reading facial expression or body language. They have problems understanding emotion in others and therefore may act or say things that seem inappropriate to most of us. If we understand that they do not mean offence then we can start to work with this person. We can help them get the best out of themself so that we can form a beneficial relationship with them. Autism comes on a spectrum, with the most severe forms easily identifiable and the milder forms barely recognisable.

The frustrated father

Some years ago when I was working in a hospital clinic, a father came in with his 18-year-old son. The father described his frustration with his son and how, although he loved him, he could no longer tolerate his son's odd behaviours. The father told me that his son would not use common-sense and would use up an entire bottle of shampoo for his hair when he went for a shower. No matter how much the father explained that this was an inappropriate thing to do, still his son did it.

The father went on to say that when he came home from work his son would bombard him with questions and, after answering as many as he could tolerate, the father would get very annoyed with his son and end up raising his voice and telling him to stop.

The more we talked, the more it became apparent that the son had a form of autism. I explained to the father that the way in which his son's brain was made up meant that the son would not always be able to work out when to stop actions. He would typically continue with these actions, such as washing his hair until all the shampoo was gone or asking questions incessantly. Once I explained this aspect of his son's behaviour we agreed on a simple and practical plan of action to help both the son and father. We agreed that the father would only put enough shampoo in the bottle for one hair wash. We also agreed that when the father returned from home the son was allowed to ask only three questions, then he was to go to his room to play on his computer. This worked perfectly because the young man would accept rules as long as they were very clear, and the father didn't get frustrated.

The important lesson here is that we need to understand who is in front of us and how they think and work. If we accept this then we can work effectively with them but we have to be willing to look at people with an open mind in order to do this. In effect, our relationships with others are very often dictated by our expectation of them and our reactions to them. Autism is an extreme example to try to drive the point home.

A danger to beware of
The second example of a very different brain is that of the psychopath (sometimes called sociopath or dissocial personality disorder). Let's dispel a common myth: not all psychopaths are violent and kill. Psychopaths *may* become violent and kill but that is exceptional; most psychopaths in society get on with life and do quite well, but they do a lot of damage to people around them en route. They are often, but not always, involved in criminal activities because they have no conscience. Interestingly there are psychopaths in practically every occupation – for example, doctors, lawyers, nurses, teachers – but they learn to contain and work with the brain they have got and stay on the right side of the law. The estimate varies, but a rough figure is that this kind of brain occurs in around 1 in 150 people.

Simply speaking, the brain of a psychopath lacks the Humanity Centre that the rest of us have, which is in the Human part of our heads. The Humanity Centre contains areas that evoke such things as guilt, remorse, compassion, empathy and conscience. Psychopaths are typically just cold and calculating individuals that use others to their advantage. So is a psychopath really responsible or not for their actions? There is a great deal of argument about this, but whatever we believe, there is a lot of evidence that this centre in the brain is either absent or asleep. It is useful to recognise the psychopath, as they are typically destructive towards us when we meet them. Learning to deal with them means that we can walk away from an encounter without being hurt or damaged.

If you find yourself involved with someone who you suspect of being psychopathic, always get advice – ask for other people's opinions and find out about their past. If you find yourself on the receiving end of their actions, do not blame yourself, cut your losses and share your experiences with a friend, who you trust. You are not alone in having been deceived or abused. Don't expect the psychopath to change – the brain is hard-wired.

What do we mean by personality disorder?

If we diagnose someone with a personality disorder in psychiatry, what we basically mean is that they have fixed behaviours and beliefs that are ingrained. These features can't be changed and are harmful or detrimental to the person with the disorder, or they are harmful or detrimental to others who come into contact with them. So it is like an extreme form of normal behaviour that doesn't shift.

There are numerous types of personality disorders. These people are arguably not ill but have traits such as obsessional behaviours or impulsive behaviours that are more extreme than most of us. There is a body of evidence to support the argument that they have different types of brains or different functioning brains than a typical human brain.

Different Mindsets

We have discussed Mindsets earlier and here are two examples that are not that uncommon. They will demonstrate how people can get stuck in their behaviours and beliefs because of the Mindset that they hold. It helps to recognise specific Mindsets (and there are many of them). Many people can display some of the features of a Mindset rather than having the full-blown picture.

Snow White Mindset

This Mindset is more common in women than in men. If we take Snow White as being an innocent, passive victim at the hands of others and circumstance, who is completely devoid of any responsibility or accountability and has no power to change things, then we start to understand the Mindset.

Here a number of Gremlins have got together and have locked the person's mind into a fixed approach to life and themselves.

Let's name the Gremlins that work together, and then look at the Mindset, and then find the way out of it. The Gremlins are a mixture of behaviours and beliefs. All or some of the following will be found:

- I am not responsible for my own decisions.
- I am not responsible for my own happiness.
- Life is really tough and life has always been tough.
- I am a victim of circumstance.

- There is nothing I can do to change things – 'That's the way it is,' is a common statement.
- Others are not helping me.
- Others should understand me.
- Falling apart and being helpless is part of my life.
- The world is a harsh place.

Snow White sufferers often make sure that you are aware of the above Gremlins by subtle sighs and gestures. They usually try to make you feel that somehow you owe them greatly and that even though they are suffering they will somehow get through despite your lack of understanding and, of course, your selfishness. They make sure that you know that they are heroic in managing what is almost unbearable to them. If challenged they either become aggressive and accusatory or they become suitably depressed and tearful and therefore use passive aggression against you (because of course they will point out that it's your fault that they are depressed and tearful).

Typical behaviours are shown when the Snow White sufferer has not got their way over something that they have probably never even mentioned. When the partner asks, 'What's wrong?' the frequent answer is, 'Nothing,' or 'I shouldn't have to tell you why I'm upset.' A Snow White sufferer is often quick to fall apart and cry or sulk, whilst absolving themselves of any responsibility or power over their own life. The feeling of being hard-done-by and that someone else owes them a favour is usually followed by acts of passive aggression, such as silence or refusing to communicate.

How does the Snow White Mindset return to a healthier stance on life? It is tough for those who have fallen into this (and even tougher for those around who have to deal with it!) because getting out means a real change of approach to life. However, this has to happen if they want to escape the Mindset.

What needs to happen is that the sufferer is helped to see exactly how they are working and presenting themselves to others. Clearly to get the best out of life you have to be proactive and make it work. You have to live with reality and live in the world that you have – this doesn't mean being resigned to suffering. It means make sure you have changed all that can be changed. Also, that you have SOUGHT OUT and ACCEPTED help, from suitable people, who can support you with the changes that YOU have instigated. You can either be a victim in life or you can get on with it with a GENUINE smile. This is your choice and no one else's. Many of us have occasionally developed a touch of the Snow White Mindset if we have allowed the Gremlins to move in – be vigilant!

Some thoughts worth considering that might help to keep the Snow White Mindset from developing could be:

- Nobody likes a victim.
- Nobody owes you anything.
- Everybody likes a positive-acting person.
- Happiness is not something to be guilty about.
- Happiness is a choice that you make.
- Looking after your happiness is not selfish.
- Life is what you make of it, not what it throws at you.
- Everybody is responsible for his or her own actions and also attitudes.
- Assertiveness is normal and what adults do.

It is important to consider therapy or seek help for those with the Snow White Mindset because often there are underlying problems that need addressing. Unless you know what you are doing then it is risky to try to change the Mindset of a friend or partner. However, if you are good at choosing the right words and showing understanding then this could lead to unlocking the Mindset and disbanding the Gremlins that are dancing together.

Alpha Wolf Mindset

The Alpha Wolf is a dominant Mindset and is more common in men than women.

The features that this Mindset displays are a mixture of the following:

- The world is a place that belongs to them and others are in their world.
- They give people a value on how they can use them to fulfil their own ambitions.
- They dominate by believing that getting the best out of a situation means showing zero tolerance to people.
- Compassion is seen as weakness.
- Others' opinions are irrelevant in most cases, as they believe that their opinion is right.
- Ignoring someone who is seen as being of little value is the best way of dealing with them.
- Any challenges are met with aggression and hostility.
- Any admissions to errors, or being wrong, are merely given lip service and dismissed quickly.

The Alpha Wolf has varying degrees of being a dictator or a control freak and genuinely believes that this is the best way forward as they are best at decision-making and doing things. The people who they hurt along the way are seen as weak. Popularity is never an issue, as their success and ego are paramount.

This Mindset is often found in business and they can be quite high up in the organisational structure. Whilst some managers would be praising and helping others to fulfil their potential (thus the business performs well), Alpha Wolves 'chew up' the pack, using aggression to prove and use their position. Good managers will utilise their staff, whereas the Wolf will not delegate and will get irritable when deadlines are not met (usually ones they have set without discussion).

In nature, the Alpha Wolf's power is respected and feared but the Alpha Wolf itself is not respected. Similarly, the Alpha Wolf Mindset is unpopular and there is always another Wolf waiting to take over the prime position. Beware the Alpha Wolf Mindset – it makes people around it extremely unhappy and it is only a matter of time before an attack brings down the Wolf.

The probability of changing this Mindset is not so good! The Alpha Wolf either has to recognise that they have a problem or realise that they are having difficulty with others, something that doesn't come easily with this Mindset. Dealing with them is a matter of pragmatism. You either accept their ways or you get away from them.

Accepting their ways doesn't mean rolling over. It means learning not to personalise attacks, understanding that they are very unlikely to change, being assertive (which they will usually respect), avoiding confrontation (where you are unlikely to have a good outcome), staying at peace within yourself and, finally, wisely recognising when it is time for you to move on.

There are lots of different Mindsets and these are just two examples to demonstrate how people can get locked into dancing with Gremlins. Understanding a Mindset helps us to understand others and how to deal with them.

Meeting others

When we meet other people there are three approaches that can help us to understand them better:

- Try not to make assumptions about others.
- Try not to have preconceived expectations of others.
- Beware of prejudice.

For example, if I meet someone for the first time and they are quiet and seem disinterested in the conversation, I may see them as rude and decide I don't want to know them or meet them again. However, I have made many assumptions and judgements without knowing the full facts and taking time to find out the truth. For example, I have assumed that this person is not distracted in any way and that there is no reason why they should not engage fully with me and I have also assumed that they know that their lack of engagement is agitating me. I am sure that you can add many more assumptions!

However, this person could have just received some bad news, are in pain or there may be another reason that is making them distant, which has nothing to do with me or the conversation. If I had taken time to check on the facts, then I wouldn't have judged the person in the same way.

It is always useful to remember that every person is living within his or her own world and at times it may not be a pleasant one. Finding out about the world they live in, or accepting that there may be influences on them that you are not aware of, can help to stop assumptions being made.

Key Point
A golden rule for understanding people and situations is to ALWAYS try to establish THE FACTS before you make your assessment.

A word of warning: don't base 'the facts' on hearsay or gossip. Hearsay is when someone starts telling you what somebody else said or thought and this then can influence your view of him or her.

Whenever possible, get in touch with the person and ask them what they really said. Don't accept information about somebody else's opinion unless it comes directly from that person.

Having preconceived expectations of people can on occasion be reasonable. For example, it would be reasonable to expect someone to be civil with you but don't bank on it! It would be unreasonable to expect someone never to make a mistake. There are lots of expectations that we place on people that cause us to get unsettled. For example, having an expectation that a friend is someone who will never let us down or never have cross words with us is a ridiculous expectation. Someone who holds this expectation is unlikely to have many, if any, friends for long.

Sometimes expectations can be linked to prejudice. Prejudice doesn't have to be a negative belief. For example, you might believe that older people are wise and therefore hold a positive prejudice towards older people if you are looking for advice. Sadly, this prejudice may cause problems because although some older people are wise, many are not. If you meet someone and do not have any preconceived ideas about them, or hold prejudice or expectations, then you are more likely to engage constructively with them and to find out who they really are.

First impressions

First impressions are known as the primacy effect. When we meet someone, we pick up on many things including their demeanour, how they are dressed, their attitude, the intonation of their voice, what they say. In new situations the blood supply in your brain will be directed to the Chimp because there is a potential danger. As your Chimp meets the person it interprets these clues as to the type of person that you are dealing with. Research shows that if your Chimp gets this first impression wrong then it will take it about seven more meetings with that person before it changes its mind!

If your Chimp is inflexible or holds a prejudice, then it can take even longer, because you are holding onto Gremlins that keep the Chimp fuelled up to hold that belief. This is the reason some people never change their first impression, even when it was wrong. For example, let's say that you believe that fair-haired people are not very clever. You meet a man with fair hair who doesn't understand a bus timetable that seems quite simple to you. Your first impression might be that he is not very clever and your belief is backed up by his inability to read the bus timetable. He meets you a second time and seems quite clever and he tells you that he is a lawyer. Your first impression was that he was not very bright and also he has fair hair, therefore you are surprised he is a lawyer and your conclusion is that you now know a 'not very bright' lawyer! It will take you some time and some experiences with him before you will think that he is actually very bright, but the day you met him he just happened to be struggling with that particular bus timetable. (We all have our moments!) However, because you still believe that fair-haired people are not clever, it is likely that you will struggle for a long time before you can reach a conclusion that you are wrong in this assumption about fair-haired people. Or of course, you might think he is the exception to your rule!

The difference between the Human and the Chimp in using evidence

Humans look for evidence and then draw up conclusions. Chimps draw up conclusions then look for evidence to support them. The Chimp's error, therefore, is to make a decision on someone and then look for evidence to prove its point. It has self-fulfilling prophecies. This is purely emotional thinking.

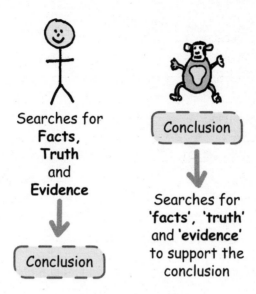

Searches for
**Facts,
Truth**
and
Evidence

Conclusion

Conclusion

Searches for
'facts', 'truth'
and '**evidence**'
to support the
conclusion

Why do you want to understand others?

Before you try to understand others, first ask yourself why you want to do this and what you want to achieve.

I am assuming that your Human is wanting to understand them in order to have a better relationship with them, which means that you are going to be tolerant and probably compromise, to some extent, some of your own requirements or demands of them. Read that bit again! You are going to be *'tolerant and compromise to some extent'*. It is unlikely that you will get to understand anyone if you allow your Chimp to follow its agenda. Your Chimp's agenda is more likely to be about judging them and being intolerant of anything that doesn't agree with your beliefs of what should happen and how they should be. Chimps are characteristically inflexible and highly intolerant of others.

Humans on the other hand are typically tolerant and flexible and understanding of others. So where do you stand? *More to the point, where do you want to stand?*

Same question, but two agendas

To get a better understanding of others you will also have to be open-minded and be prepared to look at them in a different way, otherwise nothing will change.

This next point is a very important one. If you want to build bridges with someone then it is you that has to build the bridge. Don't expect them to build it with you, because if you approach someone with that attitude it is very likely to fail. This is your choice and your decision. Think about what I am saying. If you enter a relationship with demands or expectations that the other person should do something towards this relationship then you are likely to have a stormy passage. It would seem reasonable to expect a two-way relationship, but don't bank on it.

I am not saying that you should do all the work and roll over. However, I am saying that once you expect something back then there may be problems. Most people will return the bridge-building once you start the process. However, if they don't, then either call it a day or keep going without expectations or demands on them, until you think you have had enough. It is your decision to decide whether a relationship is worth investing in.

Building a bridge means you do all the work!

> ## *Key Point*
> *Successful people don't make demands of others but set the scene so that the Human in others can respond, rather than their Chimp.*

It does take effort and patience to get the relationship that you want and there is no guarantee that it will work, as it depends on them, as well as you. Remember that when we engage with people, how we approach them and interact with them will affect the way that they will interact back with us.

Have realistic expectations of people

One of the worst things we can do to disrupt any relationship is to have unrealistic expectations of the other person. For example, it would be fair to expect someone you meet to show respect towards you by listening, being pleasant and cooperative. However, it would be unfair to expect them to be interested in you or in what you have to say, by showing enthusiasm, asking lots of questions and encouraging you. That would be a bonus! Check that the people in your world are able to be themselves and that you are allowing them to do this without judging them by expectations that are unrealistic.

Here is an example to demonstrate this point. Recently, a friend asked me for some help with his girlfriend. He said that the problem with his girlfriend was her terrible time-keeping. He went on to explain that no matter where they were going, or what time they were going to meet, she would always be about 20 minutes late. This was driving him mad and he asked how he could help her to be more organised and on time. I asked if she had commented on this and he said she hadn't and seemed happy with being late but, he continued, she does need to 'sort this out'.

Wow, how inappropriate were his expectations of this woman? It is not her problem. She has every right to lead the life that she wants to and if she wants to turn up late for every date, then that is her right to do so. He doesn't have to stay with her, that is his decision. What you can't do is to impose your expectations and conditions on to someone and then say that they have a problem. Of course, you can explain that it frustrates you and you might even want to say that you can't live with it, but you can't demand a partner to be the way you want them to be. The bottom line is that it is **your decision** to remain with them and to accept them as they are or to leave them and it is **their right to act in the way that they want to**.

Have a think about key people around you and spend some time to work out if you are doing this to others in your life. If you have frustrations with people then have a look at your expectations of them and see if they are reasonable. Do not measure 'reasonable' by your own standards and then impose them on to others because everyone has different standards. Measure 'reasonable' by objective measures such as 'is this person bullying me?' If the answer is 'yes' then this is unreasonable. Clearly, bullying, intimidating and humiliating behaviours are unreasonable. However, how someone wants to use their time or chooses to behave in their personal relationship with you is up to them. You always have the right to walk away.

If you want a painting then search for an artist

While we are looking at expectations of others it is worth considering their limitations. Very often we ask people to be something that they cannot be or do something that they cannot do. If you want a picture painted then you would be wise to ask an artist or accept that the painting may not be as good as you would like. If you pick a person at random and ask them to paint you a picture it is not their fault if it is not good. It is your problem for asking for something they can't deliver.

A common example is that a lot of men struggle to read body language and it frustrates some of them that they don't pick up on moods or unhappiness in people. If you have someone in your life like this, then it is pretty unreasonable of you to expect him to suddenly develop this skill. It is unlikely to happen. He doesn't have the problem, it is how he is built; it is you that has the problem if you don't accept this. Of course he is trying to read your body language, but he needs you to explain or express your feelings verbally so that he can understand. It doesn't help him if you expect him to be a mind reader!

Remember: if you want a picture painted find an artist. If you really want a partner who can read body language and is sensitive to your unspoken needs, then go out and find one but if you choose to stay with one who can't, or possibly even won't, then don't complain. It's your choice to accept a painting not painted by an artist!

Being tolerant means understanding how we are all different and the easiest way to be tolerant is to have little, if any, expectation of the people that you meet but to just accept them as they are and to work with this. Again, you don't have to stay with someone who refuses to try or who can't meet your expectations. It is your choice to stay but you are being unreasonable if you complain or make demands of them.

Cats can't speak

Imagine a scenario where a friend of yours calls you one night to explain that their cat is starving to death. So you ask why this is happening. They say, 'Well, every night I ask the cat if it wants chicken or fish to eat and it just won't answer. So it doesn't get anything.' It isn't the cat that's lacking intelligence! Sometimes people just can't do what you are asking them to do and getting annoyed isn't helpful. Think again if you are annoyed with someone, and check to make sure that you are not asking a cat to speak.

At this point it is wise to remind ourselves of some obvious truths when it comes to expectations of people. These include:

- Not all people are going to be friendly.
- Some people never change.
- Some people never understand.
- Some people are not going to like you.
- People and Chimps vary from day to day.
- No one is all bad.
- No one is all good.
- No one is going to agree with everything you say, every time.

The 'one in five' rule

None of us likes to be unpopular or misunderstood. However, in the real world, being misunderstood or not liked is going to happen. If you took five people from the population and asked them if they liked you or understood you then you are likely to get the following response.

One of them will love you and understand you regardless of what you do or say. They will be on your side.

One of them will dislike you and not understand you, no matter what you do.

Three of them will be more balanced and will weigh you up in an objective manner.

This means that you really have to accept that there are a few million people in each of these categories, so expect to have enemies who are against you and don't like you and criticise you no matter what you do. Often these people are very unreasonable and very vocal and there is nothing you can do to change this. Try to ignore unbalanced and opinionated criticism of you. Rather, listen to the balanced majority who will be supportive and have constructive comments, even though at times they may be critical.

Summary key points

- Getting the best out of people depends on how you approach them and what you understand of them.
- Having preconceived ideas about people or expectations of them may prejudice how you relate to them.
- The best relationships are the ones where you accept the person as they are and work with this.
- Walk away from people whose behaviours or beliefs you cannot accept.
- Invest a lot in those whom you care about.
- The one in five rule means that you need to accept that some people you will never please and they will never like you and it may have nothing to do with you.

Suggested exercise:
Assessing your impact on others

Your effect on others

Ask yourself what effect you are having on others after you have interacted with them. Are you building them up or knocking them down? Are you coming across as an energiser or are you sapping their energies? Work out what effect you want to have, and then work on doing this with each interaction during the day. Monitor your progress by reflecting at the end of each day. Remember that sometimes people can be uncooperative no matter what you do, but count the successes that you have.

Chapter 8
The Troop Moon
How to choose the right support network

- The purpose of the troop
- Selecting the troop
- Maintaining the troop
- Partners and the troop

The Troop Moon represents the people that support you. It is critical to have the right people in your troop and also to understand what the consequences are of having the wrong people in the troop. Having a supportive troop will stabilise how you work with everybody else outside the troop.

The purpose of the troop
What is a troop?

The troop is a small band of people. These people will help, nurture and develop you, but most importantly you can trust them to stand by you and protect you. This doesn't mean that they will always get it right or never let you down. However, when your back is against the wall, they will stand with you.

Why do we need a troop?

Apart from wanting companionship, both the Human and the Chimp welcome the troop but for different reasons. The troop is something that virtually all Chimps **need**. The troop is something that nearly every Human **would like**. So there is a difference. This is important because the Chimp and Human select the members of the troop for different reasons. As they may choose different people for the troop there may be dire consequences.

As well as helping you to get your troop together, this chapter will answer some frequently asked questions:

- 'Why do I always feel the need to please others?'
- 'Why do I worry so much about what others think?'
- 'Why do I always feel the need to impress others?'

Why the Chimp needs a troop

Let's start with the Chimp. A wild chimpanzee belongs to a troop. Without its troop a solitary chimpanzee is unlikely to survive. This is because it would be easy for predators or a foreign troop of chimpanzees to catch it. If it is part of a troop then there are lots of ears and eyes keeping vigilance to keep it safe. Therefore, the instinct for a chimpanzee to make sure that it belongs to a troop is very high indeed. This is one of the most powerful drives that the chimpanzee possesses.

The drive within your inner Chimp to find a troop is equally as strong and it will search for people who can act as protectors. The need to belong to a group is so powerful that we will often compromise our lives and lifestyle in order to remain as part of the group. Think of how teenagers act when they reach a stage where they decide that they don't need adults. They typically gather together in groups of individuals that have similar dress or codes of conduct. If the leader of the group wears orange socks then everybody feels it is cool to wear orange socks and they all wear them. If the leader decides that green socks are in, then everyone changes to green. The group may have a struggle for leadership and the group frequently divides and reforms. Anyone who falls out with the group is usually devastated and distressed. A person that causes trouble in this 'troop' is likely to be excluded, so it is important for the person to conform and to be accepted. The inner Chimps therefore groom each other and make friends, especially with high-ranking Chimps, in order to be safe. They make friends by appearing strong, so impressing others is very important. To be excluded from the troop would mean almost certain death to the inner Chimp.

With this in mind, you can appreciate how important, and how strong, is the drive to be accepted and approved by the troop. Your inner Chimp is telling you that there is danger everywhere and you must be part of a troop. To stay within this troop you must be seen as strong (and impress others at all times), you must be sure to be popular (keep everyone happy) and above all you must ensure that others think highly of you (you must care what they think). This now gives answers to the three questions posed at the beginning of this chapter. The result of this troop drive is that the Chimp puts a few Gremlins into the Computer. These beliefs are things such as, 'I must please everybody,' 'I need to prove myself all of the time,' 'I mustn't fail anything,' 'Everything is important,' and so on. We unconsciously start to believe them and then try to live up to them. The troop drive is the main factor behind these beliefs but they can be learnt and reinforced as an unhelpful habit.

Why the Human wants a troop

As a Human we base our beliefs on society values. We enjoy sharing and working with others and most Humans want to build a society, where everyone is looked after, especially the vulnerable. The Human enjoys the company of friends and has respect and compassion for them. The Human would like to be popular and gain approval by others, but recognises that you shouldn't be worried about what others think and you should not be concerned if others are unhappy because it is their responsibility to make themselves happy and not yours. So the Human actually shares a lot of the desires of the Chimp but for very different reasons.

The twist to the story!

But we have a problem. The twist is that the Human has misled the Chimp. The Chimp knows that most of the people it meets in its world act like Chimps and when people are in Chimp mode they can be very dangerous. It knows that in order to keep you safe it must reject outsiders. The Chimp knows that everyone in the world can't be in your troop and that you can't impress or please people who are not in your troop and are intent on criticising you.

However, the Human brings society's values and beliefs to the Chimp. The Human bases these beliefs on the principle that it is living among Humans and not Chimps. So the Human logically reassures the Chimp and says we don't live in a jungle but a society and therefore we should look after everybody and please everyone because everyone is in our troop. The Chimp now listens and then makes everyone into a member of its troop. This then has disastrous consequences, because sadly, it isn't a perfect world and a lot of the time people don't act in Human but in Chimp mode.

Now the Chimp is very vulnerable because it hasn't got a selected troop. It will get attacked and bitten frequently by Chimps that are definitely not in its troop but that it feels it ought to include. Clearly we need to resolve this problem. Effectively the Chimp has been misled by the Human and got the interpretation that it must accept everyone into its troop. The Chimp was right originally and we need to listen. There are only a few Chimps in your troop (a few people who are truly with you). All other Chimps (people) are not part of your troop and they may attack with force and aggression. Therefore, what the rest of the world (alien Chimp troops) thinks about us is unimportant.

The Human misleads the Chimp!

However, we need a balance because we do live in a society and it would be unreasonable not to treat everyone with respect and some Human warmth. This balance can be struck by allowing your Human to make a rule to be ***personable and approachable*** to everybody. However, accept the Chimp's rule that not everyone is in your troop, ***do not become personal*** with everybody and thereby protect yourself from emotional harm. This time listen to your Chimp!

Getting the troop drive under control

So check that you have not got an out-of-control troop drive. The Chimp does need to be reassured and nurtured. It does need a troop that it can please and it needs the troop to reassure and give approval back. However, if the Chimp fails to recognise who is in the troop, and tries to please and gain approval from everyone, then the troop drive is out of control. So if you are stuck with thoughts such as trying to keep everyone happy, always trying to impress others, always needing to get approval or worrying about what others think, then it is likely that your troop drive is out of control. Sit down and redefine your troop (see the exercise at the end of the chapter). Decide who is in it and then work to please them and get your reassurance from them. Other troops are unlikely to welcome you! Of course, it helps to be friendly towards everyone and to be civil. Just recognise the danger of an out-of-control troop drive.

Selecting the Troop

Chimp selection – who the Chimp needs in the troop

Your Chimp is looking for strong individuals who can make the troop secure and safe. If your Chimp is a natural leader (and research suggests that one in four of us have Chimps like this) then it will look for strong followers. If the Chimp is not a natural leader then it will look for the natural leader or parent figure. It is no surprise then that most Chimps look for heroes or for those who are popular.

Your inner Chimp is also likely to look for those Chimps with influence and wealth because the Chimps that possess these qualities are the Chimps that can boost the strength of the troop and offer you safety. The Human may also want to meet wealth but for different reasons!

The Chimp will therefore select its members based on what they can offer it, or on what it can offer them in order to get Chimp fulfilment. The Chimp selects on looks, and frequently on other fairly superficial qualities. Chimps also look for familiarity. Familiarity offers a sense of security and reassurance. For example, if you meet someone from the same town as you, or who have experienced something similar in life to you, then your Chimp will draw you towards them. Your Human may have very little in common with them but if the Chimp feels secure with familiarity and common ground then it will accept them. Our Chimps will be very wary or reject people who are dissimilar to us or who have very different backgrounds. Shared experiences and backgrounds are factors that help us to form a troop but they may lead us to form a faulty troop.

If we find someone we admire, or whom others hold in high esteem, our Chimps tend to forget about their personality. The Chimp might draw them into the troop, overlooking their personality. When we finally get to know them, our Humans may think, 'I may admire their ability, but they are not a pleasant person,' so we change our minds and reject them from the troop.

Beware of allowing the Chimp to decide on the troop. Just because somebody lived in the same town as you, shared a similar experience, is admirable or wealthy, doesn't mean that they belong in your troop. The Chimp works on feelings to select its troop and they can be unreliable. It is therefore important to realise who we are bringing in to the troop and why – what role do they fulfil? Remember first impressions are made by the Chimp and can be wrong (though they can also be correct). We may be excluding valuable troop members or including disruptive and inappropriate troop members

Human selection – who the Human wants in the troop

The Human has quite a different agenda. The Human within us would like to be surrounded by people of like mind, who can offer friendship and companionship. The Human chooses these people on the significant qualities that they possess that are found in the Humanity Centre. These qualities are things such as integrity, honesty, selflessness, remorse, positive outlook, a sense of humour, and so on.

These people will nurture and develop us as people by understanding us, looking out for us and at times confronting us with a reality check on our outlook and behaviour. We also look for Humans that are reliable and predictable. Predictable Humans usually mean that they have good management of their Chimps and we don't see their Chimp get out very often. If their

Chimps do get out then the chances of attack from them are slim. The Human is therefore looking for soul mates, spiritual companions and friends.

Getting it right and getting it wrong!

As we can see, there are two of you trying to select your troop, the Human and the Chimp. The Human works with logic, and looks for people with Humanity and it chooses the troop members on significant qualities that they possess. Conversely, the Chimp uses emotion and feelings and looks for people who possess fairly superficial qualities such as looks and power. Getting the balance right is therefore not that easy.

Bringing into your troop people that are going to hurt you is not a wise thing to do, so it is worth spending some time defining your troop. The troop size will depend on who is available and who fits the bill. Some people feel comfortable with just their partner in the troop. Others have very sizeable troops. It is your choice on the size of your troop – there are no rules.

The problem arises when the Chimp chooses someone for the troop and the Human disagrees. For example, an unreliable and selfish person is unlikely to be chosen by the Human but if they are fun to be with and seen as the life and soul of the party then the Chimp may cling on to them. Another flaw that often occurs when the Chimp chooses the troop is when a person uses flattery on us. Our Chimps are taken in by flattery and apparently kind words, and they allow the person to enter the troop. In its severe form, this is not uncommonly seen when a person has such low self-esteem that their Chimp allows their partner to beat them up, physically or psychologically, and then remain with them. The Chimp then offers excuses such as 'but they are a kind person' and 'you don't know them like I do'. (Thank goodness we don't.) Any woman or man who is being abused in this way could learn to recognise what is happening and work with their Chimp's emotions and learn to build self-esteem and self-respect to replace insecurity. This is not an easy task and professional help is often needed.

We can have friends who are friendly Chimps from other troops, who will not be hostile to us, but are not part of the inner circle of the troop. Typical members of the troop would include partners, some family members and close friends. We usually decide our troop automatically, whereas if we use a little bit of thought and care, we can save ourselves a lot of emotional turmoil by recognising and differentiating a member of our troop from a friendly person. If you get this wrong then this is like a chimpanzee that goes to the wrong troop and gets attacked and may even be killed. You may know from experience of a time when you have included the wrong friend in a close circle, who has ended up attacking you; this is why we need to get our troop right.

Troops are not fixed. Members can move in and out without your control. Clinging on to friends, who may have moved out of the troop, often hurts people who do not realise this; letting go and realising who is in your troop at any given time is the key.

Maintaining the troop and roles within the troop

The troop needs maintenance. It is important that you look after the members of your troop. To do this, you have to recognise their needs and try to meet them. Each member of the troop will play a role in your eyes and also in the eyes of your Chimp. One of the problems of maintaining the troop is to make sure that you don't impose a role onto someone who cannot fulfil that role. For example, most people have a need for a father or mother figure and their parents usually fulfil this. However, in some circumstances our parents are not there, so we impose this role onto someone else. This could be a caring boss or a professional figure such as a doctor or nurse. Imposing the wrong role with expectations on to the wrong person rarely works! When we impose a role on someone with an expectation of what they should be doing in that function and it does not get fulfilled, it can lead to frustration and even anger, or it can risk people crossing professional boundaries. Conversely, others can impose a role on you that you do not want. It is important that when roles are being established with people that you are both on the same page. This especially applies to partners. Trying to make them something they are not can be disastrous, for example, trying to give them the role of being your parent or child to meet your own needs.

When roles get confused there is usually conflict. One common example is seen in families where there is a clash between mother-in-law and daughter-in-law because they are competing for the son/husband. The mother and wife have totally different relationships with the man; both are unique and both fulfil a mutually exclusive role. This mixing of boundaries creates competition between roles that does not need to exist. If you can understand the role others take, and the role that you take for them, then there is a much greater probability of relationships, family-units, work-colleagues etc. working harmoniously without emotional responses and clashes.

A very important role within the troop is that of leadership. Both the Chimp and Human want and need a leader but for different reasons. The Human may want someone for support, a mentor and facilitator, whereas the Chimp needs a strong and dominant leader to protect it and lead the troop into battle. Clarify the role of your leader!

Partners and the troop

When two people fall in love, it can be easy for them to expect their partner to fulfil all of the roles in their life. This is highly unlikely to work. Usually a partner cannot fulfil all of our needs. There are some drives such as female bonding or male bonding that our partner cannot fulfil (unless they happen to be of the same sex). Trying to make one person fulfil all your needs and roles can be very dangerous, because if the relationship falters we are left with nothing.

However, this is an individual decision and there are circumstances where it might work out.

Summary key points

- Establishing your troop is critical to reassure your Chimp.
- Recognise the different ways that the Human and Chimp choose the troop.
- Opinions from outside your troop are not important.
- Clarifying the roles of those in your troop helps it to function well.
- The troop needs time spent on it to make it function.

Suggested exercise:
Creating your troop

Establish your troop
Redefine your troop. Think carefully about who is really in your troop and make sure that the Human has chosen these people. List the members of your troop. Importantly, recognise who is not in your troop and whom it is unwise to rely on or open up to.

Clarify the roles of the members of your troop
Think about what each person in the troop is offering you and what you are offering him or her. Try to recognise when you are asking a troop member to fulfil a role that is not suitable and find someone appropriate to meet your needs. Writing out your needs first is a good starting point.

Invest in the troop
Once you know who the members of your troop are, prioritise your time to engage with them. Look after your troop, as neglected people often leave. Ask yourself what you have recently done for each member.

Chapter 9
The Planet Connect
How to communicate effectively

Communication
- Four ways of communicating
- The Square of Communication

- Preparing yourself for significant conversations
- Dealing with unresolved conflict

Now that we have looked at how the Psychological Mind works, we can look at how two minds interact with each other.

An inability to communicate effectively can often lead to frustration and conflict; therefore it is worth investing some time in improving your communication skills. Let me state the obvious: If you don't set time aside and work on communication then don't be surprised if you don't improve.

Four ways of communicating

There are four ways in which two people can communicate together. Each person can either be in Chimp mode or in Human mode. Chimp mode means the conversation is going to be emotionally charged and not necessarily logical. Human mode means the conversation will be logical and not emotionally charged. Each person can move between Chimp and Human mode very quickly.

The ideal conversation between two people would be Human to Human because this will be logical and contained. The nightmare scenario would be a conversation between two Chimps. Here the 'conversation' will be highly emotionally charged and could involve a lot of attacks and counterattacks. If one person is in Human mode and one is in Chimp mode then it is unlikely that the conversation will be too helpful either.

Four ways to communicate

The key to communicating well is to prepare yourself. So let's first look at the basis for communicating and then draw up a checklist for preparing for a significant conversation. Finally we can briefly consider how to deal with unresolved conflict.

The Square of Communication

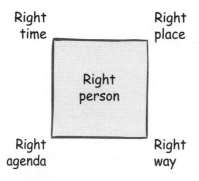

The Square of Communication is the basis for communicating and it has four corners and a centre. To promote effective communication it would help to remember this square.

The 'never-ending wrong person trail'

If you don't get the centre of the Square right then you are probably wasting your time and doing yourself no favours. The 'never-ending wrong person trail' is very common. If someone has a complaint or discussion involving a specific person, it is amazing that they go to everybody but this person to sort it out. The result is that instead of sorting out the problem by approaching the right person, they end up going down a trail of wrong people, who can never satisfy or resolve the situation. Hence they moan and complain to lots of people. They themself may now have become the problem and can quite legitimately come in for some criticism.

Talking to the right person would save them a lot of time, effort and emotional stress. The usual reason that we don't talk to the right person is because of a lack of assertiveness, so I will address this next.

Assertiveness or aggression?

Being *assertive* means explaining to someone else what is acceptable in your world and what isn't acceptable and why. This is explained in a calm manner without expressing emotion. By contrast, being *aggressive* is expressing emotion and behaviours that are attacking in manner in order to convey your message.

ASSERTIVE COMMUNICATOR	AGGRESSIVE COMMUNICATOR
Removes emotion from speech.	Full of emotion.
Chooses words carefully.	Evokes emotion in other person.

If you stop and think about the Chimp within the other person, you can easily work out exactly what emotional response they are likely to give to these two very different presentations. An aggressive approach to someone will definitely wake up their Chimp and it is likely to do one of two things. It will either attack back or it will recoil. Either way, the person will be unlikely to hear the message because their emotions have taken over and their Chimp will now have an agenda of its own. If you are assertive, then the Chimp in the other person is much less likely to come out and they are much more likely to hear the message and respond appropriately.

So what are the simple rules of how to be assertive? There are three parts to being an assertive communicator, *and all three parts must be used, in order to be effective.*

The three parts to assertiveness are:

1. Say to the person what you don't want, using the word 'I'.
2. Say to them how it is making you feel.
3. Say to them what you do want, using the word 'I'.

To help to convey your message you can also add that you would like to be heard uninterrupted and you can state the facts as you see them. It always helps to thank them for listening.

Here is an example to demonstrate how this could be done.

Let's assume you have turned up late for a meeting for whatever reason. The person you are meeting is very angry when you arrive and starts raising their voice, saying that you are rude for arriving late. Remember to remove emotion from your voice, otherwise you will evoke an emotional response in the other person and the situation will probably just get worse. It is better to wait until they stop shouting, because interrupting them may also make it worse. So let their Chimp finish its scream but don't react to it!

1. State: 'I would like you to listen to what I have to say and I would like you not to interrupt me. Thank you.'
2. State 'The facts as I perceive them are that I am late and the reason is that I misjudged the time, and for this I apologise.'
3. State 'I don't want you to shout at me.'
4. State 'When you shout it makes me feel intimidated.'
5. State 'I would like you to speak to me in a quiet voice. Thank you.'

Notice the use of the word 'I'. It is very important to use 'I' and not to say something like, 'Please don't shout at me.' If you think about it, there is nothing wrong with saying 'Please don't shout at me.' It may work well. However, assertiveness with the word 'I' is making a statement that tells somebody very clearly that you are not happy with the situation and that you have an opinion about it. 'Please don't shout at me' is a request not a statement.

If you look at the three assertiveness statements above, and say them into the air in a quiet but firm voice you will get the hang of it. Now try to say them again into the air but this time express them with strong emotion. This will drive home the difference between aggression and assertiveness. It is not what is being said, it is the way that it is being said. Also think about how you would feel being on the receiving end of the aggressive approach and what emotions it would evoke in your Chimp.

So why are a lot of people lacking in assertiveness? Lack of assertiveness is usually based in Gremlins. The commonest beliefs are based on ideas such as 'I am not as good as others' or 'I can't be as confident as others' or 'my feelings don't matter'. Very often the troop drive of needing to be accepted has turned into a Gremlin of belief and behaviour. 'I must be liked', 'I must always please others' and therefore 'I have no rights'. This is a lack of self-esteem and is worth addressing. If you are not assertive, but would like to be, you must try to work out what is stopping you. Other common destructive thoughts include, 'This isn't my world, I am in a world belonging to others,' or 'I'm not allowed to express my opinion,' or 'I cannot say 'no' to people (because I have to keep them happy).'

The corners

Now let's return to the Square of Communication and put the corners in place:

- The right time
- The right place
- The right agenda
- The right way

The right time

If you choose the wrong time, for example when the person can't listen to you or the conversation has to be rushed, then the communication is less likely to work. We also need the right amount of time to get our points across. Getting this aspect wrong only compounds issues and makes them worse, as we feel frustrated by only partly addressing the issues and agendas. Make sure you have the right amount of time to listen to the other person and express what you want to because if you don't have time it may be more difficult to return to the conversation later. It also helps to make sure the time is right within the context of events. Sometimes keeping quiet until things settle can be very helpful.

The right place

If we get the wrong place (too noisy or busy) then it is hard to concentrate on what the message is. It also agitates both Chimps and this is not good news! Also make sure that if the conversation is a difficult one that the place is private enough to do this. It isn't helpful to have someone nearby eavesdropping on your conversation if you are talking about something very personal. A neutral place, which is not on either person's territory, is often the best location.

The right agenda

There are often two flaws to getting the right agenda. One is that we go in with a hidden agenda; the other is that we address the wrong agenda by getting distracted and moving from the point. This leaves people frustrated and still feeling agitated.

Getting the right agenda clear in your mind is very important because if you aren't entirely certain about what it is that you want to discuss then the chances of success are diminished. It is also very easy to get distracted and taken onto another agenda. Try to recognise this and stick to your original agenda. It is helpful to state what your agenda is at the start of the conversation – even have it written down to remind you. (Don't forget that the other person may have an agenda and it is useful to ask them before you start.) Be sure that you address what is on your mind and don't dress it up and then present something else because the true agenda is too difficult to address. It is obvious that this is likely to lead to confusion and frustration in the long run.

The most significant point to establishing your agenda is to recognise that there are two of you entering the conversation: yourself and your Chimp.

The Chimp's agenda

The Chimp's agenda is based on emotion and typically has a 'win or lose' mentality. This refers back to jungle rules and is either black or white; there is no middle ground. So as far as the Chimp is concerned, it will come out of the conversation as having either won or lost. The Chimp will want to express its emotion and it will attack any fault in the other person and also defend itself against any possible criticism or even perceived criticism. It will also want to come out looking good and being innocent. If it isn't innocent then it will want to justify why it was provoked or put into an impossible situation and thereby justify anything it did say or do.

Frank and Peter and the four agendas

Frank and Peter are neighbours and about to meet to discuss a hedge that Frank owns that is cutting light out of Peter's garden.

Let's begin by looking at Frank, and divide up his mind into the Chimp and the Human. The Human will want to have a peaceful resolution and leave the conversation with both men happy. The Human will understand that there may need to be a compromise and also a need to keep things in perspective. So although Frank might like the tall hedge he might reasonably see that this is fairly unpleasant for his neighbour.

However, Frank's Chimp will have none of this. If it is a typical Chimp it will already have decided that the hedge represents its territory and it has no intention of conceding. His Chimp will see the fact that Peter is approaching him as a challenge to his power, ego and dominance. Therefore the Chimp must see the conversation as case of winning or losing. There will be little compromise and no backing down. It will just be a case of selecting the right facts to support the Chimp's beliefs and sticking to them. If necessary, using emotional threats or body posturing to gain dominance.

Chimps and Humans fight for control

Peter will also approach the conversation with two minds. The Human will probably have a similar agenda to Frank's Human and want a compromise and amicable discussion. The Human will want to hear the other person's viewpoint, try to understand it, and then if necessary, change his own stance. However, the Chimp will be ready to do battle, see the hedge as an affront to its territorial rights and also that another Chimp is dominating it. With this interpretation of what might typically be happening in the minds of the two men, we can see that unless they recognise the different agendas, it could go horrendously wrong by their Chimps hijacking them.

Common Chimp agendas

A Chimp will want to:

- Win
- Express emotion
- Attack the other person
- Defend itself
- Get its point across
- Not give way or change stance
- Come out looking good and being innocent
- If guilty, use excuses of being provoked and being a victim

The way in which the Chimp will do this is to try to dominate the other person by speaking first and shouting above them. It will use words and behaviours to do this. It will not usually listen to the other person but just wait until it can get its point across. It will not change its stance but refer everything to where it stands and what it believes. It will have great difficulty in changing either its stance or beliefs, because in the eyes of the Chimp this will be seen as losing the battle, which it has no intention of doing! So it won't give way. The Chimp will focus on the problem and how it feels and not on the solution.

Chimp's method

In a confrontational situation, a Chimp will:

- Shout and be emotional
- Interrupt inappropriately
- Use emotive words
- Dominate with speed and volume
- Dominate and intimidate with body language
- Focus on the problem
- Work on feelings
- Be devious if necessary

The Human's agenda

Conversely, the Human's agenda is not to 'win or lose' but to reach a sensible outcome where both people are happy and satisfied. The Human doesn't work in black or white but typically works with shades of grey. The Human accepts that it may be wrong or there may be a different explanation. So the Human can change its stance and wants to listen to make sure it has understood the situation properly. Therefore, the Human looks outside of itself to other people or the law, to discover what is correct, factual and acceptable. The Human might not necessarily agree with that ruling, but it can accept it. The Human can give way by realising that an opinion is only an opinion, it doesn't mean someone has won and someone has lost. The Human will do this by containing emotion and listening to the other person FIRST and seeing their point of view. The Human will focus on the solution and not on the problem. The Human speaks slowly and calmly, and tries to understand the other person by listening to them.

Common Human agendas

A Human will try to:

- Understand the other person first
- Allow the other person expression
- Gather all the information by listening
- Look for a solution
- Use facts not feelings or impressions

Human's method

In a confrontational situation, the Human will try to:

- Remain calm
- Use 'gentle' non-emotional words
- Listen first
- See a different point of view
- Be open to changing stance
- Recognise opinions are not facts
- Reason and discuss
- Find common ground
- Use reasoning to try and reach a joint decision
- Compromise to try and satisfy everybody
- Accept differences

You have a choice

What typically happens, if we let nature run its course, is that the two Chimps do battle first and a lot of unpleasant exchange takes place. Then, when they have calmed down and if not too much damage has been done, the two Humans take over and try to reach a solution that both are happy with. At any point while the two Humans are having a constructive conversation, one or both Chimps can wake up and start the attack again and destroy the conversation.

The most constructive way to have the conversation is for each Human to first have a discussion with their own Chimp and find out what it wants to say and why. Then for each Human to tell their own Chimp that some of what they want is destructive and not going to happen and some of what they want is reasonable. The Human will then represent the Chimp's reasonable points and will do this in a constructive manner to get a good outcome. This is the ideal first step to approaching a difficult conversation but it is unlikely to happen! This is because most people don't recognise that they even have a Chimp, or they may recognise it, but still choose to let the Chimp have its say, rather than be represented by the Human.

The right way
Before you decide on having a conversation just consider if it could be better to communicate via letter or email? Although there may be disadvantages to doing this, there are two clear advantages. The first is that it gives you time to construct carefully what you have to say and the second is that it also gives the person time to think and digest what you have said before responding. On some occasions it could be appropriate to communicate via a third party.

Assuming that you have decided to have a face-to-face conversation with the person, then let's look at how you can go about this in the right way. Think about how you are going to approach and work through the conversation. Before you begin, you must get into the right frame of mind by making sure the right way is the Human way of conducting the conversation.

Key Point
Preparing yourself is the best thing that you can do to enhance your chances of success in an important conversation.

The presentation and packaging of communication

How we present our message is critical to a successful outcome. It is a bit like selling a product or offering a gift. So much can depend on the presentation and how it is packaged. It is so critical that we will now spend some time considering the types of packaging and the types of presentation that are available.

Whenever we communicate, the message is always packaged. So let us say, for example, that you have been drinking a cup of coffee in a coffee bar and gone over to the counter to get a spoon to stir it with. When you return to your seat someone has taken it. You now want to tell them that they have taken your seat. This is the simple message. There are multitudes of ways in which you can package this. You could shout and raise your voice; you could smile and talk quietly; you could tower over the person to impress your authority; you could have eyes that are looking gentle or menacing; you could use 'please' or you may just be confrontational and start with a statement 'this is my chair'. In all of these options a number of packages were chosen. To make it easier to work with, I will divide the package types up into four groups:

- Body language
- Intonation
- Use of words
- Ambience

Body language

There is no mystery to body language; everybody assesses body language every day. Research suggests that females are far better than males in reading a situation by using body language cues. As said in earlier chapters, it is our Chimps that read other people's body language and they do this often without the Human even knowing they are doing it.

Body language is simply the term used for a message that we convey without speaking. Instead of speaking we use facial expression, positioning and movement of our body. A simple example is shown when a person wants to disengage with you and they look away from you, cross their arms and sigh. These three body language signs are all very clear messages.

Body language always has to be put in context, and cultural differences also play a huge part in the way we act. This topic has been studied in depth by various researchers and will not be explained here in any detail. However, it is important that we recognise the body language we are using, as this will definitely colour our interactions with others.

Examples of body language

If we **tower over someone** when talking to them, most people would find this very intimidating and threatening and any message offered might get interpreted with a negative feeling attached to it. It is the same as having your body space invaded. We all have a space around us that we feel belongs to us and if someone gets too close and is unwelcome then we immediately feel uncomfortable. Body space is different from culture to culture and person to person but the general rule is that we are programmed to feel comfortable at arm's length from another person. Any closer leaves us uneasy unless we are welcoming it.

Crossing our arms generally means that we feel attacked and are being defensive. It can also mean that we are being overloaded with information or are not sure we want the information being given. Then again we might just be feeling cold or cross our arms out of habit! The important point is that if you cross your arms the other person is likely to have a negative interpretation.

When we talk to people we generally look at their face, and their **expression** tells us what the person is feeling. When we meet someone we like, our pupils dilate and others recognise this in us and feel more at ease with us. If we don't like someone that we meet, our pupils tend to get smaller and again they might recognise this and feel less at ease with us.

Our faces also use what are called **micro-expressions**. These are defined as facial expressions occurring in very high emotional states that last for less than a quarter of a second. It has been argued that some people can read micro-expressions and be able to tell when others are lying. In reality, research suggests that very few people can do this with any amount of accuracy. However, as the micro-expressions are involuntary, if we video someone who is talking, we can slow the frames down to watch for certain signs that seem to correlate with lying. All aspects of the face, involving the lips, eyes, eyebrows, nose, mouth and muscles, are monitored.

What we can say is that typical brains can recognise when someone else is showing strong emotions such as being angry, bored or stressed. According to some researchers, body language can account for over half of the message that is being conveyed and we read this naturally so you don't have to learn anything! The point to note here is not to overrate body language, even though it is still worth considering how you are using your body when interacting with others. As body language is generally Chimp-to-Chimp, you don't want any miscommunication with the other person's Chimp.

Intonation

Around one-third of our communication focuses on voice intonation and this can be broken down into three parts: speed, volume and emphasis.

Speed

The speed of speech can portray many feelings and emotions: urgency, irritation, excitement, uncertainty, etc. When somebody speaks quickly they will alert the Chimp in the other person. The Chimp will interpret this rapid speech depending on what is happening around it. Conversely, when we speak slowly the Chimp is more likely to relax and therefore the Human in the other person will be able to respond more easily. It is also true that we mimic what we hear and see. If someone is speaking quickly then we are more likely to respond with rapid speech. If someone speaks slowly then we are more likely to respond in a slowed-down manner.

Key Point
Speaking steadily will help us to get messages across in the way that we intend and help the other person to listen.

Volume

The volume of speech has the same effect as the speed of speech in terms of alerting the Chimp. The Chimp will also mimic the volume and tone set by another person.

I borrowed a friend's three-year-old son for a few minutes to demonstrate an impressive example of volume imitation to some of my medical students. I simply asked the boy where he had been that day. We then had a conversation about his visit to the zoo and I deliberately began to raise my voice. The boy soon followed and we ended up virtually shouting at each other. It was also interesting that at this point he invaded my body space in order to make sure I could hear him from a few inches away! After being almost deafened, I deliberately reduced the volume down to a whisper, over a few sentences. Like magic, he followed me down the volume scale and pulled away from me. However, when we reached whispering point, he again moved into my body space to make sure I could hear him. Finally we returned to normal volume and he was none the wiser as to what had happened.

Think about this when you are talking to someone. You may not get such a dramatic response but think what effects you may be evoking in their Chimp.

Therefore the best way to get a Chimp in someone else to remain calm and for the Human to hear is to speak slowly and with a normal or quiet volume. As with body language it is important to put things into context. Sometimes when a person speaks slowly and quietly in a deliberate way that is not appropriate, it can be very irritating and can be a form of passive control of others. In these circumstances you are almost guaranteed to see their Chimps appear.

Emphasis

Emphasis is very interesting. Changing the emphasised word in a sentence can completely change its meaning. For example, take the sentence, 'I think you have a very good voice.' The meaning of the sentence alters by emphasising different words. Here are four versions.

When the stress is...	It could mean...
I think you have a very good voice...	It is only me that thinks this.
I *THINK* you have a very good voice...	I am in doubt but I could be right.
I think *YOU* have a very good voice...	You are better than others.
I think you have a very good *VOICE*...	This is your best aspect.

We only have to raise or lower our voice at the end of these sentences and it can change the meanings again. Generally, raising the voice means asking a question or challenging something but in some cultures it is just customary. This demonstrates that the emphasis in all of our sentences needs to be placed into context.

Use of words

The chimpanzee in the jungle uses branches, teeth and fists as weapons to attack other chimpanzees. If it wants to send a message of friendship then it might offer food or groom another chimpanzee.

As people, we mainly use words to communicate. Words can be an offer of friendship or kindness but we also know that they can be the most severe of weapons. **Make no mistake, an attack by words from one person to another is exactly the same as an attack from one chimpanzee to another, using teeth and fists, and the damage can be equally as savage.**

Let us look at two very different uses for words. The first use is as a communication tool. The second use is as a dangerous weapon.

The first use as a communication tool requires some thought. If you want to chop some wood you wouldn't pick up a screwdriver to do it. Picking the wrong word to use in a conversation can have big consequences. One of the reasons for this is that both the Human and the Chimp in the other person pick up the word. The Human hears the logical aspect of the word used and the Chimp hears the emotional aspect of the word. All of the words that we use have an emotional content attached to them. When we hear words we also associate emotions with them and we release chemicals in our brain that influence how we feel. Some words such as death and love are very emotive, whilst other words, such as apple and table have little emotional content. Of course this is a very individual thing because the same word can have a different response to different people. So if you said to someone, 'I hate one of my neighbours,' the use of the word 'hate' will evoke a response in them and also in yourself. The chemicals released will give you both feelings. However, if you had said, 'I am not too keen on one of my neighbours,' then you would have a very different response chemically within your own brain and so would the person that you are talking to in their brain. This would result in different feelings for both of you. There is a very different response to the word 'hate', compared to the words 'not keen'. The words that you choose will evoke emotional responses in both yourself and others. If the Chimp doesn't like the words then it will be straight out of its box to have an opinion.

Choice and reaction

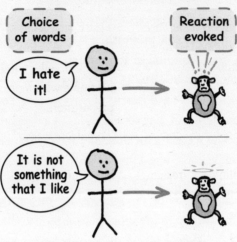

Choose your words carefully

Often it may not even be others on the receiving end. A lot of people use words that attack themselves. If you go around saying 'I am a useless person' expect the chemicals in your head to be bad news! It's your choice.

Here are a few common examples of how changing a word can have a large effect on your Chimp.

Recall from an earlier chapter how 'should' and 'could' have dramatically different effects on the meaning of a sentence and emotions evoked when interchanged. The word 'should' implies a standard or expectation. If you fail to reach that expectation then you have failed in your own world. The word 'should' is typically associated with such feelings as failure, blame, guilt, threat and inadequacy. All because we chose the word 'should'. If you had chosen the word 'could' then this does not evoke feelings of failure or set standards. Instead it is associated with feelings of opportunity, choice, possibility and hope.

Should	Could
'I should have won that race.' Puts pressure on self and states failure.	*'I could have won that race.'* Gives room to look at the situation, reflect and try better next time with more preparation.
'I should lose weight and be healthy.' Evokes feelings of pressure and obligation with possible judgement.	*'I could lose weight.'* Gives feelings of hope and opportunity.
'You should say you're sorry to her.' Evokes Chimp feelings of resistance and guilt.	*'You could say you're sorry to her.'* Evokes reflection and choice without confrontation.

Of course, there are times when the use of the word 'should' might be appropriate, and there are times when the use of the word 'could' might be inappropriate but it is worth considering the difference when you do choose.

Try looking at these next two sentences and reflect on them for yourself:

- 'I want you to make me a cup of tea.'
- 'I would like you to make me a cup of tea.'

The first is a command. The second is a suggestion and request, on which you are free to make a choice.

Very few Chimps like being told what to do. Nearly all Chimps like to be able to decide for themselves. Saying, 'I want you to', usually implies power and authority over someone else in order to give that command. This could lead to some resentment or confrontation from their Chimp.

Think carefully about the words that you choose and the effects that you will evoke in others. By taking time to think about and sometimes change the words we use, we can alter the way people react to us and alter feelings we take from situations.

A word of caution

Sometimes the use of 'I want' would be correct. For example, when you need to be assertive, then 'I want' is correct.

Assertiveness in situations is sometimes called for. If, for example, you wanted to end a relationship and you said: 'I want to end this relationship because I don't want it,' there is no discussion because you have stated a fact.

Whereas, if you tried to be polite, saying: 'I would like this relationship to end because I don't think it is working,' then you have left the topic open to discussion.

The point here is that there are **no hard and fast rules**; try to think a little deeper about the effect your chosen words will have on you, the message you are conveying and others around you.

The second use of words as a dangerous weapon is fairly self-explanatory. Words can be very damaging and using them to hurt others is an attack. It is worth reflecting on this before you do damage to someone inadvertently. Words are weapons!

Ambience

The ambience of a person is a mixture of their demeanour, stance, mood and the way in which they interact with others. The Chimp works this out for us. If we get it wrong and approach a person who is not friendly or in a good state of mind it could have serious consequences. Reading ambience is very useful for us but often we don't consciously think about it unless warning bells sound. The ambience of a person comes from both the Human and the Chimp and can change quite quickly.

Recognising ambience is easy in children and dogs; they do not have the mask that adult humans can often use. Children and dogs are open and transparent; they have nothing to hide. When we meet a dog it soon lets us know how it is feeling and it gives off an ambience. It may come across as friendly and relaxed or hostile and agitated. Children likewise have an ambience about them that they do not try to hide. We soon know how they feel.

When we pick up on the atmosphere that an adult creates around them and the way in which they are interacting, or not interacting, with us, it will evoke large responses from your Chimp within. Chimps must know when to approach other Chimps and when to stay clear.

It is worth thinking about the ambience you have because it may well out-weigh any message that you are trying to get across.

Ask yourself two simple questions:

- What kind of ambience would you like to meet in someone that you have to talk to?
- What kind of ambience, in that person, is likely to put you at ease and help you to listen to them?

These two questions are almost rhetorical. It is obvious that we all prefer to meet happy, relaxed and pleasant people who engage with us and listen well.

Ambience is something that can be chosen. Working on your own ambience is about making an effort to check yourself and deal with anything that is causing you not to be where you want to be. Often it means giving some attention to Chimp Management. Think about what ambience you present to others and then make sure it turns into exactly how you would like it to be.

> ## Key Point
> *Working on your body language, intonation, use of words and ambience will help to significantly improve the effectiveness of your communication with others.*

Preparing yourself for significant conversations

We can now pull together this chapter by looking at how we can employ the previous concepts when preparing for a significant conversation. Here are some suggestions in the form of a checklist with steps.

Checklist
Step 1: *Check that you are talking to the right person for your agenda.*

Step 2: *Make sure it is the right time to have the conversation.*

Step 3: *Check that the place for the conversation is appropriate.*

Step 4: *Establish the agendas of your Chimp and Human.*
You need to start by clearly defining to yourself what you want out of the conversation. In other words: what is your agenda; what do you want to leave the conversation having achieved?

The most important thing to think about here is that when you enter the conversation there will be two of you trying to speak, you and your Chimp, and they may have very different agendas. Your Human will probably want solutions and your Chimp will probably want expression. So start by defining the agenda of your Chimp and also the agenda of your Human.

Step 5: *Remove the unreasonable parts of your Chimp's agenda.*
Explain to your Chimp that it is very understandable and reasonable

to be emotional or upset but expressing this inappropriately is unlikely to help in the long run. How the Chimp feels is very reasonable FOR A CHIMP, but it may be unhelpful. So, accept that the feelings that your Chimp has are normal but recognise and remove those agendas that are unacceptable to your Human, such as 'I must win' and 'I must get revenge'.

Human represents the Chimp

Step 6: *Approach the conversation in Human mode.*
You must exercise your Chimp if necessary before you enter the conversation. Ensure that you are in Human mode and employing the Human's method of communicating.

Step 7: *Remind yourself to present the conversation with the right packaging.*
Before you enter the conversation think about your body language, intonation, use of words and ambience.

Step 8: *Help to manage the Chimp in the other person.*
When you enter the conversation it is likely that the other person's Chimp will begin the interaction. Try to allow their Chimp to exercise and listen but don't interact or respond to anything it says. Allowing them a few minutes of what might be uncomfortable comments will help to settle their Chimp down. As you listen to them and hear what they have to say, you may change your mind on the way that you are seeing things and appreciate that they might

have some good points to make. Try to remember that the Chimp in most of us is not very pleasant at times. We usually regret what we say or what we do, and wish we could turn back the clock. If someone has had Chimp activity, and regrets this, then it may be harsh and unhelpful to hold them to it and remind them. At some point you have to forgive people for losing control of their Chimp and give them chance to become Human again, if you want to work with them. Notice I have said *IF* you want to work with them.

Step 9: *Find the agenda of the Human and Chimp in the other person.*
When the other person's Chimp has settled, their Human can now begin to work with you. It is at this point that you can try to elicit what they really want.

Step 10: *Clarify your own agenda.*
You can now explain what you would like to achieve with the conversation. Remember that it is important that your Chimp remains silent if you want the best chance of success.

Step 11: *Agree any common ground and outcomes aimed for.*
It helps to start with things you do agree on. Also to establish what you agree to try and achieve before you begin.

Step 12: *Try to meet the other person's agenda first before your own.*
Letting the other person achieve their agenda will really help them to listen when you want to cover the areas you want to talk about. Otherwise they may find it hard not to keep interrupting and trying to get their agenda heard first.

Step 13: *Try to meet your own agenda.*

Step 14: *Summarise what you have agreed.*
It is best to get the other person to let you know what they have understood and agreed. When you do have an important

conversation or pass a message on to someone else, it is always worth checking that they have received it correctly and understood it. It is helpful at the end of any important conversation that you take time to do this. The best way of checking is to ask the person what they have understood from what you have said to them. Everyone can misunderstand or not hear parts of a message, and very often the message or parts of it need to be repeated for it to sink in. If the message is very important then you can also check for understanding by asking the person to explain to you why you have given the message and why it is important. This way you have a chance to fine-tune any slight differences that may still be present.

Key Point
Never assume that because you have told someone something that they have heard it or understood it.

Step 15: *Smile and thank the person.*
Letting someone know that you are grateful for the conversation, and his or her time, is not only polite but also acknowledges that you are respecting him or her. People are not mind readers, and often damage is done not by what we say but by what we don't say.

Dealing with unresolved conflict

Even with the best methods possible, conflict and differences can still continue. Sometimes when there is strong emotion involved it helps to involve a third person. The best person would be someone neutral to solve the dispute or conflict. When two people get into conflict with a difference of opinion, there are basically three levels of dealing with this. These three levels are negotiation, mediation and arbitration. The last two involve the third person.

Negotiation

This is the first step to sorting things out. Approach the person yourself and try to find common ground by listening to each other, respecting opinion and agreeing to differ if you can't agree.

Mediation

If you can't agree but want to sort things out, or you both find it hard to even sit in the same room together, then mediation would be the next step. Mediation is basically where an independent person, agreed by both of you, comes in to help you to resolve your differences. The mediator doesn't decide but just facilitates the conversation and provides the best setting for getting what you both want. They are effectively a calming influence that manages the conversation and both Chimps!

Arbitration

This is the next step when you want a decision made but just can't agree. The arbiter is a person, agreed by both of you, to come in and listen and then to be the judge with a final decision on what will happen. You both have to accept to abide by the decision of the arbiter whether you agree with it or not.

Summary key points

- Effective communication is critical to effective functioning.
- There are techniques that you can develop to improve your communication but it is a skill to use them.
- The skill of communication is no different to any other skill and takes time and effort to develop and maintain.
- The Square of Communication has the right person in the middle with the four corners being the right time, place, agenda and way.
- The way in which you package a message is critical to its success in being received.

Suggested exercise:
Effective communication and negotiation exercises

Choose the right words

Make a conscious effort to choose the right words to describe what you want to say. Remember that your Chimp is very likely to use emotional words with extreme emphasis. Try to moderate the words you use instead of extremes. For example, 'I can't stand this music,' could be replaced with 'I am not keen on this music.' This change of statement will evoke less of a change in emotion in the person listening and also in the atmosphere of the conversation.

Prepare for an important conversation

Try to follow the structure below, taken from this chapter, to engage in an important or difficult conversation. Remember to choose your words carefully!

Checklist summary

1. Check that you are talking to the right person for your agenda.
2. Make sure it is the right time to have the conversation.
3. Check that the place for the conversation is appropriate.
4. Establish the agendas of your Chimp and Human.
5. Remove the unreasonable parts of your Chimp's agenda.
6. Approach the conversation in Human mode.
7. Remember to present the conversation with the right packaging.
8. Help to manage the Chimp in the other person.
9. Find the agenda of the Human and Chimp in the other person.
10. Clarify your own agenda.

11. Agree any common ground and outcomes aimed for.
12. Try to meet the other person's agenda first before your own.
13. Try to meet your own agendas.
14. Summarise what you have agreed.
15. Smile and thank the person.

Chapter 10
The Planet of the Real World
How to establish the right environment

The Chimp's world
The Human's world
The Computer's world

We are now familiar with the concept that your mind is composed of three different working parts – the Chimp, Human and Computer. Each brain perceives a different world and it is important to understand these worlds and work with them. It is also very important to get these worlds, or environments, right for you, as this has a massive impact on your ability to function and be happy.

As we go about our daily routines we exist in three very different worlds.

- Your Chimp exists in a jungle. It sees danger and territory everywhere and lives by the rules of the jungle.
- Your Human exists in a society with people in it, abiding by laws.
- Your Computer makes sense of both the Chimp and the Human perceptions, and interprets these, and comes up with the real world that you live in: a mixture of society and jungle that is forever alternating.

There are three aspects to the worlds that you live in and each needs addressing.

- The first aspect is to recognise the different worlds of the Chimp and the Human.
- The second aspect is to make these worlds into friendly and appropriate environments for both of them to live in by considering their needs.
- The third aspect is to merge the two worlds so that they are compatible with each other, which is the Computer's world.

The Chimp's world

Your Chimp enters its jungle every day with a jungle mentality. We know that Chimps have a strong sense of territory and of belonging to a troop. So as the Chimp begins its journey into its jungle it will look for familiarity to make it feel secure. It will search out its troop and it will crave routine. It will fiercely defend its territory and troop and it will see any advances by Chimps outside of its troop as potential dangers and will attack them or run away as necessary.

Boundary disputes

The Chimp therefore needs to know its part of the jungle and its boundaries. This means it needs to be looked after by recognising its need for structure, familiarity and reassurance. However, if it has a strong troop with it, then it will become confident, adventurous and inquisitive and is less concerned with the environment.

The danger of the Chimp's interpretation of being in a jungle rather than a society means it can use its drives inappropriately. So boundary disputes involving conifer hedging or rights to pathways can literally lead to murder. Try to recognise how your Chimp is interpreting the world it is living in as a jungle and then acting on this with the principles of the jungle. Silly disputes, such as someone taking your parking place, can lead to serious conflict if the Chimp works on the basis that its territory is being invaded.

In any form of boundary dispute let the Human represent the Chimp to resolve it. Chimp mentality over boundaries can also be seen when it comes to job roles. If you are in dispute and your Chimp believes another Chimp is on its patch, then let the Human in you take the lead to sort it out. The problem when the Chimp leads is that it drives with strong, and often out of perspective, emotion.

The right part of the jungle

There are certain rules to follow if your Chimp is going to be happy in the environment. You can't override the Chimp if it cannot live in a certain world. If you try to force your Chimp to live in an unfriendly part of the jungle then you must accept the consequences. In these circumstances it is very likely that the Chimp will become anxious and give you feelings of unhappiness and unease. The jungle is a frightening place, but if you put the Chimp in a part where it is happy, then it will calm down. This means that your Chimp must be able to handle the **emotional** environment that it is living in.

For example, some time ago, a friend called me to ask for advice. She had been offered promotion and was flattered and excited by it. However, the new role would mean that she would spend considerably less time at home and also have some additional responsibilities at work. All I could do was to ask some questions and let her decide. The question that I asked, relevant to the topic of the Chimp in the jungle was, 'How much emotional stress is involved at work and at home with the change in job, and can you manage this?'

She went away to think about it and decided that it was too much for her to handle. She could recognise that her Chimp would never be at ease with the new situation and although it was flattering and exciting, it wasn't sensible. She declined the promotion. One day I asked her how she felt about her decision years earlier. She replied that she was very happy because she didn't go chasing after something that at the end of the day she couldn't handle emotionally. Of course, she might have taken the job and then learnt to manage her Chimp within the new setting, but sometimes we have to accept that our Chimp has its limitations and only you can decide for yourself what these limitations are and how to get a balance in your life.

A second example demonstrates something very different! A colleague called on me one day to express how miserable they felt in their current role. Their Chimp clearly wanted to move into an authoritative role but had grave fears and concerns in case it didn't work out. When we discussed this it became clear that the Chimp needed help to settle down the insecurity it felt and the Human needed help to present a rational argument to the Chimp and to work through any consequences the new job entailed. After some discussions the Chimp settled its fears and became excited by the prospects of a new life and the challenges it would present. The colleague moved jobs and the Chimp became very happy and the person's quality of life improved.

Some people spend their lives in the 'wrong' place. Realising that your lifestyle is not matching your Chimp's needs, and doing something about it, is one of the keys to being at peace within yourself. The right part of the jungle is where your work and home environments are happy places to be.

The territory itself

Having established the right part of the jungle for your Chimp to live in, you need to consider what it wants within that jungle area. Here are a few suggestions that will keep it happy within the territory and stop it from wandering or becoming distressed.

Right finances and possessions

Learning to live within your means is an excellent way to stop the Chimp from fretting. Borrowing money to improve things is a decision you need to make with your Chimp. Some people can deal with borrowing large amounts of money and their Chimp will be fine with it, while others cannot. Therefore, if you are constantly going to worry about owing money, then don't borrow. Your Chimp is telling you what it can and cannot cope with; take the time to realise what you can and cannot handle emotionally.

Right friends

Your Chimp will feel comfortable with some people and not others, so it is about recognising this and surrounding yourself with the right people as often as you can.

Right job

Even in the right job make sure the Chimp receives constant reassurance as to its exact role and responsibilities. It needs to feel competent and confident in order to perform its work.

Right food

The right food for your Chimp is emotional food. It needs satisfaction and peace of mind. Don't give your Chimp indigestion by asking it to accept and live with inappropriate emotions, for example, stress or unhappiness.

Right time out

If you are not giving your Chimp enough rest then it will not be happy in its world. Your emotions are no different to any other part of your physical body. They need time out and repair time. Giving yourself this emotional rest is very important to your Chimp. You will inevitably come back feeling better.

In summary, you need to put your Chimp in the right part of the jungle with the right things within it to keep it happy. If any are missing, it will become very unhappy and create problems for you until you put things right.

The Human's world

Your Human lives in a society and therefore sees the world as a place based mainly on logic and compassion. This world supports the weak and the vulnerable, and gives equal opportunities to all. It works on the principle that within this world are law-abiding Humans who live fairly and morally. They experience guilt, remorse and atonement.

Given these assumptions, it is no wonder that the Human experiences frustration and disillusionment. What Humans don't appreciate is that there are lots of Chimps living in the world who have no intention of following any of these practices and the Human must come to terms with this. Once the Human accepts this then they must learn to accommodate it into their world without their Chimp getting out and taking over.

Human environmental needs

One of the differences between the Chimp and the Human is that the Human is usually keen to develop and learn, and have opportunities to be creative. Humans need social stimulation and intellectual challenges to a greater extent than the Chimp, who is more concerned with survival. Therefore, when it comes to the Human, it is not so much about *nurturing* the Human but *developing* the Human within you. It is allowing time for your Human to have quality of life. We can therefore look at the same areas as the Chimp and work out what suits the Human within you. Where is the right place to be? What finances, possessions, friends, job, food and time out are needed to develop your Human? But most important, what social stimulation and intellectual challenges have you got in place? Having no purpose is soul-destroying to a Human.

The Computer's world

The Computer has input from both the Human and the Chimp. It is quite clear that there is conflict between the two worlds that the Chimp and Human want and believe they inhabit. There are clear differences in values and attitudes. They can't both be right and satisfied at the same time. If we lived in one of these worlds then we could adapt to it. The problem is that we don't live fully in either world. Somewhere in between there is the Real World.

2 different worlds

Human	Chimp
Society	Jungle
Society rules	Jungle rules
Quality of life	Survival
Humanity	Primitive drives

The Computer is receiving information from two different worlds

The Computer records what the Chimp says is happening and it also records what the Human says is happening and then makes sense of these two inputs. An effective Computer merges these two worlds and helps a person to switch between Chimp and Human constantly throughout the day, as is appropriate. Hence the Computer helps the person to live in the Real World of fluctuation.

Summary key points

- The Chimp lives in a **jungle** and needs looking after.
- The Human lives in a **society** and needs looking after.
- The Computer makes sense of these two worlds and comes up with the **Real World**.

- The Real World is a fluctuating existence between two parallel worlds that change frequently.
- Living in the Real World is learning how to survive and be happy.

Suggested exercise:
A defined purpose

Check that your Human has a known purpose for each day. This doesn't have to be profound; it can just be a short-term goal to achieve. The important point is that your Human is aware of the direction for the day. Therefore, start your day by asking yourself what you would like to achieve by the end of the day. The goal for the day could be to complete a task at work, or it could be some chores at home. The goal doesn't have to be work related, it could be to have a day out or just to socialise. The Human relishes and thrives on having a purpose, whether this is short-term or long-term.

Chapter 11

The Moon of Instant Stress

How to deal with immediate stress

Managing instant stress:

- The purpose of, and reaction to, stress
- An Autopilot for dealing with instant stress: 'Change'

- Diffusing stress
- Common examples of stressors

This moon is going to stabilise the Planet of the Real World by dealing with instant or sudden stress.

The purpose of, and reaction to, stress

Stress is a healthy reaction that is meant to be uncomfortable. It's nature's way of telling you that something is wrong and that you need to act to put it right. Stress can manifest itself in many different ways such as aggression, impatience, low mood, anxiety and so on. These are some of the symptoms of stress. Recognising that the symptoms are a result of some stressor is the first step to removing stress.

During stress the body releases lots of chemicals to alert you, with adrenalin and cortisol being two of the most important ones. Stress can be physical or it can be psychological. One example of physical stress is when we become dehydrated. The body reacts by making you uncomfortable and thirsty. You drink and this corrects the situation and removes the stress. Psychological stress should be dealt with in a similar way, so that when you experience stress you should search out a constructive way to deal with it properly. You do have a choice: either you can react to the stress or you can deal with the stress. No matter what stress hits you out of the blue, there is a way of dealing with it.

Key Point
Don't just react to stress; deal with it constructively.

When stress hits, the Chimp will definitely act first, because all input must go to the Chimp for screening. It isn't possible to stop this and in some circumstances this could actually save your life! So the first reaction that you will get is a Chimp one. It is very important to recognise this and to accept it as normal and healthy, although sometimes it is not helpful. Recognising the reaction is a Chimp one will hopefully stop you from criticising *yourself*.

Under stress, the Chimp will go into Fight, Flight or Freeze mode, depending on what it thinks is best. You need to recognise how your Chimp reacts to stress, as everyone is different. An aggressive Chimp that goes into Fight mode can turn its stress-related aggression or irritability on others nearby. A Chimp that Freezes under stress is just basically denying that the stress exists and hoping that the problem will go away on its own. The Chimp that uses Flight will avoid the problem, refuse to face it and run away; often hoping that someone else will solve it for them. None of these are ideal ways to deal with stress, even though occasionally they work!

What we want to develop is a way to stop the Chimp from taking over. As the Chimp looks into the Computer before acting, we need to have an Autopilot, an effective Computer programme, which is **well rehearsed** and **ready to run**. Remember: the Computer is

20 times quicker than the Chimp, so if the Computer is ready with an Autopilot then the Chimp will not get a chance to act.

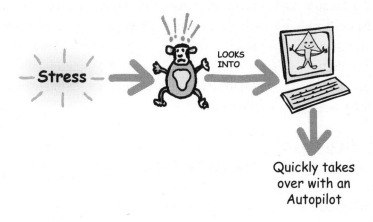

Key Point
An Autopilot is the way to manage sudden stress.

The things that will make you stop your Chimp in its tracks when it is suddenly stressed are:

- Recognising that the Chimp is reacting
- Slowing down your thinking (to allow the Human to get involved)
- Stepping back from the situation
- Getting a perspective
- Having a plan

An Autopilot based on these points above will help to deal with the stress.

Whenever we get suddenly stressed we react emotionally and sometimes we have time to think and sometimes we don't. The following blueprint needs modifying to suit you and your circumstances but the principles are the same for dealing with any type of stress.

An Autopilot blueprint for dealing with instant stress

There are seven steps that will help you deal with stress. We are going to take a look at these one by one, but here they are, in the order in which we will be dealing with them.

1. Recognition and change
2. The pause button
3. Escape
4. The helicopter and getting perspective
5. The plan
6. Reflection and activation
7. Smile

Step 1: *Recognition and change*
You must first recognise that you are suddenly stressed. This is not always as easy as it sounds. The best warning of being stressed is the Chimp offering you feelings that you don't like, whatever they may be. For example, feelings of anger, unease, stomach churning, apprehension and so on. As soon as you realise you are stressed, you must activate the Computer.

The best way of setting off an Autopilot is to have a word or action to wake the Computer up. For example, saying the word '**change**' as soon as you get the feelings. This word will wake the Computer up and set off the Autopilot, which is '**I intend to** *CHANGE* **my immediate reaction to stress**'. So the word '**change**' reminds us that we are going to do something different this time and not just go with the Chimp and Gremlins but choose to go with the Human and Autopilots.

Step 2: *The pause button*
After you have woken up the Computer by using the word 'change', you must stop your Chimp from thinking and allow yourself a moment to calm down. One of the easiest ways to do this is to imagine a big pause button in your Computer that causes the

Chimp to freeze and then press it when you realise the Chimp is reacting. This will allow your Human some time to get involved in the decision-making process for dealing with the stress.

Key Point
Whenever you want to stop the Chimp, always actively slow your thinking down. This will work in ALL situations. It is another excellent way to manage the Chimp.

Step 3: Escape
If possible, distance yourself from the situation. This helps to give you space. If you can do this physically then leave the area and gather yourself. If you can't leave then try to relax and go into your own world within your mind. For example, if you are with some-one, who has said something upsetting, then explain to the person that you would like some time out to think before you respond. Don't be afraid to be assertive if you need time to think.

Step 4: The helicopter and getting perspective
Imagine you have climbed into a helicopter that has taken off and is now hovering above the situation. You can now look down and get some perspective on what is happening. Imagine your whole life as a timeline from start to finish and see where you are at this particular point in time. Ask yourself, 'How important is this situation to the rest of my life?'; 'Is this situation going to last for ever or will it pass and things change?'; 'What are the really important things in my life, and is this one of them, or has it changed them?'

Remind yourself that everything in life will pass. You will soon look back on this moment as a distant memory. Very little in life is important in the long run.

Step 5: The plan
Now move on to form a plan to remove the stress. Remember that you want to think with the Human so always start with yourself!

Ask what you can do to react differently and would this help? Can you change the way that you are seeing this situation and would this alter it? Then look at the situation and the circumstances and see if these can be changed. What can you do practically to alter things and what things do you have to accept and work with?

Always leave engaging with the other people involved until you have sorted out yourself and the situation. Finally, look at any people involved and ask if they can help you or if you can support them.

Work out what you can control and what you can't. Generally, you can control everything about yourself and reactions, you can control a little of the circumstances, but you can't control other people. Accept this!

Step 6: Reflection and activation

If you have now created the time and space to allow the Human to think, you can reflect before acting. Ask who would you like to put in charge? Do you want your Chimp or your Human to think and act? This is a choice that you have. Activate your plan. Change what can be changed and control what can be controlled. Don't sit back and be passive. There is nothing less constructive than a self-appointed victim – don't allow it. If you really can't manage, then call on someone appropriate to help you.

Step 7: Smile

Smile when you can. Depending on how serious the situation is, try to see the lighter side of it. Laugh at yourself if you have overreacted.

Key Point
Laughing at yourself, or situations, is one of the most powerful ways to remove stress from the Chimp.

Clearly if the situation is very serious and life-changing, then you must allow yourself to grieve and you must allow yourself to receive the support of your friends. There is nothing wrong with grief; it is a very healthy way of coming to terms with disasters and heartbreak.

An example of the steps in action

Imagine Eddie is waiting at a bus stop on his way to an interview for a job that he really wants. The bus is 30 minutes late and he is getting anxious. The bus finally arrives but is full and passes the stop. Taxis rarely pass this point and Eddie's mobile is not picking up a signal. The Chimp within him is now going hysterical and getting angry. His Chimp is taking over and responding naturally and doing its job. However, it really isn't helpful. So we can now try out the steps to managing this immediate stress.

Step 1: Eddie recognises that the Chimp is reacting and accepts that it is very reasonable for it to do this but it is unhelpful. He says to himself '**Change**', a reminder that he will change his automatic behaviour from a Chimp reaction with Gremlins to a Human reaction with Autopilots.

Step 2: Eddie now visualises a large pause button in his head and presses it to actively slow down his thinking to allow the Human to get involved.

Step 3: In his head, Eddie retreats and distances himself from what is in front of him.

Step 4: He imagines a helicopter taking him above the scenario and he is looking down to get perspective. Although it may be distressing at this moment in time he can see that whatever happens life will go on and whatever happens now may have little relevance in ten years' time. Up in the air, above the situation, he asks if it is really the end of the world if he doesn't get the job. The answer is 'No, it isn't' and although it is very disappointing, he can deal with the disappointment and consequences because he is an adult Human and not a Chimp or child. He also knows logically that he may still be able to do something about the situation and must not allow the Chimp to think catastrophically.

Step 5: He now goes into Human mode and asks himself, 'What can I do about the situation?' He answers: 'I can choose the emotions I want and I can choose to act like an adult. Being emotional isn't going to help anything, least of all me. I can't think of anything practical to do at this point in time – this I must accept. I can choose to accept the situation rather than keep on saying "what if" or "this shouldn't have happened" or even worse, "life should be fair".'

Step 6: Eddie **decides** to put his Human in charge and **decides** to actively change his emotional approach to the situation. On a practical point he considers his options to either wait in the hope that another bus appears or to go home and phone the interview organiser.

Step 7: Despite his disappointment he might manage a smile and be thankful that the sun will still rise tomorrow. *He remains focused on the solution and not the problem*.

Of course, you may want to react differently or deal with the situation differently if you were in his position. It is just an example of how it might go. Clearly there are endless possibilities. The main point is that he has decided to act as a Human and not as a Chimp and to choose positive emotions despite the setback.

Choice despite seriousness

The scenario above was not so serious but what happens if a real crisis occurs?

Imagine a young man who has had an accident on a motorbike and has been left paralysed from the waist down. Sadly this is not an uncommon event. How does he deal with this type of crisis?

This time when he gets up into the helicopter and tries to gain perspective the answer is not so good. His whole life has just changed and not for the better. It would be totally unreasonable for anyone to say to him get a perspective and smile. He will need to go through a grieving process.

All of us respond differently to the same situation, so there are no rights or wrongs when responding to a severe crisis. It is about understanding your response and making choices about how you want to manage it. The simple steps described are helpful for minor crises and immediate and transient stress but they need modifying for major stress and serious incidents. Being allowed to grieve in your own time, and the way in which you want to do it, is very individual to you. It is best to work with your grief because there are recognised stages that you are likely to pass through and all of these take time. However, there will come a point when you will emerge from the grief and then, when the time is right, you can move on again. You will reach the stage where you must confront the situation and make a decision, no matter how hard it is. For this young man, the decision will be a tough one. He can be angry or upset and end up living a bitter life, or he can choose to move on, despite the setbacks, and still enjoy life with happiness and fulfilment, as many young people in this situation have done.

Over the years of seeing people suffer some terrible life events and situations, I am struck by those who chose to make the best of it and come back smiling and positive. Cruel as it may seem, you are still left with a choice to accept and move on into happiness or remain where you are and live with bitterness or anger. Anger is usually easier to hold on to than going through grief but anger doesn't help anyone.

Diffusing stress

AMP – the power of electricity

Sometimes it is not that easy to move on because your Chimp will not agree to move on, and it won't, unless you help it, and you give it a new direction. Being able to move on can be seen as a three-part process. I call this the power of electricity. AMP. This is the power to **A**ccept, and then **M**ove on, with a **P**lan.

AMP is dealing with something unpleasant that you have to accept. It may be a wrongdoing or just an event that you wish had never happened or some emotional or physical damage.

Accept – in order to accept something unpleasant, it helps to get it off your chest. This means exercising your Chimp and expressing the emotions that the unpleasantness has made you feel. You need to do this as many times as it takes and not bottle up your emotions. Bottling emotions (trying to box an upset Chimp) is probably the worse thing that you can do because it will come back to attack you and others. It isn't clever; it is foolish. When you have got things off your chest it will ease the stress and you will start to unwind. Remind yourself of the first 'Truth of Life' and live by it – 'Life is unfair'. Don't just say it, live by it.

Move on – decide when you think you have exercised your Chimp enough and want to move on. Don't stop until you are ready to move on. When you are ready, ask yourself what you want to do now. You only have two choices: stay where you are and keep the same problem alive or cut your losses and form a new plan and go forward. It is, as ever, your choice.

Plan – this is CRITICAL to moving on. You can't move on without a plan, otherwise you will just return to the same problem, with the same emotions and the same situation all over again. The plan will take you forward and out of the cycle of trying to accept something that seems unpalatable. The plan must address how you will alter your emotions as well as practical issues.

Always start at the starting point

Starting at the wrong place is very stress provoking. Starting from **where you are** and **what you have got** and then moving forward is very encouraging and rewarding as you see progress towards your goal. However, many people start from **where they want to be** and **what they want to have** and then look to see how far off they are and become demoralised. To them, every day is measured as still being behind and lacking. For example, suppose you have broken your leg and have been told by the doctor that it will be three months before you can start using your leg fully again. If you accept that you are starting from where you are and what you have got, then you will say, 'Every day I am improving and the healing process moves forward.' The Human will be in charge and positive chemicals get released in your head.

If you start from where you want to be and what you want to have then you will be saying, 'I want to be fully well again and have no problem with my leg.' Every day you will realise just how far away you still are and this will cause your Chimp to take control, negative chemicals will be released in your head that stress you and the three months will seem like for ever.

If things go wrong or you have failed at something, all you can do is to *start from where you are and what you have got* and then begin again.

Time travel

One imaginative way of dealing with stress is to use a time machine. If you are worried or stressed about something, imagine you are going forward in a time machine to ten years ahead from now and you are looking back at the current situation. Ask yourself how you would have liked to have acted, and what you would have liked to have said. Ask yourself if getting stressed about the situation helped? Having established this in your mind you can now return to the current time and act in the way you want to.

Some common examples of stressors

Stress is a very individual response because we all have different things that stress us. *These individual stresses are nearly always related to the way in which you perceive the situation and the beliefs that you are holding*, which lead to an interpretation of threat. This is the main reason why people experience different levels of stress when confronted by the same problem. Ironically, the biggest source of stress and problems that you will face will come from you, and the biggest source of help for solutions to these problems will also come from you.

Decision-making

Not making decisions is one of the commonest causes of stress on a day-to-day basis. Learning to make decisions and sticking to them is not hard to do, provided you recognise that you are being hijacked by your Chimp when you can't make a decision and you learn to get firm with it. It can help to sleep on the decision. Remember: if you have to make a decision **and there is no more information to gather** then the time is right to make it. It may help to explain to your Chimp that it is reasonable for it not to want to make mistakes, but it is not realistic to think that it will always make the best decisions. It may also help to tell your Chimp that although Chimps and children can't live with consequences, adult Humans can live with them and also deal with them.

Some Chimps tend to find decision-making particularly hard. This is normal, unless the Chimp then goes further and starts beating itself up with unhelpful statements such as, 'I must be stupid,' or 'There is something wrong with me,' or any other derogatory statement. Thankfully, Humans are able to make decisions easily if they can manage their Chimps.

Decision-making – the sweet dilemma

Imagine you have two sweets in front of you. One is green and one is yellow. You are asked to choose one and there is no consequence. This is easy: it will take a moment to pick one of the sweets.

Now imagine that you are asked to choose again but this time there are consequences. If you pick the right sweet you will be given any one thing that you ask for. If you pick the wrong sweet then you will lose the one thing that you love the most. Now it becomes very difficult to choose. The reason is obvious: because the consequences are severe and will have a life-changing impact. The stress is coming from the consequences and not the decision-making.

The problem now is that logic is going out of the window as the Chimp takes over. There is no more information to gain and waiting is going to make no difference because your choice will always be random. The Chimp is not allowing you to choose because it is looking at the consequences. It will keep going over the same consequences and won't allow you to move forward. Using logic, the Human can easily make the choice because it has reasoned that, as there is no more information to gather, I may as well choose and stop suffering and then deal with the consequences.

In circumstances such as this, the Chimp will do two things. It will stop you from making decisions for fear of getting it wrong and it will also make the consequences seem catastrophic, even if they are not, in order to stop you moving. The best way to solve the problem is to establish a routine for decision-making so that it becomes an Autopilot.

Decision-making path

- First gather all the information possible to make the decision.
- Accept that some information may never be available and some will arrive too late – so ignore this because you can't do anything about it.
- Look at the consequences of making each choice and see if one is serious – accept that both choices will have consequences.
- Tell your Chimp to stop making it into a catastrophe and get some perspective – be firm and remove or contain emotion.
- If appropriate try laughing at yourself or at the situation – it's better than crying.
- If you still can't decide then there can't be much difference between the choices, so toss a coin and go with it and deal with the consequences.

Trying to keep everything the same

One way that stress occurs is when people do not accept that life and the world is in a constant state of flux, and things never stay the same.

Relationships are a good example of this. Every day your relationship with another person changes slightly because your circumstances, and you, have altered a little. If you expect your relationship to stay exactly how it was on the day you met, then you may end up feeling upset or disappointed. We often put unrealistic expectations on relationships and don't acknowledge that they will change over time.

Jobs are similar. You cannot expect a job for life or even the same job to remain constant. People often get upset or angry when they are not offered job security or a fixed job role but this is very unrealistic.

Your Chimp and its insecurity are driving this need for fixed elements in your life. Your Human needs to educate the Chimp. *The main point here is that if you hold an expectation that anything in your life will remain constant then it is very likely to be a source of stress when it doesn't.* To remove stress you need to live in the here and now and accept that changes are normal and work with them for the future.

Unrealistic expectations

Alongside accepting that nothing is static in life is to develop realistic expectations of people and events. We have covered this concept before with the Gremlin of unrealistic expectation and it is here as a reminder. A common source of stress is when a person holds fixed expectations of what *should* happen or what *should be* done. Having realistic and helpful expectations of the world that you live in and the people that you share it with will reduce stress levels considerably.

Not knowing the difference between chicks and goslings

Some stress needs discovering! Picture this:

A hen was placed in a pen along with her chicks and then a fox was released. The fox circled the pen to try and grab the chicks. The mother hen knew instinctively what to do and spread her wings and faced the fox. With her wings spread, the chicks ran beneath them and were protected. The hen then continued to threaten the fox by lowering her head and warning him with a pointed beak. The fox couldn't get the chicks and the hen stood her ground. All was well and the fox was removed.

Later that day some goslings were added to the pen. Being a mother hen, the hen immediately took responsibility for their protection and mothered them. The fox was released again. This time as he circled the pen, the goslings also tried to get underneath the outspread wings of the mother hen. However, there were too many chicks and goslings to get underneath and so many ran around blindly. The hen tried to chase after them to get them all under her wings but of course couldn't manage this. At this point, realising that it was hopeless, she left both the chicks and goslings and flew to try and get out of the pen, leaving all of the young birds vulnerable to attack.

There is a lesson to learn from this. When it comes to dealing with problems and responsibilities in life, it is very important to make a distinction between problems that are your responsibility (chicks) and problems are the responsibility of others (goslings). If you start taking on other people's problems and taking responsibility for them, then expect to become stressed. Not only are you likely to fail to help others but you will also fail to sort your own problems out. **Beware of the goslings in life!**

Clearly I am not saying that we shouldn't help others but I am saying be careful not to start owning other people's problems. For example, trying to take responsibility for someone who has an eating or alcohol problem is not a good idea, as you are trying to control an uncontrollable; their commitment. By all means support them *as they help themselves*.

Summary key points

- Have realistic expectations and remind yourself of the obvious: life is not fair; stress will happen; things will go wrong.
- 'Change' represents a behaviour change and means that you will change your automatic response to stress from Chimp and Gremlins to Human and Autopilots.
- Being proactive means looking ahead and avoiding obvious stress when you can.
- 'AMP' represents Accept and Move on with a Plan and helps you to get over a stressful situation.
- When stress appears, actively look for solutions to remove it.
- Nearly all situations are only emotionally stressful if you allow them to be.

Suggested exercise:
Planning for stress

Your well-rehearsed plan
Write out your plan of action for dealing with sudden stress. Try to rehearse this by using your imagination to think of stressful situations and how you will now respond with your new plan. Work through them in your mind and also think about how it will all conclude with a more productive outcome.

Practice makes perfect

During any form of stress, deliberately practise slowing down your thinking as a way of managing the Chimp. For example, if someone says something that evokes an emotional response in you, try to slow down your reaction to this by using the 'change' and 'pause button' as explained in this chapter and then move to calm rational Human thinking. Slowing down your responses will allow the Human to have a chance to operate and it will also prevent impulsive Chimp responses. Making this process a habit will establish the Autopilot in your Computer.

Chapter 12
The Moon of Chronic Stress

How to deal with long-standing stress

Chronic stress:
- Responsibility
- What is it?
- Checking for
- Preventing
- Dealing with
- Arising from self

- Arising from circumstances
- Arising from others
- What if I keep getting it wrong?
- To catch a monkey

This next moon will help to stabilise the world in which you live by looking at how you can deal with chronic stress.

Responsibility

This chapter is challenging you to have *a good look within yourself to find the solutions* for dealing with chronic stress. Take responsibility for finding solutions to your stress. The starting point is to look at yourself and not to blame others or circumstances.

What is chronic stress?

When someone has been stressed for a long period of time they learn to live with the stress and it becomes chronic. The body can actually make changes to its systems and some hormone and chemical systems are altered. This can result in damage to the person's health, resulting in a lowering of the immune system and illness developing. Chronic stress also quite often leads to depressive illness and anxiety. If you are going to look after yourself properly then removing chronic stress is a must. If you are seriously stressed then you should see your doctor for help.

Checking for chronic stress

The symptoms of chronic stress are easy to recognise once you know where to look.

Some common symptoms of chronic stress include:

- Constantly feeling tired
- Short-tempered
- Lacking a sense of humour
- Anxious or worrying for no apparent reason
- Anxious or worrying for trivial reasons
- Unable to relax properly
- Paranoid ideas
- A sense of urgency with everything
- Tearful or depressed
- Unable to face work or friends
- Small tasks seem large
- Disrupted sleep patterns

Some of these are also symptoms of other things but if you have any of them constantly then you really ought to be addressing the cause.

Some common areas to look at for preventing chronic stress are:

- Using your time sensibly
- Being assertive
- Having realistic expectations

- Taking responsibility for things you are responsible for and nothing else!
- Addressing problems as they occur
- Regularly settling your Chimp down by nurturing it
- Recognising a potential problem
- Recognising your limits
- Seeking appropriate help early
- Talking out stressful situations with others

When any of these areas are out of control, you can almost guarantee to find a mixture of Chimp activity coupled with Gremlins.

Preventing chronic stress from occurring

Just as there are ways of helping to prevent sudden stress appearing, so there are ways of reducing the chance of chronic stress developing. Chronic stress occurs when we don't deal with stressful situations and start to accept them as normal. This 'normality' becomes an accepted way of working and dealing with stress but is destructive and unhelpful. In other words, we now have Gremlins of resignation and poor coping strategies in the Computer.

For example, imagine a person at work who is meant to finish at five o'clock. One night they are about to leave and the manager asks if they wouldn't mind staying on to complete a job. They agree and work until six. The next night the job they are doing isn't quite finished, so they stay on until seven o'clock to complete it. This pattern now becomes an accepted norm instead of a one-off exception. The problem is that if the person then says I would rather go home and finish the job tomorrow, they start to feel guilty. Their Chimp is now saying, 'You can't let the troop down, what will they think?' Well as we now know, it isn't the troop at all. It is work and work colleagues. Looking after the Chimp by getting it home on time and looking after the real troop is more important than working to please work colleagues.

However, the Chimp looks into the Computer and sees a Gremlin. The Gremlin tells the Chimp it is expected to work late and it is acceptable, therefore the Chimp feels even more pressure. The Chimp builds resentment as it realises it is trapping itself. Stress rightfully enters the picture trying to tell the Chimp to go home because it is in the wrong place. The Chimp, of course, remains with the false troop and under the watchful eye of the Gremlin.

Time passes and the Chimp is continually stressed and sees no way out of this. Clearly, if we step back from the scenario, something must be done to stop the stress. It started because the person didn't do something about the immediate stress. To remove the chronic stress the Gremlin must be replaced by an Autopilot, and the Chimp needs to be boxed with the truth.

Dealing with chronic stress

If you are stressed then it is useful to write down anything that you can see that is causing or contributing to the stress. Trying to unravel complicated scenarios in your head is not usually very successful. You tend to go round in circles, instead of dealing with and eliminating specific factors contributing to the problem.

Key Point
Write down the problems on paper and don't try to deal with them inside your head.

As a simple rule of thumb, when you have a problem causing stress, divide up the solution areas into three parts:

1. Your own perceptions and attitudes to the problem
2. The circumstances and setting for the problem
3. Other people involved in the problem

By looking at these areas individually you could come up with a number of reasons as to why the stress has occurred in the first place and then find solutions to remove the stress.

3 **areas that are sources of stress**

If you are feeling stressed and are not prepared to change your behaviours or beliefs then it is very likely you will continue to be stressed in the future; so you are going to have to accept that you need to change. You also need to get rid of any excuses and rationalisation as to why you can't remove stress. Sometimes no matter what you do, you can't have what you want, so you must accept this and live with it. Some individuals can't do this, as they have a sense of rights, fairness and entitlement that they cannot get over, and therefore live their lives in a state of constant battle against the world and others. Chronic emotional stress often arises from your own expectations and perceptions of the world, of other people and of yourself. Let's look at these three potential sources of chronic stress:

- Chronic stress arising from self
- Chronic stress from circumstances or events
- Chronic stress arising from others

Chronic stress arising from self

Chronic stress from yourself is usually based on Gremlin activity. These Gremlins are learnt unhelpful behaviours, such as poor coping strategies, or learnt destructive beliefs, such as seeing yourself as less than others. Some problems can be boiled down to very simple observations. Here are some examples:

Creating your own misery

It is very common to meet people who create their own misery and can't recognise what they are doing. Eddie is rude to people that he meets. He then complains that he feels lonely and that no one cares about him, which is making him stressed. He is not recognising that his own behaviours are causing the problem. A simple rule: friendly people have friends.

Red herrings

Sandra is feeling stressed as she is struggling to complete a degree course and keeps failing exams. She says that it is because she has to work part-time and that the tutors are not good. This may be partly true, but she is not recognising that these are excuses and that she is either not putting in the work required and/or the course is beyond her capabilities and/or she doesn't know how to study effectively. Here excuses are stopping her from facing the real source of the stress and then dealing with it. Sandra must start with herself and remove the Gremlins and the stress will go.

The Mushroom Syndrome

When you grow mushrooms they compete for the space available. One will inevitably try to take over. It becomes the largest mushroom, so when it has matured, you pick it and there is a gap. The next largest mushroom then takes its place and grows to fill the space. You pick this one and so the story continues. There is always a mushroom ready to grow to fill the gap.

Some people suffer with the 'Mushroom Syndrome'. Instead of

mushrooms they grow worries. If there is nothing to worry about then they find something. They are unable to stop this very destructive Gremlin. It is a learnt destructive habit. It is not only tiring for them but also enormously tiring for others around them. This is because they keep making things into worries and then presenting these to others. Sadly the response from others is usually irritation and this leaves the Mushroom sufferer feeling alone to worry again and in a state of chronic stress.

Recognising that you suffer with the Mushroom Syndrome means that you can stop this Gremlin of behaviour from continuing and remove it. It needs to be overwritten with a programme that rationalises what is going on.

Some useful Autopilots to replace the Gremlin could be:

- Humans learn to live with concerns but do not allow worry to take place, as this is an unhelpful emotion.
- Humans accept that solutions to problems take time and worrying your way to the solution is unhelpful.
- Most worries are trivial in the long run and often take care of themselves.
- Worrying never does any good.
- Worrying is an option and we can choose not to worry.
- Learning to get perspective and to laugh at yourself is the most powerful thing you can do.
- Relaxing is a powerful worry remover.

Relaxation techniques

These can be very helpful and you can find different methods online, at your library or from talking with friends and colleagues to hear what helped them. It is worth investigating these and trying them out.

Conflicting drives from within

A common example of conflicting drives is the working mother who is trying to balance work with running a family and is stressed as she feels she is failing in both. Here she has a maternal Chimp drive doing battle with a Human fulfilment desire. If this is addressed properly then there is no need for the battle and she can do both really well.

Possible reasons for her stress could be that she:

- is not being realistic about what can be achieved in these two areas of her life
- has not got the balance right
- is not asking the right people to help her
- is not accepting that there may need to be a compromise in both areas
- is actually doing fine but is unable to accept this, as her Human or Chimp is on an inappropriate guilt trip

All of these examples demonstrate that chronic stress is often from within your own mind. The last one particularly demonstrates that there are multitudes of reasons why you might be stressed and it is very individual. What is important is to start by looking inwardly to see if you are being too harsh on yourself or you are not looking after yourself.

Emotional limit and training

Physically there is a limit to what each of us can do and we accept this. Emotionally there is a limit to what each of us can deal with and we ought to accept this too. However, just as we can train our physical body and improve our fitness, we can also train our inner selves and improve the way we respond to our emotions.

Chronic stress from circumstances or events

When events have put you into a stressful situation then it is wise to have a plan to address them. As always, start with yourself and check that you are approaching the situation with realistic expectations. Be proactive and change what you can, or see if there is someone who can help and then ask them for help. If all fails, then move into AMP (Accept, Move on, Plan). Learning to accept a situation is always going to be difficult but sometimes you have little choice. For example, having a bad back is a difficult problem to face but accepting that recovery will follow an unpredictable course, and working with this, is the only constructive option.

Chronic stress arising from others

People in our lives can cause us to be chronically stressed and there are lots of ways that they can do this. As always, look to yourself first when dealing with others, and revisit the Planet Connect chapter for advice on communication. Remember that the Chimp enters discussions with a win or lose attitude while the Human enters with a plan to engage. Set time aside to think through your plans and make sure that they are solution focused. Most people are reasonable if you approach them in the right way. However, accept that some people are not pleasant and won't work with you to resolve any differences.

Don't forget to engage support from your troop. They can offer objective advice and encouragement, provided you ask them for this. When you cannot resolve the differences with a person, see if any form of mediation or support from a neutral third person would help. If you really can't get along, then be practical and try to minimise any contact.

What if we keep getting it wrong?

Nearly everybody gets stressed and responds poorly to it at some point and most of us frequently don't deal very well with stress. We're all in the same boat. However, we can all learn to improve on how we deal with stress. Some things that we do create further stress. So here are a few of these things.

Beating yourself up and guilt

Never beat yourself up if you handle stress poorly. This is a useless and damaging bad habit. As a bad habit is just a Gremlin we can remove it. Try smiling, relaxing and coming back with enthusiasm. You can only do your best, so accept it. Beating yourself up and feeling guilty are two very useless and destructive Gremlins. They never have anything constructive to offer. Remember, if you are not getting it right then it is a hijack by the Chimp. It is not you failing!

'How' not 'why'

Try not to keep asking 'why' and then giving spurious explanations, e.g. 'Why do I feel miserable all the time?' 'Why' questions can be useful but generally they are backward-looking and unconstructive.

Instead ask the question 'How'. These questions are planning questions and tend to be constructive. For example: 'How will I deal with my own feelings and become happy?' is a constructive question and much better than 'Why do I feel miserable and stressed?' 'Why has this happened?' could be replaced by 'I accept that this has happened, now how do I move forward?'

Talk!

Talking through your stress with those who are able to listen and understand (and maybe offer advice) is a very powerful way of finding out what is stressing you and sharing it. This can help enormously in coming up with solutions. Rely on the troop; that is what they are there for!

Some constructive ways to diffuse chronic stress

- Learn and use relaxation techniques.
- Be able to delegate and share problems.
- Ask for help from the appropriate source.
- Get perspective.
- Look beyond the problem to solutions.
- Be realistic.
- Remind yourself you are in charge of your own feelings and direction.
- Share your feelings with someone who cares.

An analogy – how to catch a monkey

Finally, one hidden cause of stress is when we have trapped ourselves and don't recognise it. Here is an analogy that I hope will help you to see how sometimes we cause ourselves distress by not letting go of something or someone in our life.

If you try to catch a monkey it is very difficult as they can easily out-run you, and unless you can swing around trees pretty well, you don't stand a chance; so here is a solution.

Start by cementing a vase into the ground. Now push a stone into the vase, which only just pushes through the neck of the vase, so it can't be taken out of the vase again.

The monkey will come along and put its hand in to grab the stone and try to pull it out. Of course the stone only just fitted in. Now with the monkey's hand around the stone, it definitely won't come out! The monkey cannot let go of the stone because it wants it. *Even though the stone is of no value* to the monkey, the monkey is not going to let go and remains stubborn. It is easy then to throw a net over the monkey, who threw its freedom away for a worthless stone.

Think what this means to you. If you allow yourself to hold on to 'worthless stones' you may end up giving your freedom away. If you continue to allow stress to dominate your life because you are clinging to things that are not good for you, then you must accept that you will lose your happiness. Have the courage to let go of any 'worthless stones' in your life. Don't cling on because of fear or familiarity or just plain stubbornness. Your freedom and happiness are worth more than any stone.

Summary key points

- Check regularly for signs of chronic stress.
- Deal with chronic stress and do not allow yourself to accept it as normal.
- Recognise your emotional limit for dealing with things and don't exceed it.
- Develop ways of dealing with stress.
- Don't be caught in life by holding on to a worthless stone.

Suggested exercise:
Remove the stress

Meet a friend
Be proactive and meet a friend and talk through your current stressors. It is best to write down the list of stressors on a piece of paper so that it is clear how many you have and what needs addressing. Having written them down, make action plans to deal with each one of them. Make sure you then allocate time to carry out your plans. It is wise to arrange to meet the friend again to report back!

Lifestyle stress
Check your current lifestyle and behaviours and see if you are holding on to any worthless stones. Look for these stones, which may be things like routines, familiar patterns of working, jobs, hobbies, places or relationships. In fact anything that is preventing you from being happy. Again using someone else as a sounding board is often more powerful than trying to do this yourself. Good friends can often offer home truths.

Part 3
Your Health, Success and Happiness

Chapter 13

The Planet of Shadows and the Asteroid Belt

How to look after your health

Physical and mental health
- Malfunction and dysfunction
- Being in shape physically
- Being in shape mentally
- Recuperation and rehabilitation

Malfunction and dysfunction

This planet system covers physical and mental health. Illness and poor maintenance create shadows in our lives but we can remove them.

Let me state the obvious. If you have an illness this needs addressing, because trying to employ the Chimp model with a machine that isn't working properly is going to be much more difficult, if not impossible.

Malfunction means you are ill. The machine is not working properly and you need to see a doctor for treatment. The asteroid belt that encircles the planet represents malfunction and all the physical and mental illnesses that you can suffer.

Dysfunction is when the machine is working fine but it is not being used properly or is not being looked after: it needs maintenance. The Planet of Shadows represents this dysfunction. We are all dysfunctional to varying degrees! This whole book is about minimising this dysfunction.

Malfunction -
machine not working

Person ill
- needs treatment

Dysfunction -
machine working

Person not functioning
correctly
- needs maintenance

Being in shape physically

This topic is vast and cannot be covered within the space offered in this book. However, here are some guidelines.

If we look at physical maintenance, it could be divided into nutrition, diet, weight, exercise and fitness. Without going into any detail, let's look at what happens to cause dysfunction in any of these areas. I will take an extreme view to emphasise the differences.

Your Chimp and your Human have very different agendas for any of the topics. Basically the Human knows what it wants in each area and takes great pleasure in being fit, in shape and eating sensibly. The Chimp, however, would rather not take any responsibility, go with the pleasure aspects, have immediate gratification and dismiss the consequences.

The Chimp's default here is indifference and an easy life. Therefore most of us who have found this to be the case will now have a permanent struggle trying to manage our Chimps.

Don't wade through treacle

I will offer two golden rules to help you to get in shape physically. The first rule is not to wade through treacle. By this, I mean don't start with the problems and then try to find solutions. Instead start with a blank slate and define exactly what you want. When you know what you are aiming for then state how you will do it. For example, state how you want to stay fit, what you want to eat and so on. Set down the ideal and then with this as the benchmark implement it by removing anything that prevents it from being reached. Wading through treacle is demoralising because it means looking at all the past failures and reasons why it just can't happen. Wipe that off the slate and begin again with a plan.

Proactive and responsive

Successful people are *proactive*, in other words they have a plan. They are also *responsive*, which means that if the plan fails for whatever reason, they respond by regrouping and immediately bring in another plan. They are very resilient and don't give up.

Unsuccessful people tend to be *reactive*. This means that they base their plans around reacting to problems and are constantly trying to fight back. They see life as a struggle. Chimps tend to be reactive; therefore they give up easily and take the line of least resistance. Humans tend to be proactive; therefore they constantly plan.

Fitness class

Apply these two concepts to your physical maintenance and recognise the Chimp and deal with it. For example, we might say that you are looking at getting fitter and a lighter weight. Start by stating what you want. Now make a plan of action without thinking of the hardship. Clearly the plan must be realistic. For example, you march your Chimp down to the local leisure centre and enrol in a fitness class. You are aware that your Chimp is likely to default each week with a myriad of excuses, so you must have a plan to counter this. You might therefore speak to the instructor of the group at the end of the first session and say how much you are looking forward to seeing them next week. This comment will help to unsettle the Chimp, which is unlikely to want to look bad and there-fore will reluctantly push you along to the next session. Sometimes very simple plans like this can be very effective. We will cover these topics in greater detail in the Planet of Success chapter.

Being in shape mentally

Humans need healthy minds. There are a number of ways to keep your mind healthy. Some examples include intellectual stimulation and challenge, laughter and fun, purpose and achievements. Making these happen will bring your mind into a healthy state as long as you don't overdo it and stress yourself! Laughing and having a sense of humour can be the best tonic that you can give your mind. Try to see the funny side when things don't go accord-ing to plan. Learning to laugh at misfortune and at your self is a learnt behaviour, a strong Autopilot, and one worth developing.

Recuperation and rehabilitation

Recuperation is possibly the most neglected aspect when looking after your machine. If you think of recuperation existing at three levels then you can see why most of us do not allow our bodies to gather themselves before we go back into the routine of life.

The three levels of recuperation could be seen as:

- Relaxing
- Resting
- Sleeping

Sadly, most of us neglect all three levels. This is all about getting the work and play balance right. Your mind and body need to have time out in order to recover from the day-to-day stress that life brings. If you are going to look after yourself then this is a priority.

Relaxing is about taking a few minutes out of your day to wind down and take a breather. **Resting** is about stopping for a significant period of time during the day, typically the evening to escape work and stress, and to completely unwind. **Sleep** speaks for itself.

What are the consequences of not allowing yourself any one of these three levels of recuperation on a regular daily basis? The answer is frightening. Your brain will start sending the blood supply and all decision-making to your Chimp. It takes no imagination to predict what will happen. The sad part of this is that we all know this. Whenever we get tired we often become irritable, make silly mistakes and rash decisions or have unstable mood swings. So if this is obvious then it is incredible that we can neglect this critically important area of maintenance for our bodies and minds. It is well worth spending time on a practical plan of action to make sure that you get your relaxation, resting and sleeping in order.

Recovery from emotional injury

Everyone is aware that following a physical injury, such as a broken bone, there is a period of rehabilitation where you will gradually increase your muscles again and eventually return to full functioning. Emotional injury is just the same. When you have experienced a traumatic event, such as a loss or break up of a relationship, you need to have a period of emotional rehabilitation.

The general time period for this is between three and six months and there are very specific stages of grief reaction that you will go through. Accept that it takes time to get through an emotional injury and don't be harsh on yourself. Return to normal functioning in your own time. An excellent way to rehabilitate the injury is to talk through the event with friends, as often as it takes. This way the Chimp is being exercised and will come to terms with the injury and recovery. Some people find it difficult to talk through emotions or express their feelings. It can help to write down feelings and thoughts or to just take time to think them through.

In the middle of the night

Imagine that you have gone to sleep with something on your mind that is really concerning you. You wake up in the night and your mind starts racing. At this point the Human is fast asleep and the Chimp is now in full control. Therefore, your thinking is irrational and emotional.

The Chimp will think and see things catastrophically and worry you for however long you are 'awake'. Eventually, you will collapse asleep and come round again in the morning. You now get out of bed and wake yourself up and wonder why you were thinking so emotionally during the night.

The answer is simple: during the night your brain changes its functioning and the Human no longer gives any check to the Chimp. In the morning the Human is now rational and puts things back into perspective. Nothing seems as bad, once you return to Human functioning. There is a simple lesson to learn and a golden rule to follow.

The simple lesson is that, unless you're a night-shift worker, during the hours of eleven at night and seven in the morning you are in Chimp mode with emotional and irrational thinking. You rarely think with perspective and this will only return after seven in the morning.

The golden rule therefore is:

If you wake during the night, any thoughts and feelings you might have are from your Chimp and they are very often disturbing, catastrophic and lacking in perspective. In the morning you are likely to regret engaging with these thoughts and feelings because you will see things differently.

Try to develop an Autopilot that says I am not prepared to take any thinking seriously during night-time hours when the Chimp is in charge.

During the rehabilitation phase, only take on what you can emotionally withstand and use some 'emotional painkillers'. Emotional painkillers are things such as spending time with friends and family for support; allowing close friends to share your pain by letting them know how you feel; accepting help where it is offered; being kind to yourself; and giving yourself permission to deal with the injury in the way that you want to.

> ### *Key Point*
> *Sometimes emotions are very irrational and you have to work with them rather than constantly trying to understand them.*

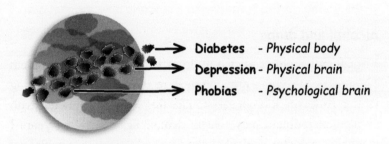

The Asteroid Belt

The asteroids represent malfunction (illness)

Just a brief word on illness: don't forget some illnesses of the body disguise themselves and present as mood changes. For example, hormone shifts, such as pre-menstrual syndrome (PMS) or thyroid disorders are very treatable. Trying to manage your Chimp when you are experiencing severe PMS or a thyroid disorder is very difficult and you can only really take a little responsibility for the Chimp's behaviour! The only responsibility that you do have, as with any illness, is to get professional help.

Mental illness

Most mental illness occurs when neuro-transmitters (chemical systems) in the brain get out of balance. Neuro-transmitters that are implicated in many mental illnesses include, serotonin, nora-drenaline, dopamine, acetylcholine and GABA. If you are suffer-ing with any signs of illness it is very probable that this is a neuro-transmitter problem that can be treated. Sadly there is still a stigma attached to mental illness. You would not be embarrassed to go to a doctor if you had broken your leg, so why should you be embarrassed if you have a serotonin receptor problem, that we happen to call depression? Mood disorders, anxiety disorders and other states of the mind should always be assessed and treated by experts.

Alcohol and drugs

Virtually all people addicted to drugs know they have a problem and most people with a drink problem recognise there is something wrong. However, it is not easy to face this and often someone with an alcohol problem may live in denial. For nearly ten years I worked as a doctor in alcohol services and the patients explained to me that there was a difference between someone who is drinking habitually and someone who was 'an alcoholic'. The common view was that 'an alcoholic' can't stop once they have had their first drink. It was a useful point that they made. If you find you have to restrain yourself after one drink, think carefully about getting help. Sadly, there is also still a stigma about this devastating condition but thankfully there are whole teams of experts that can help. Most drugs, and certainly alcohol, can affect not only your mood state but also the way that you think.

Summary key points

- The simple message is to look after your body and mind in a serious way if you want to get the best out of yourself.
- Work on maintaining your physical and mental health.
- Make sure that you have enough recuperation: relaxing, resting, sleeping.
- If you are ill, take responsibility to seek out help to get yourself better.

Suggested exercise:
Looking after yourself

Recuperation helps Chimp Management

Consider the time that you allow yourself to recuperate. Look at all three levels: relaxing, resting and sleeping, and keep a diary for one week to check on how much time you are allowing for each on a daily basis. Your Chimp is very hard to control if recuperation time is not implemented. Poor recuperation management will definitely impact on your relationships and work. Good recuperation management will definitely enhance the quality of your relationships and work.

Chapter 14

The Planet of Success and its Three Moons

The foundations for success

Defining success

How do you define success? Pause for a moment and remember that both your Human and Chimp will have answers and they may be very different. As a rule, to define success, Chimps look for material belongings and achievements, whereas, Humans look for personal qualities. For example, your Chimp may answer, 'Being a millionaire defines success to me,' but your Human may answer, 'Being happy defines success to me.' Of course the Human might argue that if you had a million pounds then you would be happy! Don't be influenced by others, but work out what your Human and your Chimp define as success. Then decide if your Chimp's ideas are truly acceptable.

There is little point in chasing after success, as defined by the Chimp, only to discover, on finding it, that it wasn't what you really wanted in the first place.

Measuring success

There are always different ways to measure success. For example, if you want to take an exam course, there are two ways with which success can be measured. Of course you want to pass the exam, however, you could approach it from different angles.

The first measure of success is passing the exam, which is more likely to be the Chimp's definition of success, to which the Human may agree.

The second way might be by completing the course, or even just trying, which is more likely to be the Human's definition of success. This is because logic says that if I have done my best I can hold my head up and deal with the consequences.

If you choose the Human's definition, then as long as you try, you cannot fail to be successful. Of course, it would also be great to pass the exam! However, if it doesn't work out, it doesn't imply anything more than you tried your best (and you can't do more than this) and therefore you can celebrate your successful effort.

Your Chimp will still insist this is a failure. Think carefully, you have a choice here. If you always wish to measure success in life by what level you attain, then you must accept the emotional consequences when you do not reach this level. If you measure success in life by effort and doing your best, then it is always in your hands to succeed and to be proud of yourself. You can then deal with any disappointing level of attainment as an adult Human.

So first define success before you start on any venture and also work out what that success will mean to you. There are choices. Success can be attainment or it can be effort or it may be both. Success can be a material gain or it can be a spiritual or personal gain. Don't forget the Chimp and Human may differ considerably in what they define as success.

Partial success

Another point worth considering is that success does not have to be black and white. There can be levels of success and stages of success with shades of grey. It may be that you can consider partial levels of success and be happy with these. For example, you may decide to attack the garden because it is neglected. So you have a go, but don't manage to do it all. You can sit back, call it a partial success and be pleased with what you have done.

Partial successes are often reality checks on what you can realistically achieve. Learning to accept that you have a made the effort, and rewarding this, is far more constructive than criticising yourself for failing to reach total success. Try to recognise when to accept and celebrate partial success.

Success can often be broken down into stages and celebrated at each stage. Your Chimp is very good at either rushing you to succeed, or procrastinating and stopping you from moving. Recognise this and deal with it by staging success.

The Three Moons of Success

There are many fundamental stabilisers that you can put in place to enhance the chances of success. The Moons surrounding the Planet of Success represent three of these stabilisers.

The Regal Moon

Your Realm
- Wearing the crown
- Regal rules
- Advisors
- Subjects

The joint Realm
- Personal or professional relationships
- Personal relationships
- Teams

Other people's Realm
- Being a subject

This first moon is about recognising who is in charge in the different areas of your life and then acting accordingly. It is one of the major factors that contribute to increasing your chances of success.

The problem is in dealing with differences of opinion

Any system that runs effectively, involving people, will have clearly defined philosophies, procedures and 'rules'. In the Human's world this is no great problem because it works with logic. In the Chimp's world we have major problems because it works with emotion and does not always abide by the 'rules'. The problem arises when differences of opinion occur between people about what should be done and how. If we establish how these differences are to be resolved then we can start to function happily. Humans discuss ideas and typically come to a joint opinion. Chimps give opinion, criticise others and rarely give way. If they have to give way, they typically challenge and undermine.

The Human and Chimp will both reach a settlement if there are clear rules and a definite agreed leader, who has the ability to make the final decision. Effective leaders listen to and respect the opinion of others.

Therefore, what we need to do is to establish:

- Who is in charge in any given situation in your life
- What the rules are
- Whether you are going to live by the rules

We can consider any situation as having a Monarch. This Monarch will wear the crown and have the final say, inside a defined 'Realm'. To make it simple, we will look at three different leaderships or Monarchs:

- You
- Another person
- Joint leadership

Your Realm

Wearing the crown

Make sure the crown
is on the right head

There are obvious situations where you are in charge and therefore you are the Monarch. For example, when you are at home you are the Monarch of your Realm. You decide who enters and you decide on the rules. When you enter somebody else's home, you have entered their territory and therefore their Realm, and he or she is the Monarch. In their home, if it were very warm, you would politely comment and perhaps ask if you could open the window. You wouldn't just get up and open the window. This would be seen as rude and inappropriate, unless you had a very special relationship with the person. Likewise, if they entered your home, you wouldn't expect them to say 'I don't like the colour of your walls,' open a tin of paint and start changing the colour. This is because our home is our Realm. Another example of your Realm could be at your place of work. Here you will have a role and responsibilities. It is important to know exactly what your role and responsibilities are so that you can act appropriately.

Allowing someone to enter your Realm, who then starts taking over, will upset the Human and agitate the Chimp. Inevitably, Chimp activity is going to take place within you and this may not be a good thing. Recognising your Realm *and acting on it* can prevent Chimp activity. For example, you may not tolerate people shouting at you and you need to enforce this. In order to act, you must be assertive or have ways of avoiding conflict yet still enforce your rights. As a Monarch, you need to make sure that you have set the rules, and that people entering your Realm know and understand the rules and that you enforce these if necessary. It would be expected that as a Monarch you would act regally! So enforcing the rules means doing so in a regal way via your Human and not your Chimp.

Regal rules

Monarchs need to
act regally

Regal rules

The 'regal rules' are the behaviours and attitudes that *you have decided to abide by* as a Monarch. They are not for other people to abide by! Spending time on thinking about this with your Human, and making it happen, will really help to increase the chances of being successful in whatever you do. The rules are set as a reminder to your Chimp. Your Chimp needs to be brought in line and managed so that it lives by your rules. For example, you might set a regal rule that you will always be pleasant to other people, regardless of how they might treat you. This is a commendable but difficult rule to get the Chimp to abide by. Again, the bottom line is being able to manage your Chimp.

Advisors

Monarchs don't know everything; therefore they have a responsibility to appoint their advisors. The expert advisors will now offer advice (NOT commands) to the Monarch. It is very important when you are out of depth, or uncertain, to seek out the person or people who can help you. In order to be successful it is important, if not critical, to have the right support. One of the factors that differentiate successful people from unsuccessful people is the ability to recognise when they need help and then get it from the best source.

It's your responsibility to check that your advisor has the credentials to do the job. Have they got the skill and ability to advise you or to do some work for you? It's worth looking at the qualifications, experience or track record that people have before taking advice from them or allowing them to help you. Once you have established your expert advisors then remember it is very unwise to reject their advice.

Having selected your advisor, don't forget that you chose them! You can't blame them later if they didn't come up to the standard you expected because of your own poor choice! Successful people take full responsibility for whatever they do and look to improve next time. They do not allow their Chimps to blame others.

Advisors

Choose your advisors
very carefully

For example, let's assume that you want to lose some weight, a very common scenario for many of us. You are wearing the crown and in charge of your plan. The fact that you are looking at losing weight means that you didn't do so well in the first place with controlling your weight! (No problem, just a reality check). Therefore, it would be wise to get advice from 'an expert' in weight control. The expert could be a dietician or just a friend who has successfully lost weight. If it doesn't work out because you feel the diet or advisor was 'wrong' then don't blame them. It was your decision to follow their advice. The message from this scenario can be applied to many areas of your life: you must learn to be responsible and accountable for your choices.

Subjects

Other people in your Realm are the equivalent of your subjects and need to understand two things. The first is that you are the Monarch and the second is there are some rules. As the Monarch it is *your duty* to make sure that you politely make your subjects aware of these two things. It is no use blaming others if they are taking over your world or are acting in a way that you do not accept because you were not assertive enough to make these things clear. Treating others with respect regardless of how they behave is more likely to get your messages across. Make sure it's your Human who is doing the talking and not your Chimp.

Having subjects also means looking after them and respecting them at all times. The more that you show respect to others, the more likely it is that they will show respect back. However, there are always Chimps on the loose, so beware and recognise that it's very unwise to engage with a Chimp.

Other people's Realms

Sometimes you don't
wear the crown

Being a subject

If you recognise that you are not the person who is wearing the crown then it is reasonable to show respect to the person who is.

Disrespecting someone or their decisions will ultimately reflect on you, and is very likely to cause your own success to be compromised. Being a subject doesn't mean rolling over or being a doormat. It is about respect. If you recognise that somebody else is in charge and has the final decision then it is wise to find out what their rules are and to abide by them.

Fighting against the system may not always be inappropriate if the system or person is corrupt, but there are ways of doing this without losing your own integrity. If the system is not corrupt and the person just happens to have a different opinion to you and you still fight them, then expect the consequences of being disrespectful. If it is a Realm that you don't want to be in, then the answer is to move on as soon as possible and into a Realm with a Monarch that you do respect.

The joint Realm

Personal or
professional?

Professional or personal relationships

In life we encounter two different kinds of relationship. The first relationship is a professional one and the second is a personal one. These types of relationship often overlap or become confused. This can be dangerous ground. Recognising the difference between the two relationship types, and when each is appropriate, is very important because crossing boundaries usually leads to trouble.

Every relationship has a purpose, so consider what it is you want from each relationship that you have. Also consider what the other person wants from their relationship with you. This can be critical to the success of the relationship.

The purpose of the relationship is distinct from the person. For example, sometimes you have to work with someone but this doesn't mean that you have to like him or her. Being *personable* and being *personal* are two very different things. Personable means that you are friendly, approachable and amenable; you can be this whether you like the person or not. Personal means that you are forming a friendship or more with the person.

Personal relationships have no prescribed boundaries. You and the other person decide how you will relate to each other and decide how intimate it will be.

You share confidential moments, so the relationship is emotionally based with a lot of positive emotions invested in it from the Chimp. You will both express and share personal feelings and ideas so both have personal gains. The relationship will bring emotional satisfaction and that is its primary purpose. It involves a two-way intimacy whereby you also expect the other person to gain emotional satisfaction. You will judge each other on ethical, moral and emotional grounds and have flexible boundaries within the relationship that will change with time.

Professional relationships have prescribed boundaries especially interpersonal ones. Confidentiality is paramount and there are no emotional judgements made. There is no expected emotional agenda in a professional relationship because it is based on professional duties and responsibilities.

The reason that we often get our professional relationships moving across boundaries into personal relationships is because our Chimps, and at times our Humans, forget the boundaries and start looking to the other person to fulfil our more personal needs. It is wise therefore to establish what your emotional needs are and to seek out an appropriate person *outside* your professional circle to fulfil them. Avoid trying to fulfil your emotional needs from a fellow professional. Likewise, do not displace personal negative emotions, such as frustration or anger, into a professional relationship.

For success in your relationships, try asking the question 'what am I wanting from this relationship and what is the other person wanting?' Make sure that what you want is appropriate for the type of relationship involved, professional or personal.

Personal relationships

A personal relationship with someone involves a relationship with both the Human and the Chimp. So think carefully before you commit! When you have committed, every personal relationship is based on a daily decision to continue. Nobody nails your feet to the ground when it comes to relationships; they are pure choice.

When you enter into a personal relationship with someone it is important to recognise that some part of the relationship is in a joint Realm where decisions are therefore necessarily joint ones. Other parts of the relationship are not in the joint Realm and need individual decisions. For example, let's say a couple have met and have made a commitment to each other. Nobody owns anybody else and nobody can tell somebody else the rules for their own personal life. Each person is still the Monarch in their own Realm and will have full say in what they want to do and how they want to act.

One of the partners might decide that they want to spend every weekend with other friends and are not prepared to give this up. That is their prerogative and they have every right to decide this. Their partner likewise has every right to say, 'This is unacceptable to me and the consequence of you going away every weekend is that I do not want this relationship.' However, the partner might decide that accepting them going away every weekend with friends is better than ending the relationship. In this case the partner cannot complain at a later date because it was made clear at the time that these are the conditions for the relationship to continue.

What can happen in relationships is that one partner imposes rules onto the other and then gets upset when the rules are not obeyed. They have effectively put on the crown in somebody else's Realm. Imposing rules onto someone in their Realm is a form of passive aggression. The crown needs to be placed back on the right person's head by recognising what has happened and allowing each individual to decide on how they wish to conduct their life.

The joint Realm occurs in the relationship when the couple have to make a joint decision. For example, buying a house between them. Here, both have responsibility for the house so no one wears the crown; they share it.

Teams

Teams operate with either a leader who wears the crown or with a democratic group decision. These are the two ends of a spectrum. An important factor for groups to work successfully is to know who, if anyone, is wearing the crown, and also how rules will be made. Democratic groups in joint Realms all agree that there is no Monarch but a Government instead.

The Core Moon

The CORE principle
- **C**ommitment
- **O**wnership
- **R**esponsibility
- **E**xcellence

The CORE moon addresses the preparation to undertake a task. There are four areas to cover that will enhance the chances of success and these are collectively known as the CORE principle.

The first area is commitment

When you are serious about undertaking something, you need to start by checking that you have a real possibility of achieving what you are setting out to do. There is no point in starting if you have not thought through whether you will be able to commit to the challenge. In order to do this you can put yourself through a 'Commitment Screen'. It is important that both you and the Chimp sit down together to do this because it won't work if only one of you decides to commit to the challenge. So the first possible error is to allow just the Human, or just the Chimp, to speak for the other one. Here are two examples to demonstrate this point.

Emma and her jogging plans

Emma decides she is going to get fit and join a jogging club. When she decides this, she is sitting indoors in the warmth. Her Human says, 'This makes logical sense and I will run twice each week with the club and this will get me fit,' and her fickle Chimp joins in and says, 'Great, I will really enjoy the feeling of being fit.' However, by winter the Chimp has changed its mind. The Human is still saying, 'I want to get fit and do this,' but the Chimp is having none of it.

Emma has made a great mistake by planning to simply overrule the Chimp in the winter by willpower. You can't arm-wrestle the Chimp! Willpower won't work if the Chimp doesn't want to do something. If Emma really knew her Chimp well, then she could be honest and say that in the winter the *feeling of being fit* won't be enough, *emotionally*, to make my Chimp commit to jogging in unpleasant conditions. Of course Emma could make plans to coax the Chimp with other measures, such as jogging with friends, but the bottom line may be that it's unlikely to happen because the Chimp will overrule Emma's plans. Emma might be better off with a different way of getting fit; one that the Chimp will tolerate.

Notice how Emma could have recognised that the Chimp was joining in the decision-making by the statement, 'I will really enjoy the FEELING of being fit.' However, feelings come from the Chimp and can be very transient and unreliable. They are useful at times, as a guide to help us, but they are not useful to build plans on. In order to plan fully Emma needed to ask what the Chimp would feel when winter came.

Feelings from the Chimp – easy come, easy go
– not a foundation for the future!

John's football dream

John decides to start an amateur football club. He is wild about football and has always dreamt of being the manager of a club. His Chimp is excited, full of enthusiasm and is determined to make it work. He knows that the Human has the drive and ability to do it so he announces to his local council that he has plans and is looking for backing from them. It all sounds good and it could work out.

What is the problem here? The problem is that this project is being Chimp-led. The Chimp in John will probably always enthuse and have the ability and energy to do this but has the Human engaged with some truth and logic? The potential pitfall with this project is that it needs some down-to-earth business plans drawing up.

One of the biggest problems will be that the venture definitely needs commitment *from other people*. No matter how keen John might be, he can't do this alone: he also needs capital and time. Has he really thought through what time and money will be needed? Of course we don't want to curb his enthusiasm but it won't go far without some solid business plan to support it.

The Human needs to get on board with some logic, and work out what he needs for success, otherwise the dream could end up becoming a nightmare. When John has got firm commitments from others and financial backing in place, he now has a firm basis for progressing and his Chimp will give him the energy to successfully complete the project.

These two examples demonstrate the need to work out what both your Human and your Chimp can commit to. There is no point in the Human being 'successful' if your Chimp is not happy, and vice versa, so you need a balance. Many people commit everything to their jobs and are very successful but are not happy, as they never see their friends and family. Success has to be worth the price you have to pay for it. What can you physically and emotionally handle? The Chimp needs to let you know what it feels and the Human needs to let you know how practical it is. There needs to be cooperation between the two of them and then the probability of success increases dramatically.

Motivation versus commitment

Motivation is Chimp-driven. It is a feeling based on emotion. Motivation generally happens when there is a great reward to gain or when you are suffering so badly that you want things to change. Motivation is helpful to drive us on but it is not essential to success. It is unrealistic to expect to 'feel motivated' every day, no matter what you are doing. The problem with motivation is that it works on feelings from the Chimp and these can shift very quickly.

Commitment, on the other hand, comes from the Human and does not depend on feelings. Commitment means following a plan even if you don't feel like it that day. For example, a surgeon can't say halfway through an operation, 'Do you know I just don't feel motivated to finish this, so I'll stop now!' Motivation doesn't matter; it is commitment that will finish the operation.

Key Point
When you decide to do something, remind yourself that it is commitment not motivation that matters.

The Commitment Screen explained

In order to assess your commitment in a structured way, use the 'Commitment Screen', which is a list of questions to answer. The screen is composed of two aspects. The first aspect is working out what you will need to do the job. The second aspect is preparing solutions to overcome anything that might stop you from succeeding.

The two aspects of the Commitment Screen

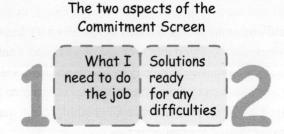

> What I need to do the job | Solutions ready for any difficulties

First aspect: What is needed for the job?

We can break these requirements down into three types:

- Essential
- Significant
- Desirable

Essential – these are the things that are critical for the venture to succeed. So, for example, if you want to start a business then you must have access to a certain amount of money. If you want to become a professional opera singer then you must have a good voice. If you want to get fit jogging then you must run regularly. Essentials are both physical and emotional in nature and this is where it is worth doing two lists every time you consider doing something. The first list is for you the Human and the second list is for the Chimp. The Human covers the practicalities and truths and the Chimp covers the feelings and emotional skills needed.

Significant – these are the things that will definitely have an influence on the final outcome and therefore must be considered. For example, if you want to do some gardening then it will help to have a number of different tools to work with and not be limited to just one or two. If you want to study for an exam then having a quiet place to study would help considerably. If you want a good relationship with someone then having enough time to develop it will greatly improve the chances of success.

Desirable – these are things that may or may not help, but they will make things more comfortable. For example, if you want a good night out, then having some money to spend would be welcome. If you want to lose weight, then it helps to have a friend on board to encourage you. If you want a successful and happy company, then it is pleasing to have a social gathering now and then.

You have to work out for yourself what is in each category because it will be different for different people. This all depends on what your Human and your Chimp think. The same criteria may end up under a different category for two different people. For example, one may believe that it is *essential* to have high intellect to learn a language, whereas a second person may believe that this is only *desirable,* and everyone can learn no matter what their intellect is.

As we can get these things wrong, it is always advisable to run your list past a friend who can help clarify that everything is considered and in the right category.

Second aspect: What are the challenges you might face?
We can break these challenges down into three types:

- Hurdles
- Barriers
- Pitfalls

You need to work out what you may have to overcome to be successful in your plans. If we consider the challenges as three different types, it will help to look at them from a Human perspective in practical terms and then a Chimp perspective in emotional terms.

Hurdles – these are things there is just no getting round and you have to jump them. There are always unpleasant or difficult things that you have to do in anything that you undertake. Your job is to work out what these are and then have a coping strategy to deal with them. Poor coping strategies may include ignoring, running away or fighting them, and these will definitely jeopardise your chances of success.

Not working out potential problems before you start is a virtual guarantee for failure. Here are some examples:

- If you want to lose weight you have to change your eating habits.
- If you want to get fit you have to exercise.
- If you want to work successfully with people you have to learn. to cope with their Chimps.

There are no choices here, so you have to learn how to jump these hurdles.

Barriers – these are things you can get around with good planning. This doesn't mean ignoring the difficulty, it means dealing with it by removing it. Hurdles can't be removed, barriers can. So it is very important to recognise the difference and then remove the barriers. For example, trying to deal with something that you don't have the experience or expertise to do can often be delegated to someone who has these qualities. Wanting to go on holiday with limited money just means choosing an affordable place to go, not stopping the holiday.

Pitfalls – these are areas that could easily be your downfall if you are not looking out for them. An example is letting yourself become emotionally exhausted before recognising the need for time out. Other examples are: entering a difficult conversation without preparing for it; or deciding not to eat junk food but keeping a small stock of it in the house! Drinking excess alcohol has recognisable pitfalls, such as using alcohol to deal with anxiety. This pitfall can be avoided if the anxiety is dealt with more appropriately.

The Commitment Screen questions

Here is a set of questions you can answer to cover the two aspects of the Commitment Screen. This will ensure that you are fully prepared to take on your dream.

Is it really a dream?

- How important is this to you and your Chimp?
- Do you and your Chimp really want to achieve it?
- What are the benefits of achieving your dream?
- Are the benefits worth having, compared to the cost of getting there?

The plans and requirements to fulfil the dream

- What plans have you made to achieve this?
- What have you tried in the past?
- If it failed in the past, why was this?
- What are you going to do that is different this time?
- What new strategies have you got for the future?
- What worked in the past?
- Have you made sure that your plans are watertight by letting someone else check them with you?
- What are the essential, significant and desirable requirements for both Human and Chimp for this plan to work?
- Have you got the essentials in place BEFORE you start?

Hurdles, barriers and pitfalls
- Have you made a list of the hurdles you have to jump?
- Have you got a strategy to jump **each** hurdle?
- What will you have to sacrifice?
- What are your plans for dealing with the downsides?
- What stress will you face in trying to achieve this dream?
- What barriers do you think you will have to get round or negotiate on?
- What are your plans to avoid or get round each barrier?
- What pitfalls might you need to avoid?
- How will you recognise the pitfalls as you approach them?
- If you failed to reach your dream how would you feel and how will you deal with this?

What will keep you going when you face problems?
- How will you deal with failing to meet a goal or target?
- Who have you got to help you deal with issues/problems you might face?
- Is this person clear on why and how they can help you?
- How will you measure progress?
- How willing are you to learn new strategies?
- How willing are you to change your approach?

If you find yourself wanting to give up your dream, ask yourself the following:
- Why do you want to give up?
- Can you change anything before you give up?
- Can you find a different approach?
- Who have you talked it through with?
- What are the advantages to giving up your dream?
- What are the disadvantages to giving up the dream?
- What plans have you got for when you stop working towards the dream?

Some suggestions to help you to stay committed to a plan

- Be realistic with your resources – money and time are not elastic.
- Time management is a skill worth learning.
- Work effectively not just efficiently.
- Prioritise what you need to do and don't allow yourself to get distracted.
- Doing one thing at a time, where possible, is the best way to give it full attention.
- Avoid negative people or at least let them know what they are doing (nicely) and if they can't stop, don't involve them.
- Actively listen to advice and where necessary seek it out.
- Indecision is the best energy sapper, so once you have all the information, make the decision and follow it through.

Key Point

The biggest factor for success is for you to function at your best, practically and emotionally.

The million-pound question

Be disciplined and not just organised. Anyone can organise, by making a plan. Very few people can carry out the plan because they do not have the self-discipline. If you feel you are stalling or making excuses and not getting the task done, ask yourself the million-pound question. **If you were given a million pounds to do the task before the end of the day could you do it?** If the answer is yes, I would definitely have it completed, then this means that it **is possible to do it**. It means that if you don't do it by the end of the day, then any reason you offer as to why you didn't do it is just an excuse for not being disciplined. It would suggest that you are not so serious in wanting to fulfil your dream.

Getting disheartened

All of us get disheartened from time to time and want to give up our dreams. When this happens, sometimes, paradoxical psychology works. This is where you basically say the opposite of what you want. So you can say to yourself it is okay to walk away from the dream. You don't need to fulfil your dream and it is your choice: so off you go. It is surprising how often the Chimp, who is telling us it wants to walk away, suddenly reverses and says it has no intention of giving up and gets back into the dream. The Chimp does this because it recognises that the dream is still alive and it wants it badly, therefore walking away is not something it intends to do. The Chimp just wanted a scream, which is very reasonable for a Chimp. Always remember that it is perfectly normal and acceptable to get things off your chest from time to time. Exercise your Chimp sensibly.

The second area is ownership

The second area of the CORE principle is about ownership. Imagine that you work at a factory and the owner asks a lot of you. We will assume that you are a good person, who works hard and is conscientious. You are committed to your job and have high standards.

One day the factory owner decides to retire and calls you into the office. She says that she has decided to leave the factory to you. You now own the factory. How hard do your reckon that you will work, now that you own the company and all the profits are yours? Nearly all of us, would work longer hours and put everything into it.

Having ownership of something always excites the Human and the Chimp because it offers all kinds of rewards. Human beings generally love ownership and will take things more seriously when given it. We take things personally and invest both the Chimp and Human energies into the venture.

Therefore, to increase your chances of success you need to have ownership of your plans because following someone else's plans, no matter how good they are, is not the same unless you fully agree with them. Owning the plan means that you have either formed it yourself, had a major say in it, or believe that the plan is ideal for you and you couldn't do better. If there are any parts of the plan that you do not own, that is, you don't agree with, then your chances of success are likely to diminish.

What happens if you don't have ownership? Below is a diagram to show the difference when ownership is given, or not given, and the most likely results of this. When you don't have ownership the Chimp typically disrupts the plans and decreases the chances of success.

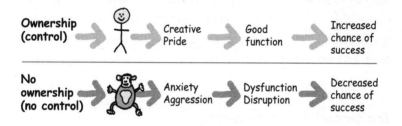

Having a plan and having ownership of this plan
is all about being organised

The third area is responsibility

In the CORE principle, responsibility introduces accountability. Owning a plan is a great step forward towards success. If the plan has been carefully prepared then all that remains is to carry it out. Carrying out the plan is about having responsibility and being disciplined. This is where most people fall down because their Chimps begin to work on feelings and this stops them from being disciplined and doing what they know they need to do. Being organised is the easy bit. Most students will tell you that they are excellent in sorting out a revision plan before exams. They can detail down to the smallest items how and when they will study. However, most are then unable to discipline themselves and fail to carry out the plan. Each week the revision timetable is adjusted until eventually the amount of work that they expect to do is crammed into just a few days or even hours. Responsibility is all about managing the Chimp and its feelings, and getting down to business without excuses.

If you have responsibility for your plan then you must be held accountable for it. The chances of success increase when we report back to someone with a progress report on how it is all going. This is a big factor for succeeding. Having deadlines and reporting back makes both the Human and the Chimp feel obligated to act. When you become *accountable*, and it might even be to just yourself, you will audit the way things are going. Then you will step in quickly, if things are not going according to plan. So, responsibility can also be seen as accountability on a regular basis.

Key Point

Taking responsibility and accountability for implementing or carrying out the plan is all about being disciplined.

The fourth area is excellence

We have now seen that your chances of success will increase if you have:

- A thought-through *commitment*
- A plan for which you have *ownership*
- Accepted *responsibility*

The fourth area of the CORE principle, to increase your chances of success, is to set very high but achievable goals. You can only do your best in everything that you do. You cannot do better than your best; this is illogical. As long as you have tried, despite mistakes and errors, and occasional unintentional lapses, you have done your best. It is very important to accept this principle.

If you define a level of excellence and cannot reach it you may feel very deflated and see yourself as a failure. That is a choice that you are making. You set the bar at a specific level of excellence. There is nothing wrong with this but it can have serious consequences for your Chimp, who may not deal with the demand for excellence, or the failure to reach it.

There is an alternative in life. You can aim for *personal excellence*, which is doing your best, regardless of the standard that you achieve. This personal excellence is always achievable. You may still be disappointed with the level you achieve but at least you can hold your head up and say that it was your best. The Chimp is very likely to live with this. (This concept is covered in more detail in the Moon of Confidence chapter).

Key Point
Personal excellence is defined as doing your best.

The Moon of Carrots

Key topics
- The carrot and no stick
- Recognising the stick
- Types of carrots

The carrot and no stick

We all know of the old adage about the donkey pulling the cart. You can get him to move with either a stick or a carrot. Donkeys, Humans and Chimps don't like punishment (sticks) but do like rewards (carrots). Hitting Humans or Chimps with a stick will get them to move but will also make them unhappy, rebellious and unlikely to perform at their best. Chimps enjoy eating carrots but these carrots need to be big otherwise the Chimp won't move.

Imagine we are in the jungle watching Mitch the chimpanzee making his plans to become the alpha male. He 'thinks' about the way to do this. It is the jungle; therefore the jungle laws are in force. He decides to scream and shout and thrash the ground with a stick. Any chimpanzee that gets in the way will be attacked with the stick or with his fists. If Mitch becomes the alpha chimp then he will use his authority giving savage beatings to any chimp that steps out of line. If he fails to become the top chimp then he will hide, keep his head low, and wait for the chance again.

It doesn't take too much imagination to superimpose this scenario onto an office or any other place of work. The story is all too familiar. Consider a person who wants to fulfil their ambition but they do it by force, threats and domination of others in order to keep them in line. When they do become the boss they work on the principle that by beating their staff, their staff will not attack but will work harder.

Thankfully there is an alternative.

In the Human society, we don't have sticks. Here, an ideal leader is the person who develops the group and encourages them. It is based on the principle that people are doing their best and if they are failing then it means they need more support, guidance or development. People prefer to be encouraged, supported and rewarded, rather than being beaten. Of course there are standards to reach and benchmarks must be set and the consequences of not reaching them clarified. If someone has tried their best with **full support** and failed to reach the benchmark then they can accept the consequences, which may be unpleasant, but without suffering the stick. There is no place for a stick in society. There is a place for benchmarks and consequences of not reaching them, which adult Humans learn to deal with.

Chimps work with violence, threats and sticks. Humans work with compassion, encouragement, carrots and consequences

So the system is to set benchmarks for standards and use carrots to reach these. If you can't reach the benchmarks after all possible support then you must accept the consequences. Clearly if someone is being lazy then they will not reach the benchmarks set and will suffer the consequences.

Key Point
In a civilised society the stick is replaced with carrots, benchmarks and consequences.

So why is the Moon of Carrots such an important stabiliser to the Planet of Success? The Chimp in you may work best by being violent and responding to violence but the emotional damage it can bring might be devastating. Every day we suffer at the hands of other people's Chimps or even at the hands of our own Chimp. Humans work best when they receive recognition and appreciation for what they have done; also when they are rewarded in other ways. Humans like to achieve and be constructive. Chimps like to be groomed by others in the troop and to feel part of the troop. So to bring out the best in yourself you need to make sure that you are getting plenty of carrots!

Types of carrots

Lots of varieties

There are many types of carrots and it is a good idea to make sure that you try all the types. Everyone needs to learn what carrots they like best and to make sure they obtain them. Grow your own carrots!

Rewards

These can be obvious material things such as football tickets, new clothing, chocolate bars, a meal out, a car and so on. It can be anything that is a reward to you and will make you happy. Linking rewards to work that you have to do is a very good way of getting your Chimp on side. Have rewards in place to look forward to as this can give the Chimp motivation and the Human commitment to carry on.

Celebrations

It is important to look back and celebrate what you have done. Reflecting on your hard work and effort is important to increase the chances of success. It is important for both you and your Chimp to recognise this and praise yourself for what you have done, or even tried to do.

Recognition

Most Humans do not need recognition but are self-satisfied. However, most Chimps within us **do need** recognition from **the right person** and if you deprive them of this then they can become very bitter, angry and upset. Make sure the recognition happens by working out whom you would welcome praise or recognition from and make sure that they understand that this would mean a lot to you. This is a sensible way to look after and nurture your Chimp.

Encouragement

Your Chimp needs encouragement from time to time and it's not unreasonable to ask for this. Encouragement is a very good carrot to give your Chimp good feelings when it needs them. Don't forget that people around you are not mind readers. You might have to tell them that you would like to be encouraged. Sometimes we all forget to encourage others. Looking at the benefits of achieving something is one of the strongest encouragers.

Support

Getting support from the right person or people is a great boost to morale. The troop rallying to support a distressed Chimp or Human is a very welcome carrot. Don't be afraid to ask for support or help. This is one of the reasons why we have troops. Don't be foolish by cutting yourself off from support. This is unlikely to be wise and much more likely to be stupid! It's unlikely to be a sign of independence but rather a sign of stubbornness. If you had a friend who was in trouble you would not hesitate to help. Don't deprive your friends of the chance to show their friendship for you when you need it.

Recognising the stick

Typical sticks

Any form of threat, punishment or attack is a stick. Sticks can be physical or psychological.

Beating yourself up

Using a stick on yourself is more destructive than others doing it to you. Beating yourself up is a useless and damaging process and it is also a CHOICE. You don't have to do it. Ask what good is it doing? Also ask is this the way that you want to deal with yourself? You can choose to look more objectively and see what you can do to improve, or accept the way that you are, with a smile. Things won't get better by attacking and demeaning yourself. Relax and encourage yourself instead.

Guilt, blame and regret

The stick also comes in the form of guilt, blame or regret. Of course these emotions are there for a purpose. They are to let us know when we have done something wrong or amiss and we ought to make amends as best we can, and learn from our mistakes. However, once we have recognised this, and done what we can to show remorse and amendment, then they have no place. These negative emotions become a stick that we beat ourselves with for no good purpose. Living with guilt, blame or regret is a terrible stick that will destroy any chance of happiness or constructive living. It can also become a tool of self-pity to use so that we don't have to get on with life. Think carefully if you are using these against yourself and ask what purpose they serve.

The abusive reminder stick

An even worse stick is when someone has done something wrong and clearly shown remorse and change, only to be repeatedly reminded of their previous misdemeanours by another person. This very strong form of passive aggression by the stick-wielding person is abuse.

Summary key points

- Define what you mean by success and stick to it.
- Wear the crown when it is appropriate.
- Respect the crown when it is on somebody else's head.
- Commitment is the biggest part of the CORE principle.
- Take ownership and responsibility for your life.
- Aim for personal excellence.
- Grow lots of carrots and get rid of the stick.

Suggested exercise:
Success by thorough preparation

Turning failure into success

Have a look at some venture or task that you have failed to accomplish in the past but would like to do in the future. Run yourself through the Commitment Screen and answer all of the questions. Then follow through by taking ownership and responsibility for carrying out a plan. Try to implement all of the recommendations in the chapter and reinforce those that are relevant to you.

Chapter 15
The Planet of Success

How to plan for success

The Dream Machine – A plan for success

Success can happen regardless of plans. However, having structured plans improves your chances of success and allows you to know that you did everything you could to achieve your dream, so at least you can smile. Remember that life is not fair and even though you can do everything right, you may not be successful.

The Dream Machine is a structured approach to optimising your chances of success when you have a specific dream. I have used this model frequently in many different situations and implemented it to help various professionals in different fields to achieve their dream. It incorporates aspects drawn from the stabilising moons around its planet and has seven distinct cogs. Each cog will lead you through to the next one and after turning the seventh cog you will have hopefully realised your dream!

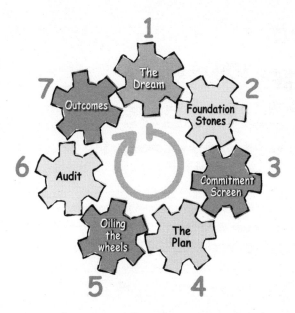

Before you start the cogs turning please remember there are two of you planning this journey: you and your Chimp. So you must consider your Chimp when you make the plans. The Chimp will have needs of its own, such as reassurance and rewards, if it is to stay on side. If you have no interference from the Chimp then you are likely to be very successful. If you look after the Chimp then it may even help you to be successful. If you consider your Chimp as a child that has little staying power, easily gets distracted, is undisciplined, disorganised, and constantly wants instant rewards, then you won't go far wrong!

Cog 1

The difference between a dream and a goal

The Dream Machine makes a very important distinction between 'dreams' and 'goals'. Don't move on until you understand the difference and can identify your own dreams.

A **dream** is something that you want to happen but it is not fully under your control. The dream has outside influences and therefore you cannot guarantee that it will happen; it is just a wish.

Goals are something that you can set and achieve because you have full control of them. Goals increase the chances of dreams happening.

Here are some examples of dreams and some supporting goals. You can add many more goals with a little thought.

Dream – wanting someone you love to love you
Goals supporting the dream
- Asking what makes them happy (and doing it!)
- Asking what makes them unhappy (and avoiding it)
- Greeting them with a genuine smile
- Being happy and encouraging
- Telling them what you appreciate about them
- Respecting their space and respecting them

Dream – wanting to win a race
Goals supporting the dream
- Regular training
- Good diet
- Correct mental attitude

Dream – wanting to be a confident person
(NB: You can't guarantee being confident all the time because it is a skill and is variable depending on Chimp Management.)

Goals supporting the dream
- Spending time learning to recognise when your Chimp is in action
- Spending time practising management of the Chimp on confidence issues

Dream – wanting to achieve a good sleeping pattern
(NB: You can't guarantee a good sleep pattern because your biological clock can play up and also external influences can wake you up.)

Goals supporting the dream
- Learning about and implement sleep hygiene
- Learning about, and be realistic about, what sleep you need

Dream – wanting to get a job when you are interviewed
(NB: Your job success may depend on what the panel are looking for and if there is a better candidate.)

Goals supporting the dream
- Preparing yourself for the interview
- Making sure you know what the job is all about
- Dressing appropriately
- Practising interview techniques

Key Point
Goals must be realistic and achievable.

Why the distinction between dreams and goals is really important

Whenever the brain recognises that it doesn't have full control of any situation it sends the blood supply to the Chimp. This results in unease and you will feel under threat, with the consequence being that the Chimp now controls the thinking and plans. However, if the brain recognises that it is in full control of a situation then the Chimp relaxes and the blood supply goes to the Human. The result is calmness and a feeling of opportunity. Then the Human thinks and makes the plans.

Don't make dreams into goals because you will set your Chimp off. You need to see a dream as **a possibility** but accept that it may not happen. It is like throwing the dice and saying I know I can get a double six, then getting upset when it doesn't happen. If you understand it is a roll of the dice that can go one of many ways then you are more likely to accept the result with a smile. If you carry out all the goals needed to give the dream the best chance of success, then you can be happy that you did your best.

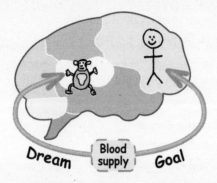

Dreams send the blood supply to the Chimp.
Goals send the blood supply to the Human

Aim for the stars not the moon

Psychological evidence says that we need to dream big and set extremely challenging goals if we want to increase our chances of success. Don't aim for the moon but the stars. The 'moon' is a goal that you know you **can achieve** by effort. The 'stars' are a goal that you **could achieve** by great effort and it will feel fantastic to reach this goal. If you aim for the moon your Chimp can get complacent; but if you aim higher for the stars your Chimp and Human commit to it and get excited by the big challenge. Therefore make sure that your dreams excite you, as you are more likely to achieve them and if you do miss the stars you might still reach the moon!

Your task for cog 1 – the dream

- Define your dream.

Cog 2

Foundation Stones are the components that you can work on to achieve your dream. For example, if you want to run a race then three Foundation Stones would be your speed, your weight, and the distance covered each week. There will be a lot more Foundation Stones and it is important to try and elicit all of them.

A dream is based on Foundation Stones

Each Foundation Stone can be given a goal that you can measure and achieve. So for example, your weight can be dropped or increased to an optimum. These specific goals are under your control and if you reach them it will make the dream more likely to happen. It is useful to divide the goals into those you are specifically working on to achieve gains (target goals) and those that you are happy with but are keeping an eye on (maintenance goals).

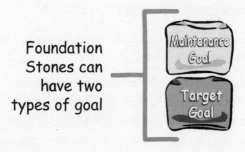

Foundation Stones can have two types of goal

So you could be at a chosen set weight and wish to just maintain it or you could be reducing your weight and therefore targeting it. Target goals are where you feel you can make gains. It is best to select just one or two target goals to work on over a fixed period of time, with the other Foundation Stones remaining as maintenance goals. You do not want to spread your effort out too thinly but concentrate on one thing at a time and achieve it. If you spread out your efforts on too many things then you are likely to increase your chances of failing.

Work on just one or two target stones until they have improved

Key Point
The fewer tasks you focus on, the more likely you are to succeed with them.

When your target goals are reached then you can swap the target goal to a maintenance goal and select another maintenance goal to become a target to work on.

Your tasks for cog 2 – Foundation Stones

- Write down the Foundation Stones that will support your dream.
- Give each stone a measurable goal.
- Divide the goals into maintenance and target goals.
- Set new standards for the target goals and a time scale to work on them.

Cog 3

The Commitment Screen is covered in the CORE moon section. We will use the checklist there to complete your next task. The Commitment Screen is to make sure that you are aware of what is needed to take on the dream, and to give a reality check and form your preparations.

Be prepared

Remember your Chimp will be involved in the plans. Try to think ahead and know what things are likely to upset it. Think particularly of the excuses that the Chimp might try to use to stop you from progressing. Stopping to think these out and writing down your strategies for dealing with them, if they arise, is time well spent.

Your tasks for cog 3 – Commitment Screen

- Write a list of all the essential, significant and desirable needs to take on the dream.
- Write a list of all the hurdles, barriers and pitfalls that may stop the dream from happening and devise plans to deal with these.

Cog 4

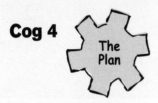
The Plan

It was Abraham Lincoln who said: 'If you have eight hours to chop down a tree, spend six hours sharpening your axe.'

> ## Key Point
> *The more preparation you make with your plan the more likely you are to succeed.*

Now that you have your Foundation Stones, and know exactly what you need to work on, you just need a realistic plan to pull it all together. The plan must be achievable in the time that you have to complete it.

The plan is best constructed in stages, based on your goals, so that you can measure how well you are doing as you move forward. Define exactly how you will measure each goal so that you can see your progress. The stages need realistic time scales to show exactly where you intend to be at these given points in time. Be realistic because being unrealistic will inevitably lead to failure and an unnecessary sense of disappointment in yourself.

The plan works best in stages

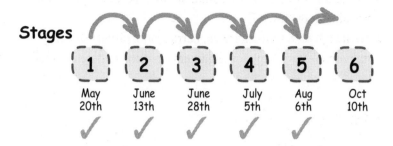

Stages

1	2	3	4	5	6
May 20th	June 13th	June 28th	July 5th	Aug 6th	Oct 10th
✓	✓	✓	✓	✓	

Your tasks for cog 4 – the plan

- Form a plan in stages with measurable goals.
- Give time scales to each stage and goal.
- Select two target goals to work on.

Cog 5

It is important to keep the process going by doing things that keep you happy, encouraged and committed. You don't NEED to be happy but it helps.

To climb a mountain

One way to think of your journey to success is to consider it as like climbing a mountain. If you imagine your dream as being the top of a mountain then you need to break the climb down into realistic camps. You can now climb to each camp, which are the stages from your plan. There are some things that you can do to make the climb more likely to succeed.

Climbing a mountain

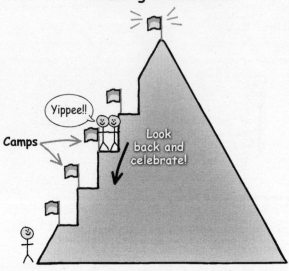

When you reach a camp (goal) make sure you celebrate

It is very important to measure your success and reward yourself when you reach the goals for each stage. (Of course you don't have to celebrate with alcohol!)

Monitor the success with a chart or some form of visible record so that you can see your progress

Keeping a record to measure the progress of target goals is very important. Making the record visible by putting it on a wall will help to remind the Chimp of what you are doing. Chimps like to win and they like to see things. It is psychologically powerful to see your progress on charts and graphs on walls or in notepads. For example, if you are trying to lose weight you can keep a progress chart on the fridge door.

Motivational reminders are also very helpful, such as a poster on the wall or a written message to yourself. This might stop the Chimp from hijacking you.

- When you reach a camp always *look back* to see how far you have come; try not to look up the mountain because this may dishearten you.
- If you look up, only look to the next camp.
- Climb the mountain with a friend whenever possible.
- If a friend can't join the climb then at least let them know when you have reached a camp so that they can share your success.

Once you start doing something it is usually not as bad as you first thought and taking a small step can encourage you to keep going. For example, let's assume that your house is in a bit of a mess and you are going to tidy it up. The task seems daunting and the Chimp looks around the house and sees a mountain to climb. The Chimp then goes into Freeze mode and refuses to engage, offering excuses or just a simple 'It's all too much' or 'I can't be bothered.' The Chimp is overwhelmed.

The Human can now form the first camp and say to the Chimp, 'What we will do is tidy just one small area of the house,' or maybe one room, or even as little as a table or desk area. Make sure the task is small and achievable within a short time. Your Chimp will be happy doing this because it is quick and the results are immediate, and Chimps like immediate gratification.

Don't look around now to see just how much still needs to be done (this is like looking to the top of the mountain), it will only dishearten you. Instead, be happy and celebrate the fact that you have started, and now form another easy camp to reach. Clean the house in small stages with a celebration at each stage. You may not finish it all but you will make progress. Remember that partial success is better than no success.

Studying can also seem like having to climb a mountain when you look to see how much there is to do. This means that your Chimp is very likely to try and stop you by distractions and excuses and feelings of exhaustion before you even open a book or sit down at a computer. Simply speaking, the main reason this happens is that the Chimp is looking to the top of the mountain and disengaging because it knows what lies ahead. Again, form a small step to an easy camp. For example, instead of saying, 'Tonight I will study for three hours,' which is a big ask of any Chimp, say, 'I will study for 15 minutes each day and then stop. If I then choose to continue, I will, but if I don't want to continue, 15 minutes is better than nothing.' On a daily basis, 15 minutes will cover some significant ground. It is not a lot to ask and nearly every Chimp will agree to this and do the 15 minutes immediately. It is important that the small study time has to happen every night and be strict with this. If you think 15 minutes is too long then try timing yourself to do ten! However, don't go the other way and commit to an hour every night because it is too much for the Chimp and it won't do it. This will again just leave you feeling disheartened. As with all plans and tactics, you must work out what will work for you.

These are suggestions that most Chimps will be happy with, but you must find out what *your* Chimp will tolerate and how they will react to what you plan. Plans should always be discussed with your Chimp! Don't forget that when you have done your 15 minutes you should celebrate or at least pat yourself on the back.

Your tasks for cog 5 – oiling the wheels

- Plan a reward and celebration for each goal achieved and each stage reached, before you start.
- Make a visible record to measure progress and put it somewhere prominent.
- Display helpful reminders and encouragers such as posters or notes to keep your Chimp on track.
- Get a friend to share your journey with; either by climbing the mountain and being as committed as you, or just to encourage you.

Cog 6

Audit

The Audit Cog is looking at the progress towards the dream and seeing if it is on track. An audit is where you can look at what is and isn't working. You then continue with what is working and change what isn't, by finding out why it isn't working. You can check on target goals and if they have reached the level you want, move them to maintenance goals. Then you can select different maintenance goals to become target goals to work on to improve standards.

When you do an audit of your progress against your plans you are really just holding up a mirror and being honest with yourself. It is a good idea to do this with a friend whose opinion you respect and who will tell you the truth, even if it is hard to hear.

Having someone to account to is a key
promoter of success

Revisit your goals and decide if they are still the right ones or whether they need to be changed. If the goals are proving too hard and affecting your happiness or well-being in a negative way, and you can see no solution to this, then try to get help from others or change your goals. It is a SKILL to recognise when you are off track and then deal with it appropriately. The audit is all about being positive and realistic. Don't see the audit in a negative light.

It is only helping you to see if changes need to be made. One of the key factors to a good audit is to **be flexible** in your thinking and with your original plan.

Successful thinking

Successful thinking is based on flexible and adaptable thinking. Successful people tend to think with their Human when solving problems; 'What have I done, or what am I doing, to contribute to this problem?' Then they ask, 'What can I do to change my own behaviours or beliefs in order to solve the problem?' After they have looked at themselves and what they can change, they then consider the circumstances that the problem has appeared in. They then ask, 'What can I do to change the circumstances that might help to solve the problem?' After trying to change the circumstances, they will finally look to others and ask, 'What are others doing to contribute to the problem and how can I help them?'

Thinking through a problem

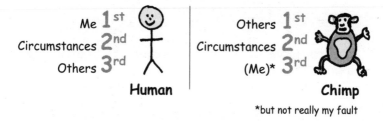

Me 1st
Circumstances 2nd
Others 3rd

Human

Others 1st
Circumstances 2nd
(Me)* 3rd

Chimp

*but not really my fault

To find the source of a problem

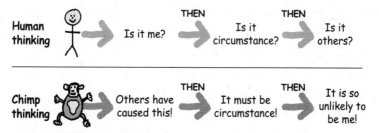

Human thinking → Is it me? **THEN** → Is it circumstance? **THEN** → Is it others?

Chimp thinking → Others have caused this! **THEN** → It must be circumstance! **THEN** → It is so unlikely to be me!

Less successful people tend to allow their Chimps to do the thinking and problem-solving. This thinking then becomes emotional and uses the following pattern.

First the Chimp starts with others and asks, 'What are other people doing to create the problem and how can I make sure that they know that they are wrong?' Then it thinks, 'What is wrong with the circumstances that have caused this problem and why is this so unfair?' Finally it then tries to solve the problem. It may or may not have an afterthought about how much it might have contributed to the problem. If it does, this is usually dismissed by rationalising any fault on its part as due to the actions of others or to circumstances. It repaints the picture, as described next.

Repainting the picture

A Chimp will analyse situations by looking back and repainting the picture of what happened in order to put themselves in a good light and with good intentions. It will also justify why it acted in the way it did in order to come out smelling of roses. This is well recognised and known as a self-serving bias.

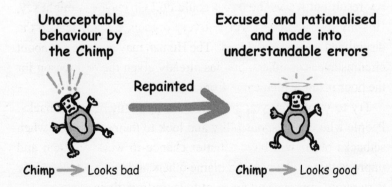

Let's take a look at an example.

The exam result

Let's go back to school days (assuming that you are not still there!). You have taken an exam in a subject that you found difficult. The exam result turns out to be disappointing.

The Chimp now starts by blaming others; we didn't have a good teacher; he never finished the syllabus; he couldn't control the class; the other pupils were disruptive and stopped me learning; my parents just weren't supportive; and so the list goes on. Having finished blaming others it moves on to circumstances. The exam was harder that year and no one got a good mark; the exam had nothing similar to previous exams; we moved house months before the exam and it was impossible to study; and so it goes on. Finally to complete the self-serving bias the Chimp absolves itself of all responsibility. I had miles to walk to school and it left me tired all day; my pet guinea pig died in the middle of the exams; I was taught in a way that didn't suit me; if I had wanted to I could have got an 'A' but there were lots of other things that I preferred to do.

Some of these reasons may not be excuses but factual; however, it is very unlikely that they prevented us from getting an 'A'.

Let's see how the Human would approach the same situation. The Human starts with itself and may say, 'I am disappointed with my result but it was the best I could do.' Or maybe it might say, 'It's my own fault as I was not very organised and I lacked the discipline I needed to succeed.' The Human may go on to say about circumstances or others, but has already given the real reason for the poor result, which came from itself.

Try to think how you approach disappointments or setbacks. People who own responsibility and look to themselves first when setbacks occur will have a better chance to work on them and improve things. People who blame others and circumstances only very rarely improve and tend not to learn from their mistakes.

There is a second point to this approach that we should look at. What would have happened if we had done really well in the exam and surprised ourselves? The Chimp would have taken full credit for the success and would reverse the thinking. Now the Chimp says, it is 'me' first, then circumstances, and finally others. Often the Chimp just stops with me first! The Human, on the other hand, often reverses the thinking and acknowledges the role that others have had in their success and the circumstances and then modestly is proud of their achievement.

The way that we deal with success and failure or setbacks and disappointments in our life becomes a habit. It can either turn into a Gremlin or an Autopilot. Look at the way that you think and consider whether it might be good to change.

Attribution error

Finally, on this theme there is another point to consider. If someone else had taken the exam and did poorly then our Chimps would immediately hold them responsible. Such a different story to when we ourselves fail. The way that the Chimp thinks is, 'If I do something wrong or make a mistake then there is a good reason. People ought to understand that reason, as I am basically innocent.' Whereas if others do the same thing wrong or make the same mistake, then the Chimp thinks, 'It is their fault and they should expect to take the consequences.' In other words, our Chimp excuses us when we go wrong but blames others if they do exactly the same thing that we have done.

Using attribution error is a learnt behaviour, so yet another Gremlin can be found in many people's Computers. If you recognise this Gremlin, then remove it and replace it with an Autopilot that is not biased towards you and biased against others.

In summary, we repaint the picture whenever we look back on events to make sure that it brings us out in a good light. We tend to do this by only hearing what we want to hear and seeing only what we want to see and remembering only what we want to remember. Our memory of events is repainted and is rarely the whole truth. Typically when we tell a story we keep on touching it up until we get it 'right'! The effect this has on others and our relationship with them is very significant. Repainting the picture usually diminishes our chances of learning and hence diminishes the chances of success.

Turning the light on and going to court

Sometimes we need to turn the light on to see what is happening. When you want to decide on whether you are working effectively you can sit down with a piece of paper and pretend you are going to represent yourself in court and put a light on the situation. Write down all of the evidence (no feelings or 'might be's, only FACT) both for and against how you are behaving and why. It can be a very interesting exercise to discover the truth! This exercise is very useful in a lot of areas, not just the area of success and audit. Sadly the court may find you guilty and this will demand change!

Your tasks for cog 6 – audit

- Recruit someone you can be accountable to.
- Regularly check your goals are realistic and be flexible if you need to change them.
- Check the Human method of thinking is being employed and not the Chimp.
- Make sure problem-solving is by the Human.
- Don't repaint the picture and deceive yourself.
- Turn the light on and go to court!

Cog 7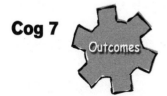

As you travel the journey to your dream it is inevitable that some things will go well and others not so well. In order to progress optimally it is very useful to have plans to deal with different kinds of outcomes. We will look at three types of outcome and how you can deal with these or see them differently. The three outcomes will be success, partial success and failure.

Success

This is obviously a great thing, and what we want, but there are some pitfalls to be aware of after you have been successful in an event.

The first danger is **complacency**. Whenever we have achieved something there is a tendency for the Chimp to forget quite quickly exactly what we had to do to succeed. Very often, therefore, successful people fail to continue with success because they fail to continue to do what they did in the first place in order to succeed. You need to be vigilant when watching for complacency. Complacency can also present if we become over-confident and start believing our own hype. Most success is achieved by hard work and there are few, if any, short cuts.

Success can also lead to **fear**: of not being able to repeat what you have achieved and of things going wrong. Focusing on this fear won't help, but focusing on what you have to do will! 'Manage the Chimp' is the message here. It is really important to look at each event separately and remember that you are starting from a level playing field for the next event. Stop your Chimp from comparing your achievements from past events to future ones as this will give you expectations that lead to anxiety. For each new situation, you can only do your best and work to the best of your ability. The outcome will be what it will be.

A common problem people experience, following a success, is to go into an **emotional dive** or **feel depressed**. There has been so much time and effort put into achieving the goal that there is a bit of an anti-climax afterwards, with a loss of focus and routine. This experience is very common and it is really just your mind demanding time out from the battle. The reaction to success is different for different people. If you do experience a dive in emotions be reassured this is within normal experience and allowing time out will usually bring you round quite quickly. It is therefore important to plan how you will deal with success and celebrate what you have achieved. Have a routine or plan ready for when something you have been working on for a long time comes to an end. Setting another goal or planning a reward to satisfy the Chimp often works well. Don't ignore your Chimp's needs at these times.

Partial success

The Chimp within us typically thinks in terms of black and white. Children also tend to do this a lot. The Human within you, and most adults, tend to see things in shades of grey. Success can be seen in this way too. If you have not been fully successful but there are some good parts to an outcome, then it is worth celebrating a partial success. Trying to aim for partial success is not usually a good thing as your Chimp is likely to become indifferent and your drive to succeed may well diminish. However, once the outcome has happened it is worth looking at accepting some success no matter how small this might be. It is a choice that you have. The alternative is to see something as a failure and then accept the emotional consequences of this.

Failure (or setbacks)

Try to see a failure or setback as a challenge. It can be an opportunity to develop yourself and your skills to deal with problem-solving.

When we fail at something there are consequences for our self-esteem and self-worth. The Chimp sees it as a catastrophic event and typically gets the outcome completely out of perspective. The Chimp often sees failure as evidence it is a worthless and useless being; that everybody is now aware of this evidence; and there is no way to recover this. On the other hand, Humans see failure as being relative; accept that sometimes we don't win or get things right; and see failure as a learning curve. Humans accept the outcome and work with it. Therefore, there are two very different perceptions of failure that can occur in a typical mind. How can you deal with this, and why is it that some people don't get this sense of conflict?

The answer is generally found in the emphasis that you have placed on failing and what this failure means or implies. It is always good to think this through.

Key Point

Anything in life is only as important as you want it to be.

An example might help to illustrate the difference in a Chimp reaction and a Human reaction. Many of us took our driving test when we were quite young. At this age if someone failed the test it could have quite devastating effects on him or her. Somehow, passing first time was critically important and got muddled up with ideas involving self-esteem. However, when you ask people who are older about their experience with their first driving test, they often laugh about failed attempts because they perceive failing first time as unimportant. It was merely an inconvenience and didn't have anything to do with their self-esteem, and probably not even how well they would ultimately drive!

Sadly, getting perspective can **take time** but can often be speeded up if you **make time** to develop perspective on life events. Try to do this by seeing what you can learn from failure or disappointment and don't take it too seriously.

So why does getting perspective take time? Your Human can get over failure quite quickly but the Chimp within is not programmed this way and you have to live with this. The Chimp has a well-recognised pattern of dealing with failure and loss and this pattern is seen in almost all people. It is commonly called a grief reaction. Usually we relate the term 'grief reaction' to dealing with the death of someone close. However, the reaction can be seen with any loss and also with any perceived failure. The reaction is the Chimp's way of dealing with something that is very emotional and hard to accept. Any bad news can therefore be compared to a grief reaction. The reaction has recognised stages and your Chimp is very likely to go through these stages, or most of them, when it suffers a failure. Knowing this, you can at least know that it is normal to have a reaction to failure and you can 'nurse' your Chimp through it. There is little point in fighting the reaction, but it is better to work with it.

Normal grief reaction from the Chimp

Simplified, the typical stages, which can occur in any order but usually follow as listed below, are:

- **Denial** − not accepting this event has happened.
- **Yearning** − a longing for the event not to have happened and for a return to the previous circumstances.
- **Bargaining** – trying to change the outcome of the event. Often starting with 'If only' or 'If I do this' (the Chimp constantly wants to go back in time and change things, whereas the Human accepts that you cannot change what has happened).
- **Anger** – frustration and blame often accompany anger, and some kind of explanation is sought to make the event seem less painful.
- **Disorganisation** – the truth is now being accepted and dealt with and a feeling of depression appears with lots of unpleasant emotions and a sense of emptiness. This is real grief.
- **Reorganisation** – you start to accept what has happened, or at least learn to live with it, and make plans for moving on.

The failure of a relationship will go through the same stages. Letting your Chimp work through these stages is important or you may get stuck and the grief process can then take longer than normal. **Everyone is different** but it usually takes about three months to go through the acute phase and up to a year to function again, possibly longer depending on how severe the event was and how important it was to you. It is unreasonable to expect yourself not to react emotionally to any failure. It helps to be more aware of how you might react and how you can deal with your reaction. Hopefully any failure can eventually be given perspective and you can move on from what you have learnt from the setback. Failure is a normal part of life's experiences and reacting to it is just as normal and acceptable.

Your tasks for cog 7 – outcomes

- Measure success in relative terms and where possible celebrate partial successes.
- Deal with failures or setbacks constructively and see them as learning points to develop yourself.
- Try to develop the ability to get a perspective on all life events.
- If your Chimp grieves, allow it to express itself. It is perfectly reasonable to grieve.

Summary key points

- There is a difference between a dream and a goal.
- To be successful you will need planning and structure.
- Oiling the wheels will greatly improve the chances of success.
- Regular audit will keep you on track.
- Dealing with outcomes is part of the blueprint.

Suggested exercise:
Implementing this chapter

Realising the dream
Define your dream and make time to go through a structured plan as outlined in this chapter. It is best to work through this with a friend. Follow the steps by doing the exercises for each cog. When you have begun to implement the plan keep reminding yourself of why you want the dream to happen and what it will mean to you to succeed.

Chapter 16
The Planet of Happiness
How to be happy

Happiness
- What do we mean by happiness?
- Three states of mind
- Moving into happiness
- The happiness approach
- Happiness promoters

Happiness is a choice. Being happy all of the time is unrealistic; there will always be adversity and setbacks. It is natural to have ups and downs but you can get back to happiness **by working on it**.

What do we mean by happiness?

You have to decide what happiness means to you because it is different for different people. So your first task is to take time and decide what makes you happy, then at least you know what you are working towards. The brain releases different chemicals when it is anxious, than when it is relaxed or than when it is happy. Therefore, it might be easiest to approach the way to happiness by defining three different states.

Three states of mind for the Human and the Chimp

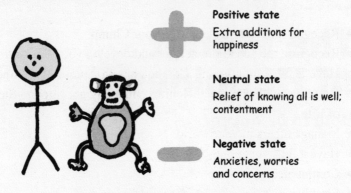

Positive state
Extra additions for happiness

Neutral state
Relief of knowing all is well; contentment

Negative state
Anxieties, worries and concerns

Three states of mind for both Human and Chimp

Removing the negative state of mind

Things that put you into a negative state of mind are anxieties, worries or concerns. This is typically because you don't have the four functional planet systems (The Divided Plant, The Planet of Others, The Planet Connect and The Planet of the Real World) running smoothly. It means you are not fulfilling fundamental things that the Chimp and Human need to feel relaxed and content.

Therefore, to get out of the negative state of mind you need to get all the four functional planet systems spinning correctly. Realistically we are always going to have some level of dysfunction, it is about minimising it and containing it, so that we can move on and use our energies to get quality in our lives.

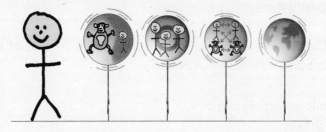

Staying out of the negative state is like spinning plates:
the planets need constant attention

Here are examples of things to address from the first four systems.

- Recognise, nurture and manage your Chimp.
- Recognise the need to look after and develop your Human.
- Have a fully functioning Computer with Autopilots, without Gremlins, with contained Goblins and a thought-through Stone of Life.
- Manage others in your world.
- Have a fully functioning troop.
- Communicate effectively.
- Establish a friendly Jungle for your Chimp.
- Have a Real World perspective in place.
- Be able to deal with immediate and chronic stress.

Make sure the common physical and emotional drives and needs of your Chimp and Human are being met. Here are some examples of what the Chimp needs:

- Troop
- Sex
- Food
- Power
- Ego
- Territory
- Security
- Inquisitiveness

The Human shares many of these common basic needs of the Chimp but also includes things such as:

- A role or purpose in life
- Soulmates
- Intellectual stimulation

We all fall into a negative state of mind from time to time, which is normal. The secret is to address it as quickly as possible and accept that it is not normal to remain in this negative state.

The neutral state of mind
This state is when the first four planets are spinning well and you are content, but this might not mean you are happy. For some, 'content' is 'happy' but for most happiness means something more.

The positive state of mind
The positive state of mind is when you *add* positives and quality to your life and not just live on basics. It has a feel-good factor and your life feels rich, productive and fulfilling. Not surprisingly this quality defines happiness to many people.

Examples of Chimp additions
- Fun
- New experiences
- Pleasurable activities
- Socialising
- Treats
- Rewards
- Mental stimulation

Examples of Human additions
- Laughter
- Satisfying activities
- Achievements
- Altruistic behaviours
- Future planning
- Entertainment
- Reminders of good things – possessed and achieved

Moving into happiness

To become happy and enter the positive state of mind *you need to add on extras in your life and bring quality to it*. You have to put things in place to have the best chance of becoming happy. So look at the lists opposite to find examples of extras for your Chimp and Human, and select from them and add to them your own thoughts. Then make active steps to try and fulfil them. Happiness comes at a price because it usually takes effort.

We can look at happiness in terms of 'having' and 'being' and these two aspects simply clarify the difference between 'what you have' and 'who you are'.

'Having'

The material aspect of 'having' includes achievements and possessions, whereas the emotional, physical and intellectual aspects of 'having' are less tangible. For example, the emotional aspect can include the need to be loved by others or to have respect from others. The physical aspect of 'having' doesn't just include good health but also feelings of well-being. Intellectual aspects include having a fulfilling life that stimulates your brain to think and challenge it in a pleasant way.

The 'having' list
- Achievements
- Possessions
- Emotional
- Physical
- Intellectual

There are many overlaps between 'basics' for survival and 'additions' for quality. The Human and the Chimp share many features on their lists. The important point here is to spend time working out what **you need** to make yourself happy and then to **make it happen**.

A potential problem with achievements

Achievements are important for Humans. We like to know that we have done something constructive or achieved something to be proud of. But there may be a problem with achievements.

Whenever we set our sights on achieving something, such as getting a promotion, we believe that when we have succeeded we will be proud and this will stay with us. Sadly, it is a very common experience that when we have managed to get the promotion, we often dismiss our achievement instead of celebrating it and then we look for something else to achieve.

I have seen this in elite sport where a sportsperson tries to get a world record. When they have achieved it they are very often quick to dismiss it and say things such as, 'Well it's not a good world record, it's just a weak world record!'

The problem is that our Chimps are never satisfied and whatever we achieve, or can do, they frequently dismiss as low-key or worthless. So we have to be careful when it comes to achievements not to let the Chimp within us dismiss our efforts and achievements. When you achieve something, no matter how small the Chimp may think it is, celebrate and pat yourself on the back. It is much more likely to lead to a happy state of mind than allowing the Chimp to dismiss your achievement.

A potential problem with possessions

Possessions are similar to achievements. It has been shown that happiness derived from possessions is short-lived. Some people think they would be happy for ever if they won the lottery. After a period of adjustment it has been found that lottery winners go back to their previous levels of happiness. It is similar to getting something new; after a period of time it usually diminishes in value to you. Beware that you don't forget to cherish precious things that you have before they are gone.

Clashes between the Human and the Chimp when it comes to happiness

Recognising a clash between what the Human and the Chimp need, particularly when it comes to emotional, physical and intellectual aspects, is very important. There are many times when the needs and drives of the Chimp and Human do not match.

Some are easy to deal with. For example, playing sport can easily satisfy aggressive and territorial Chimp behaviours. This is socially acceptable and the Human can enjoy it too. If there is no outlet for aggression then it may displace itself into unhealthy violence.

Sometimes there has to be a compromise because the Chimp and Human don't agree. For example, it's not unusual to find a couple whose sex drives don't match. Hopefully both partners would want to be respectful towards each other as their Human would demand, but yet they need to have their sex drive fulfilled. This problem can be dynamite if it's not addressed. Being honest and approaching the problem together to find acceptable solutions is the best way forward. It is dangerous to ignore a powerful Chimp drive because if you do, the Chimp will only agitate and may take you places you don't want to go.

Happiness is based on understanding the needs of your Human and Chimp and making sure that they are addressed and become compatible.

Getting the right partner

Most people want and need someone to share their life with. The problem, simplistically speaking, is that their Chimp and Human are looking for different things within that partner.

The Chimp will only see a mate to form a bond to, in order to secure a territory, have a family and produce the next generation. It is programmed to do this by looking at the physical aspects of the partner and also the emotional aspects that fit its agenda.

The Human, on the other hand, is looking for a true soulmate or companion and looks for Human values within the partner. Sadly, most people enter a relationship with either their Chimp or their Human but not with both.

You will have to make sure that you are happy with the Chimp and Human in the other person. Beware of your own Chimp's powerful emotional feelings, as they can be very fickle in the long run, no matter how right they may feel at the time. Enjoy the feelings just don't build on these alone.

Generally you can work out what the Chimp and Human in others are like. When you have done this it is a useful exercise to write three columns on a piece of paper. In the first column put all of the good points of their Chimp and their Human. In the second column, write down all of the not-so-good points that don't really bother you. Note well, I did say 'all of the not-so-good points that don't really bother you' and NOT 'all of the not-so-good points that you think **you can change** in them'. To change them is extremely unlikely to happen! (Extremely unlikely **means** extremely unlikely). So the points in the second column must be ones that really do not affect you. The third column is for things in their Human or Chimp that you do not like and will find hard to accept.

Now think carefully: you can live with anybody's good points. Therefore, remove the first column and do not consider it. Don't focus on this first column, as it will very often blind you to the bad points and hold you to that person, which may emotionally damage you. The second column means that you can honestly live with these points and that you accept them AS THEY ARE. So ignore this column. Finally we reach the third column. If you have put down anything in this column then you are really saying that you cannot live with this person. This seems tough, but research looking at lots of couples indicates that whenever there is even one item in the last column, the relationship is unlikely to last.

This one feature could be like a single drop of poison. No matter how appealing and tasty-looking a meal is, if you add just one drop of poison then it is inedible and lethal. Relationships, environments and jobs can be like this. Beware the drop of poison that is just one irresolvable or unacceptable difference. Don't be surprised if you eat the meal and take ill! Therefore, equally don't be surprised if you suffer emotionally if there is a single drop of poison in your life. Think very carefully therefore before you enter a relationship; do not look at the first two columns because they are not an indication of real compatibility. Look at the last column and be honest with yourself. Finding the right partner is not too easy but the search is worth it. Getting yourself into a stable emotional state will attract many people and then putting yourself in the right place to meet them will bring rewards.

Building fulfilling relationships

All personal relationships can be improved and bring us more fulfilment. Here are some suggestions you can consider when looking at your own approach to your relationships.

Ask yourself if you are being realistic about what this person can offer you, whether they are a friend or partner. It is unrealistic to believe that any one person can meet all your needs and that any one friend or partner can deliver all that you want. Most relationships are healthier if there are other friends and family in the picture.

Choose your friends on the basis of not only what you can offer them but also what they can offer you. An ideal friend or partner is likely to:

- Make you feel good about yourself
- Help you develop as a person
- Bring out the best in you

- Put you first before themselves
- Accept you as you are

The reverse is also true, that as a good friend you would be doing these things for them.

All partners hurt us and let us down from time to time. Getting over this and being understanding is the way to keeping the relationship alive.

If you have forgiven a remorseful partner then that means putting the incident behind you. Forgiving doesn't mean storing up the misdemeanour to use it over and over in the future when it suits you. If you are doing this then *forgiveness* is not the right word. The right word to describe what you are doing is *tormenting*. You can either forgive the partner, and don't bring it up again, or you can call it a day and let the person find someone else who won't torment them. (Notice forgiving doesn't mean forgetting, it just means not using it as a weapon. However, it is sometimes wise for you to remember an event or behaviour if the person keeps repeating it and you think it is time for you to move on!)

The handover

As our Chimps work by having a partner in mind before they actually meet them, they often superimpose onto someone what they want to see rather than seeing what is in front of them. This can cause a great deal of stress as the Chimp continually tries to make the person out to be the 'right person'. It makes breaking up from someone, who in the end is unsuitable, very difficult.

One way that may help if you get stuck in this position is to try the 'handover'. Imagine that you are going to hand your partner over to another person and you have to be absolutely truthful about your partner, warts and all. Try speaking into the air and tell the new person what to expect from the relationship. Give the good points and then give the bad points, but don't hold back. Imagine if you lie that they can take you to court!

By doing the 'handover' you may come to realise that the new person is unlikely to take your partner, and you yourself may wonder why you are hanging on to them. I have used this exercise with many people who are suffering in a relationship that really isn't going to work and it has given them a different perspective.

'Being' is about who you are

There are a number of aspects to consider when looking at 'who you are' and how this promotes happiness. We could consider them as a 'being' list.

The 'being' list is made up of:

- Self-image
- Self-worth
- Self-esteem
- Self-confidence

In order to understand how you perceive yourself it is very important that you recognise the difference between the way that your Chimp perceives you and the way that your Human perceives you. They are typically a million miles apart. You really have to make a choice here as to which one you want to go with.

A brief reminder of the way that the Chimp thinks will help you to understand why many people have a very poor relationship with themselves! The Chimp is a vulnerable individual trying hard to be accepted within the troop and trying to impress the troop. This is a permanent state and will never change. Typically, the Chimp will be very self-critical and lack confidence in its own abilities in order to eliminate errors or show weaknesses. It will be intolerant of any shortcomings or mistakes that it makes. The Chimp believes that others are constantly judging it and seeing its every fault.

The way that the Human thinks will show you the alternative viewpoint. The Human recognises that although everyone has different abilities and looks, everyone is equally valuable as a human being. The Human also recognises that trying to impress and keep others happy, in order to be popular, is not a good basis for living life. The Human believes that all you can do is your best. The Human also believes that the values that count in life are not based on looks, achievements or possessions but are based on values such as honesty, integrity, kindness and consideration.

Therefore, when it comes to assessing yourself, you and your Chimp will come to very different conclusions because they are working with very different measuring scales and values. Before you start to look at yourself, the most crucial thing to do is to make sure that you have a Stone of Life with the values that you honestly want to be measured by. Then measure yourself and others by these values and **do not allow your Chimp to hijack you**. For example, if you put cheerful, friendly and honest high on your list then measure yourself by these Human values.

The values and beliefs used as the
reference to work from.

Self-image

This is the way that you see your personality and presence.

The Human will give a balanced viewpoint and see both attractive and unattractive aspects about yourself. But it will do this by looking at Human values such as compassion, honesty and altruism to decide on the person that you are.

The Chimp will look at your physical appearance and your achievements to define who you are. Beware, the Chimp can change its mind very quickly and is very subjective. One minute it will think that you are the most amazing person around with stunning looks and the next it will believe that you are the ugliest creature walking the planet.

Happiness about your self-image is unlikely to be stable if you base it on the Chimp's opinion of what matters and is very likely to lead you into emotional turmoil on a regular basis. A true self-image will be based by how much you are living out your values.

So how you decide on self-image is a decision between going on the Chimp's values and going on the Human's values.

This is a choice and how you choose will definitely affect your happiness. STOP at this point and make sure you understand all that has been explained on self-image and then make your choice.

Self-worth

This is the value that you put on yourself as a person. Again, I hope it is obvious that the Human and Chimp will measure this against very different values. It is your choice as to how you wish to see your own worth. If, for example, you choose to weigh your worth against being a happy person who brings a lot of pleasure to others just by being pleasant and smiling, then you have a chance of seeing yourself as a very valuable member of the community. Your happiness levels will rise accordingly because even the Chimp will like this.

However, if you weigh yourself up against how clever you are and what job you do then you may well waver from day to day in your self-worth as the Chimp changes its mind.

Make your choice between Chimp and Human assessments.

Self-esteem

This is how you compare yourself to others. The same theme continues: you either use the Chimp's criteria or the Human's criteria to decide on how you compare.

The Human is likely to say that everyone is equal in value and although we possess different skills and abilities the overall belief is that all are equal as humans.

The Chimp will say that everyone is at a different level and some people are better than others, with power, looks and possessions being very important. Research suggests that the way you compare yourself to others has a major impact on your happiness levels.

If you must compare yourself then do it with Human criteria and not the Chimp's.

Self-confidence

This is what you believe that you are capable of doing. This is such a large part of our lives that a stabilising Moon to the Planet of Happiness represents it. The chapter on the 'Moon of Confidence' will go into this in detail.

When you look at all the ways in which you can assess yourself, there is a constant theme: you can either work with the Chimp and its value system, or you can work with the Human and its value system. The results then will be very different and will lead to different levels of happiness. Happiness is then greatly influenced by your own belief systems and values. In order to get this right, you need to turn back to the Stone of Life. *It is very important to know what your absolute values about life and people are, BEFORE you start trying to work out who you are*. Once you have got your own house in order you will be at ease with yourself and it is likely that your happiness levels will dramatically increase.

The happiness approach

To have the best chances of being happy you have to approach life, and yourself, in the right way.

Some people naturally have a positive, optimistic approach to life. Their beliefs and attitude are slanted towards seeing the best in any situation. They do their best and if things don't go right they can grieve but then get on with it. This approach can be learnt and culti-vated. It is an attitude of mind. It also depends on what you see as normal for you. If you think happiness is not normal for you then it becomes a self-fulfilling prophecy and happiness becomes elusive. There are a number of approaches to life that happy people seem to adopt. Here are a few you could consider taking on for yourself.

- Learning to have a realistic but positive approach to life is a learnt behaviour. Whenever a situation occurs where things are not going to plan, *try to develop the habit of looking for solu-tions rather than dwelling on problems*. This is an Autopilot that is very useful to get into your Computer.
- The thoughts in your head and the approach you take to life are your choice. *You can choose how much a situation bothers you*. Think about this. It is for you to decide what in your life is important and what isn't. If you don't want something to be important then it doesn't have to be.
- Ask yourself how long you want to brood or dwell on something unpleasant that has passed *and how long you want to stay in that frame of mind. Also ask what good is brooding doing?*
- One approach to life that is guaranteed to help you to be happy is to *learn to laugh at yourself and keep a sense of humour,* whenever you can. Again, this is an Autopilot in the Computer of happy people; it is a learnt behaviour. If you take yourself too seriously then happiness can diminish.
- Always be proactive in life, especially in relationships. Try not to be reactive to another person's moods or wishes. Decide what

you want and then negotiate but don't allow yourself to become a passive victim.

- Try to deal with the cause of a situation and not the symptom. Sometimes getting things off your chest is all that is needed (letting your Chimp have a safe scream). However, simply screaming doesn't solve the problem that caused the symptoms. Solving the problem is very helpful in the long run. Happy people will find and treat the cause!

The happiness list

I am still surprised when someone tells me they are unhappy and then can't tell me anything that would make them happy. It doesn't take long to work out some very simple things that you can do to promote happiness in your life. So one of the obvious things that you can do to increase your chances of happiness is to know exactly what will make you happy and then make sure this happens. If you are not good at looking after yourself and your own happiness, then form your own happiness list. This list can be referred to and things put in place to look forward to. The happiness list exists in two forms:

- The 'immediate happy list'
- The 'delayed happy list'

For example, on my immediate happy list would be a cup of coffee; phoning a friend; walking the dog; making plans for the future; counting my blessings; sitting back and taking a deep breath! These are things that I can choose to do at any time, more or less. Even just sitting back and thinking of good things can make me feel happier. This means that at any time I can make an effort to raise my mood and often that's all it takes, just a little effort. Try now to name ten things under your control that you could do to make you feel happier. Then ask yourself if you have done them recently.

Your delayed happy list might include such things as having friends round for an evening; going out for a meal; holidays; playing sport; and so on.

You need to take time to put these things in place so that you have something to look forward to. This is very important to most people if they are to remain happy. Within yourself you may feel fine but your Chimp will always demand something to look forward to, so nurture it by letting it know of future events. Having some future events to look forward to will help your Chimp to get through less happy moments. Happy people tend to have things to look forward to. They also make sure that these happy times are sacrosanct. Nothing stops them from happening.

Keep these lists to hand so you can refer to them and move into a happier frame of mind. Try to keep these lists in line with your values, for example if you value being healthy and active then it is better to put 'going for a walk' or 'eating good food' rather than 'eating a whole bar of chocolate'.

The happiness audit and virtual twin

It is a useful exercise to monitor your happiness. Keep a diary and record the things that make you happy and also the things that stop you being happy. Having a dedicated notebook just for this purpose will show you clearly how you can improve and look after yourself better.

One very sure way of giving yourself some honest and frank advice is to invent the virtual twin.

Imagine you are one of two identical twins. Your twin is your best friend and loves you and is looking out for you. Give the twin a name. Then imagine that you are this twin. So, for example, you have called your twin Sam. You now become Sam. In your role as Sam, give advice to yourself and tell some home truths about what you should and should not be doing with situations, your life, and your problems.

I have used this technique with numerous people who have got stuck with all kinds of problems. When they imagine being the twin they give amazing advice to themselves. It's not surprising really because you know yourself best! Sometimes it just takes the courage to tell yourself some home truths, such as 'stop being petty', 'you need to stop being harsh on yourself', 'you are a good person and you have done your best', 'you need a kick up the pants' 'you need to smile and reward yourself' and so on. If you can do it with a sense of humour, then this is even better!

Happiness promoters – replacing Gremlins with Autopilots

Putting in Autopilots, new behaviours and beliefs that will promote happiness, is an exercise that needs reinforcing regularly. Take time to think about habits and thoughts that you have that are destructive in order to find your Gremlins. Let's look at some common themes that many of us can relate to.

Battle versus lifestyle

A battle means you will have to expend lots of effort and energy to win. A lifestyle means relaxing and living to expectations without effort.

Try not to see battles in all you do but see lifestyles instead. For example, trying to diet and eat smaller portions is harder if you see it as a battle to cut down rather than seeing smaller portions as normal (and larger portions as unacceptable). Another example is

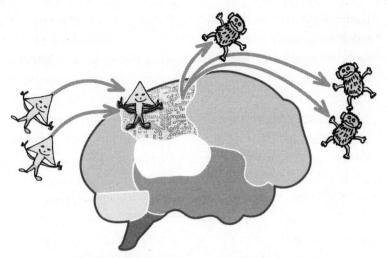

Happiness improves by finding and
replacing Gremlins with Autopilots

to believe that being happy is something you have to battle to be,
instead of relaxing and seeing being happy as normal for you. The
Gremlin is a belief that happiness is a battle; the Autopilot is that
happiness is a lifestyle.

Dichotomous thinking

Seeing everything as all or nothing, win or lose, success or failure,
is dichotomous thinking where everything is seen as having just
two options. This type of thinking is a habit, a Gremlin. It often
shows inflexibility and leads to unhappiness. Replace the Gremlin
with an Autopilot of seeing shades of grey and being flexible, as
this is more likely to lead to a happier mood.

Enjoy the roses but watch for the thorns

Life can be a bed of roses but that means there are lots of thorns.
If you want to be happy picking roses then be mindful of the
thorns. Watch out for things that you know will make you
unhappy and actively avoid them whenever possible. Avoiding
things that cause you to have unwanted feelings is a sensible way

to stay happy. If you can't avoid them, then have a plan on how you will deal with them; don't be unprepared for the thorns. The Gremlin is ignoring reality and the Autopilot is being prepared to deal with reality.

The Crystal-ball Gremlin and snow mountain

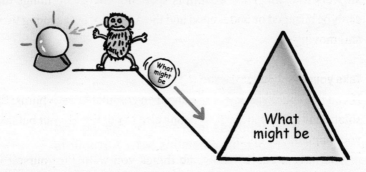

Crystal-ball gazing is looking into the future and trying to predict what is going to happen. It is usually fraught with problems and typically leads to unhappiness.

First the Crystal-ball Gremlin looks into the future and sees doom and gloom, because crystal balls rarely show a happy future. Then the Crystal-ball Gremlin makes a 'what might be' snowball and pushes it down the snow slope. As the snowball rolls down the slope it gathers more and more snow to become a mountain. The snowball forms a 'what might be' snow mountain. You now are trapped with a mountain, worrying about all these 'what might be's.

Smash the crystal ball and kick out the Gremlin. Replace it with an Autopilot of 'cross each bridge as I come to it'. The Autopilot says, 'I don't make snowballs by guessing what will happen but I will stay in the here and now, and deal with things as they unfold.'

Very often things don't work out badly and then you have put yourself through misery for absolutely no reason. If you have done this many times, then how long do you want to keep repeating this before you learn to stop?

Where the Universe ends

At this point in time, nobody knows where the Universe ends. You can spend your life thinking about this or you can accept that nobody knows. If you have worries that cannot be changed or understood then accept them and stop entertaining them; you have a choice NOT to think thoughts that don't help or don't have answers to them. The Gremlin is spending energy on things that can't be changed or understood and the Autopilot is accepting them and moving on.

Take your hand out of the fire

If you put your hand into a fire and then complain that it burns, the solution is easy: don't ask someone else to put the fire out but take your hand out of the fire.

You have a choice about the things you want for yourself in nearly all aspects of your life. Therefore, don't put yourself or remain in situations that are making you unhappy and then complain. If you don't like the rules in another person's world, don't stay. If you don't have the right job, home, partner or friends, then change them. The Gremlin is living with unsatisfactory things and just complaining about them. The Autopilot is changing your position to get happy.

Happiness promoters – common-sense thoughts

The two non-identical twins of 'Need' and 'Want'

What you need isn't necessarily what you want, and what you want isn't necessarily what you need. Learn to tell the difference between the twins.

You can't share a house with a tiger

If you are a cat lover, then you can admire and even in be awe of a tiger. However, despite its beauty, it is a dangerous animal and you will never be able to bring it into your home and share your house with it. It belongs in the wild.

Sometimes people can be like this. You can admire them and even be in love with them, or revere them, but you can never share your life with them. They are dangerous and can do some serious damage to you. If you can recognise they have some impossible-to-live-with traits, then admire them in the wild and not in your home. Find a domestic cat that suits your home if you want happiness.

Eat rubbish and have poor quality of life – what is the surprise?

It is often said that 'you are what you eat' and there is some element of truth in this. If you don't look after yourself and feel unwell what is the surprise? Likewise, if you don't look after your happiness and you feel unhappy then why be shocked?

Sometimes nobody might agree with you

Happiness is more about being at ease with yourself than it is about being at ease with others.

Biggest fan or biggest critic?

In life, we all have people who criticise us. We also have our fans that love us despite our faults. Unhappy people are often their own biggest critic. All they ever do is criticise and dislike themselves. Happy people learn to become their own biggest fan and accept themselves as they are and support themselves. It is a choice. Be happy by loving yourself, faults and all.

Summary key points

- Happiness is a choice.
- To increase your chances of happiness you need to have a plan and implement it.
- Define what makes you and your Chimp happy.
- Adding extras will lift you into happiness.
- Develop your 'having' and 'being'.
- Establish a 'happiness approach' and a 'happiness list'.
- Put in place 'happiness promoters'.

Suggested exercise:
Measuring your efforts to achieve happiness

Make happiness happen

As happiness is so very important to all of us, this chapter represents the planet that will help to make the Sun shine in our Psychological Universe. Therefore, spend some considerable time implementing the recommendations contained in it. Work through each point, and pay particular attention to those that resonate with you. Don't rush through the points, but rather think about each one on a day-by-day basis. Remember that developing happiness is like developing emotional skills. It takes effort and a lot of time, but you will get there.

Keep a diary of each day and note down just a few lines of things or thoughts that brought you happiness. Also, note down how much effort that you made to attain happiness for that day. By doing this for just a couple of weeks, you may realise how much or how little effort you are putting into ensuring your own happiness.

Chapter 17
The Moon of Confidence
How to be confident

Confidence
- Two choices for confidence
- Some important questions to help understand the concept
- Confidence and self

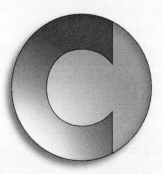

Security and confidence stabilise happiness, therefore they are important to establish.

Two options for confidence

You are about to make a choice that will decide how confident you will be in every situation. Read this chapter slowly and make sure that you follow the reasoning step by step. If you decide to change your standpoint then it will give you confidence in anything you do.

The way that most people think is as follows: 'The more I believe I can do something then the more confident I am.' These are the steps they follow:

1. What is it that I want to do?
2. How able am I to achieve this?
3. My confidence is now measured on how I rate my ability to achieve my goal.

This seems straightforward and it results in varying levels of confidence: so how do we increase our confidence?

With this thinking there are only two ways to increase your confidence: either increase your ability to do something or brainwash yourself into believing that you can do it, even if you can't.

Most people default to one of these ways of thinking because the Chimp is hijacking them into believing there is no alternative to gaining confidence. However there is an alternative way of thinking, and a small minority of people use this. The alternative, the Human way, has confidence levels remaining at 100 per cent at all times, no matter what they do. So how does this work?

The Chimp is saying, 'I am basing my confidence on **my belief in my ability** to reach certain levels that **I have to achieve** and **I cannot deal with the consequences** of not reaching them. Whereas the Human is saying, 'I am basing my confidence on **doing my best** to reach certain levels that **I would like to achieve** and as an adult **I can always deal with any consequences** of not reaching them'.

Therefore the two choices for confidence are: to base your confidence on your belief in your ability, or to base it on doing your best. You can never guarantee what you can achieve and therefore if you do this, your Chimp will take the blood supply in your brain and cause some unease, as it will constantly see the threat of failure. You can guarantee to make your best effort. Therefore, if you choose the basis of best effort, you will have full control and your Human will take the blood supply. This will mean you see life as full of opportunities and you will deal with the consequences.

With this choice we can see that the normal state for the Human is confidence because you can always do your best and deal with consequences, and therefore there is no fear. Whereas, the normal state for the Chimp is variable confidence, with a lot of fear, based around consequences and possible failure.

Liz gives a talk

Here is an example. Liz has been asked to give a talk about her role to 100 of her work colleagues.

Her Chimp will now approach this by deciding what it wants to achieve. It wants to present a good talk and be thought of as having done well. As the Chimp cannot control either of these, but can only influence them, it now senses a threat and looks to the consequences of getting it wrong. As the Chimp has based its confidence on giving a good talk and impressing people, it's now severely lacking confidence and is looking to see what could go wrong.

In contrast, the Human in Liz has decided that she will base her confidence on doing her best. The objective, therefore, is to do her best. She cannot control the level of the talk or what people think but she will be able to deal with these outcomes because she is an adult Human.

Liz knows that she will definitely do her best, even if at the time it goes wrong and the talk is not quite up to scratch. It will still be the best that she can do AT THE TIME of giving the talk. She cannot do better than her best. Therefore, Liz will definitely achieve her objective – 'doing her best' – and anything else is a bonus. With this approach she can relax and see the talk as an opportunity. Her confidence in doing her best is 100 per cent. Liz can also remember that she can reward effort rather than just celebrating achievements.

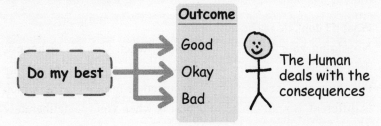

The adult Human's approach with 100% confidence

Some important questions to help understand the concept

But what if I could have done better?

Think about this logically. You cannot do better than your best. Doing your best means that, at the time you tried, you gave it everything. Some things you got right and some things you didn't get right. Therefore, the level you achieved perhaps could have been better if you had had another go. So **doing your best** is different to **achieving your best**, and they don't always go together.

But what if I fail to achieve?

Whatever you decide to base your confidence on, you will still have to deal with the consequence of the outcome. Dealing with outcomes is something every adult Human can do but something that every Chimp and child finds very difficult. So you will inevitably have to learn to deal with disappointment and sometimes that means dealing with failure.

So why choose the Human basis for confidence?

The Human basis will mean that when it is over you will be able to hold your head up, smile, and say, 'I could not have done more because it was my best at the time, faults and all.' You are also more likely to have a better outcome if you go in smiling and relaxed rather than if you go in anxious and lacking in confidence.

What if I don't do my best?

Not doing your best is, for example, when you are dishonest, deliberately lazy, indifferent or devious. Most people are not like this; however, they can be disorganised or undisciplined, which is different. So not doing your best is when you are deliberately not trying.

Let me go through an example to illustrate this very important point. You go to a park and witness a child fall from a tree. You rush across and try to help them to their feet. They are clearly distressed and you ask if they are okay. They say that their ankle is painful so you phone for an ambulance. This all seems reasonable, as you are doing what you think is right and doing your best to deal with the situation. However, the operator for the ambulance gives you a bit of a telling off and says that this is not an emergency and the child can hobble along to the nearest accident department. You then help them along to the accident department, who deal with child, and by now the parents arrive. The doctor lets you know that the child has damaged their ankle and this is probably because you helped them to get onto their feet when they first fell.

What a nightmare! You look back on the scenario and ask, 'Did I achieve a high level of competence in dealing with the situation?' The answer is clearly 'no' but 'Did I do my best at the time and with the ability that I had?' The answer now is 'yes'. So was it really your best? The answer is again 'yes' because you were **trying** your best. If, however, you had walked away from the child, knowing that the child needed help from you, then this would have not have been doing your best.

Adam's driving test and confidence

Adam is about to take his driving test. His friend asks him, 'How confident do you feel?'

Adam now has a choice on where he will base his confidence. The first choice is to base his confidence on **his ability to pass** the test. The second choice is to base his confidence on **his ability to do his best** at the time of the test.

If he chooses the first option then his Chimp will start looking at the consequences of failing and doubts will appear about his ability to pass the test. He is very likely to become nervous and all kinds of unwelcome feelings will sweep over him. The Chimp is well and truly in charge and it is not a good place to be. His confidence levels are low if not at zero. The whole experience is unpleasant.

If he chooses the second option and goes with the Human, then he will say to himself, 'I am not focusing on the outcome or consequences but on what I have to do. I can only do my best, whatever it might be, at the time I take my test. It may go well or it may go badly, but whatever happens I will deal with the outcome because I have no choice. I am an adult and I can deal with consequences!'

He now takes the test saying, 'All I can do is my best and I know that I will do the best I can at the time.' He is basing his confidence on this belief of doing his best. His confidence is 100 per cent because he will definitely do his best, **which is all he is asking of himself**. He can happily say to others, 'I did my best and I can't do better therefore I can hold my head up.' The Human has spoken!

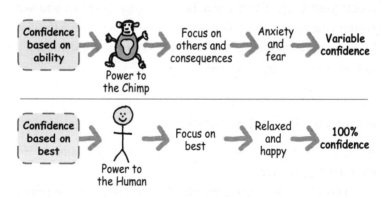

The two options summarised

Confidence and self

Self-confidence

A common problem that makes some people very unhappy is when they have an unrealistic image of themselves. For example, I have people say to me that they lack confidence in doing anything because they are afraid they will say something stupid or do something wrong that will humiliate them. Stop and ask yourself why someone would have these fears?

One very good reason for having these fears is if you have a belief that you are meant to be perfect: a dreadful Gremlin. It is impossible to live up to this and every move you make will be terrifying. You would be living with the idea that you should be error free. Trying to live up to this mythical being would give you a self-image of someone who is inadequate. In reality every human being makes mistakes continually throughout life and does something silly at times. Learning to accept the fact that you are human with flaws and faults is a great relief. It means that making mistakes and errors is normal. Learning to laugh at yourself when you do something silly or when you say something amiss is part of life and being Human. I don't know anyone who is perfect, thank goodness! Admit your mistakes and shortcomings, but do it with a smile. Also don't be afraid to say, 'I don't know.'

Go a step further and think what this belief of 'never making a fool of yourself' or 'being perfect' is doing to the Chimp within. Each day you leave your home and tell the Chimp, 'We must be perfect again today,' you will stress your Chimp out of its tree. The Chimp doesn't need this psychological torture, so think again before the animal defence organisation correctly pays you a call!

The image you want to achieve may also be based on unsuitable role models, Mr Universe, Miss World, Einstein and so on. Try to be yourself because 'attractive' is a far more powerful word than 'beautiful' or 'intelligent' when it comes to people.

Loss of self-confidence when a relationship goes wrong

Virtually everyone searches for a partner at some time in his or her life. This is such a powerful drive that it cannot be ignored. One of the problems in doing this is that we frequently try to match up with the wrong person. When this happens there is turmoil at the point when the relationship ends, whether we end it or they do.

If they end the relationship then one of the severe consequences is that we fall into a state of loss of confidence in ourselves. This extremely painful experience is sadly a natural consequence of rejection and loss. It seems to take our Chimp about three months to come to terms with such a loss and it will go through a grieving process during this time. We can't rush this, but we can prolong it by not grieving. During this time it is normal for someone to lose his or her self-confidence, but it will return. Be gentle on yourself during this period but watch for self-pity.

Summary key points

- Confidence is based on one of two ways of thinking: the Human or the Chimp.
- You have a choice to base your confidence on 'doing your best'.
- 'Doing your best' as a basis gives 100 per cent confidence.
- Self-confidence is enhanced when you have a realistic expectation of yourself.

Suggested exercise:
Making confidence happen

A choice is always made

When you next have a loss of confidence remind yourself that you are in fact making a choice. You have chosen to be a child or Chimp and are choosing to worry about levels achieved and consequences, whether this is a conscious decision or not. Remind yourself that the alternative is to be a Human adult, and to choose to do your best and to deal with any consequences you meet. Also make a mental check on whether you have an image of yourself that you are trying to live up to and whether this is not helping the situation.

In situations that involve a lack of confidence, take a few quiet moments to check which option you are choosing.

Chapter 18
The Moon of Security
How to develop security

Security
- Human, Chimp and security
- The truth around risk and security
- Practical ways to help the Chimp

Human, Chimp and security

Security is the need to feel safe in our surroundings and in our troop. Feeling secure will make your Chimp happy. The Chimp will always look to external surroundings for its security. The Human will look internally to beliefs for its security.

Your Chimp will constantly search for security and try to remove any form of risk or vulnerability from your life **because it believes that this is possible.** Of course it is not possible to live a life completely free of risk, but your Chimp will attempt to do this by trying to keep everything constant in its world, and by tending to stick with the familiar. The Human within you is far more adventurous. It accepts that nothing in life remains constant, and knows familiarity can be a helpful or unhelpful thing. The Human accepts that vulnerability and risk are part of everyday life and they cannot be removed completely.

This difference between the two beings means that there needs to be some compromise and a plan to deal with issues surrounding security. The Chimp has got a point in making you aware that there is danger but the Human must take the lead and explain to the Chimp the reality of life. The Human must also respect that you must not put your Chimp through emotions it cannot withstand. As every Chimp is different you must find out exactly what your own Chimp's needs are for security and what it can tolerate in terms of risk and change.

From this standpoint, we will begin by exploring the truth around security and risk as the Human sees it, and then go on to help the Chimp with some practical ways that can make it feel more secure.

The truth around risk and security

The Human is aware of some truths that the Chimp can find hard to deal with. Here are some of those truths:

Security and change
- Security is **relative**.
- We are **never fully secure** in life because life itself is transient.
- We live in a world that is in a constant state of change and **it cannot exist in any other way**.

Risk

- There is a risk attached to **everything** we do.
- We have to **accept** that risk is part of everyday life.
- We cannot control **all** risk.
- We can control **some** risk.

Vulnerability and fears

- It is wise to **face fears** and **address** them.
- We have to **accept** that vulnerability is part of everyday life.

Practical ways to help the Chimp

Accepting the truth

If we can get the Chimp to accept the truth around risk, vulnerability and security, it will settle down considerably. This means you need to sit down and think through the truths attached to risk, vulnerability and security, and make sure that you have registered them clearly into your Computer. For example, here are some examples of 'truths' that occur frequently.

My partner may leave me for someone else (this risk needs facing if it bothers you)

I need to accept this and get on and enjoy the time that we do have together. If I am happy and constructive then they are less likely to leave me and our quality of time together will be great. Worrying about it won't help and if it does happen then I will cope.

I may suffer illness

If this happens I will search out appropriate help and will then work with the illness. If, and only if, it happens will I use energy thinking about it because worrying before it happens is not sensible.

I am concerned about losing things that are important to me
Nothing lasts for ever. Life and people are in a constant state of flux. This is how it is meant to be and I must enjoy the journey.

When you have written out your concerns then you can write down the truths next to them. If you do not live by these truths then the Chimp will constantly become distressed and overreact to many minor risks that you put it through and search for a security that does not exist. However, the Human must accept that the Chimp is not built to feel secure and will always have its moments and need constant attention.

Key Point
Feeling insecure from time to time is normal for a Chimp, so expect it, accept it and then take care of it.

The troop

For most Chimps, the troop is the biggest factor to bring a sense of security. When we share concerns or worries, or when we go through experiences with others, it is surprising how much we can manage. If we try to go it alone we can become very distressed and get things out of perspective. Don't forget that it is wise to ask for support from a member of the troop, or a professional, if you are having difficulties dealing with a problem. One of the strengths of the troop is that members work for each other. **Rely on your troop in times of insecurity**.

Security in another person

Basing your security on one other person is usually unwise. Most people have reliable partners and sharing with a partner is one of the joys of life. However, basing your security on a partner or any other one individual is a recipe for disaster. When we are dependent on someone else for our well-being in some form or other, it tends to put restrictions on what we can and can't do and it may be that we have to accept this. Whenever possible, try to separate out your physical dependence on someone from your emotional security on them: these are two different things.

There are situations when it might be wise to rely on someone else for our security. For example, when we fall in love it is difficult for us to control our Chimps. Our brains release a lot of chemicals that basically diminish our ability to think straight. Our judgement of this person can be very impaired. And this poses a risk. So, if you are in love, remember that you are not quite in a balanced state of mind; in fact, you're a little mentally deranged! Listen to your best friends because they are not so blind!

Try to gain security from within, by basing your peace of mind on beliefs, and let your Human guide you.

Reassurance

Whenever your Chimp is feeling insecure, be practical and where possible seek reassurance. For example, if you feel insecure at work then make sure that you establish exactly what your role is meant to be, where your boundaries are, who you report back to, what their expectation is of you and how you will be assessed. You can also ask for feedback to know how you are doing and how you could improve in any areas of weakness. Being practical in this way is very reassuring for the Chimp. A Chimp that lives with unknowns and fears **that could be addressed** is an unnecessarily insecure and unhappy Chimp.

Reassurance within any relationship is also a good idea to check on from time to time. It helps to know where you stand and how the relationship is going.

Seeking reassurance is a wise thing to do whenever you need it. However, if the Chimp is constantly seeking reassurance, inappropriately, then it is likely that there is a fear that is not being addressed or the Chimp needs reminding of the truths surrounding security. It helps your partner's Chimp to feel secure if you reassure it without being asked!

Familiarity

If you have an insecure Chimp then establishing a routine that is familiar to you can do wonders to settle the Chimp. If you have to go through some new routines or experiences it may help an insecure Chimp to remind it that once you have become familiar with the new routine the fears will go. Until then it is very natural for it to feel some apprehension.

A secure future

Looking to the future and preparing plans to deal with problems or fears can be a constructive exercise. Notice that we are talking about having plans to deal with problems or fears, not just searching out fears and then not dealing with them. Searching out and confronting fears can be a healthy exercise and can often be done with a thoughtful friend or professional. Being able to see the way through and removing danger or threat is offering the Chimp great security.

Being able to deliver what is being asked of you, or knowing that you have someone who can help you to deliver what is needed, will allay the Chimp's fears considerably. The important point here is that you are addressing real fears, such as finances, work, housing and so on and being very practical about them. Avoiding facing any fears will cause immense stress and evoke feelings of apprehension in your Chimp.

Specific fears that are real

Insecurity is sometimes about death, pain or injury. These are real fears and worth confronting. There is little point in dwelling on them, but given some constructive thinking time, the concerns surrounding them will subside.

The way forward, when looking at these specific fears, is to ask yourself what is outside of your control and what is inside of your control. Your Chimp will want to control the uncontrollable and then become very distressed when it can't do this. The Human accepts that some things we cannot control and therefore we must accept them or deal with them at the time they appear.

Summary key points

- Security is one of the major stabilisers for happiness.
- The Chimp frequently seeks out security unrealistically.
- Healthy normal Chimps have fears and concerns over security and vulnerability.
- The Human needs to place an Autopilot into the Computer to steady the Chimp.

Suggested exercise:
Making the Chimp feel secure

Addressing security issues
Allocate time to consider the security you have in place to reassure your Chimp. Make a list of those things that concern or worry you and divide the list into those things that you can control and those that you can't control. Where you can control security issues then make plans to deal with them.

When working through the list of those things that you can't control, ask yourself how willing you are to accept these, as there really is no choice. In order to change your worries you must change your stance. Ask yourself directly how willing you are to move ground.

Looking Forward
The Sunrise

You have now crossed your Psychological Universe and have a comprehensive picture of all the areas you can work on. Using the Chimp model to develop yourself and improve the quality of your life will make a huge difference to both yourself and others around you. The rewards can be immeasurable.

Many people have worked with the model and put time aside to learn emotional skills and maintain them. They have applied the techniques on a regular basis and have reported that it is life-changing. I sincerely hope that you will have the same experience.

Changes within you take time and effort. They usually happen gradually and often occur unnoticed by you, but not by others. Don't be disheartened if you have setbacks; instead learn from them and always celebrate any successes. Remember: **you always have a choice**. The choices you make and how you choose to deal with life will determine your success and happiness. So what are you going to do today that will make you happier and more successful?

Your Chimp will always be alive and kicking and you must accept that fact and work with it. It is not bad, it is not good: it is a Chimp. It brings every emotion to your world. It can be your best friend and worst enemy. **It is the Chimp Paradox**.

Thank you for reading the book and sharing this journey with me.

I wish you well as you continue to watch the Sunrise.

Appendix A

The Complete Psychological Mind

The illustration below shows the complete Psychological Mind with all six working components, namely the Human, the Chimp and the Computer with its Goblins, Gremlins, Autopilots and Stone of Life.

The diagram opposite provides a complete overview of the Psychological Universe. Many of the planets have moons which have a stabilising influence on individual planets. This is why it is always important to work on the moons, as well as the planets themselves.

Appendix B

The Complete Psychological Universe

Self-Fulfilment	The Sun	

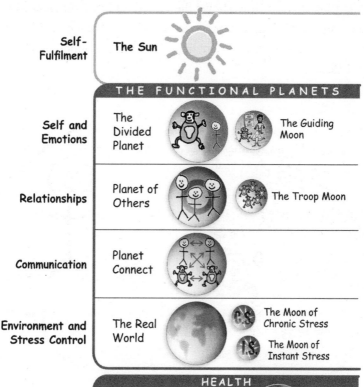

	THE FUNCTIONAL PLANETS	
Self and Emotions	The Divided Planet	The Guiding Moon
Relationships	Planet of Others	The Troop Moon
Communication	Planet Connect	
Environment and Stress Control	The Real World	The Moon of Chronic Stress / The Moon of Instant Stress
	HEALTH	
Maintenance and Well-being	Planet of Shadows and The Asteroid Belt	
	THE QUALITY PLANETS	
Success Empowerment Encouragement	Planet of Success	The Regal Moon / Moon of Carrots / The CORE Moon
Happiness Confidence Security	Planet of Happiness	The Moon of Security / The Moon of Confidence

Acknowledgements

There are so many people who have contributed in varying degrees to the making of this book, both directly and indirectly, that I would need an extra chapter just to list them. Therefore, I would rather say a massive thank you to everyone who has helped rather than miss someone out.

Special thanks, however, must go to three people who have contributed tirelessly: Ruth Banner, my niece, who has read and re-read the developing book over months and months, and offered suggestions and criticism that have been invaluable; Jeff Battista, my graphic designer, who has patiently designed and re-designed the graphics and discussed how best to represent my ideas; and Susanna Abbott, my editor, who has encouraged and guided me, tolerating my Chimp's outbursts with patience, through the mine-field of publishing this book.

Therefore, to friends, colleagues, patients and students, many, many grateful thanks.

Finally, I would like to dedicate this book to Chimpanzees and other Great Apes, who in the future may read this book and come to realise, for better or for worse, that they have a Human inside them!

Index